WORKING
MUSICIANS

■

Also by Bruce Pollock

In Their Own Words: Lyrics & Lyricists, 1955–1974

Playing for Change (novel)

The Face of Rock & Roll: Images of a Generation

Me, Minsky & Max (novel)

When Rock Was Young: A Nostalgia Review of the Top 40 Era

It's Only Rock and Roll (novel)

The Disco Handbook

When the Music Mattered: Rock in the 1960s

Hipper Than Our Kids: A Rock and Roll Journal of the Baby Boom
Generation

The Rock Song Index: 7500 Most
Important Songs of Rock and Roll

Edited by Bruce Pollock

Popular Music: An Annotated Index of American Popular Songs,
Volumes 7–24

WORKING MUSICIANS

■

Defining Moments
from the Road, the
Studio, and the Stage

■

Bruce Pollock

HarperEntertainment
An Imprint of HarperCollins*Publishers*

FIRST EDITION

Designed by Lisa Stokes

Library of Congress Cataloging-in-Publication Data has been applied for.

ISBN 0-06-107606-6

02 03 04 05 06 ❖/RRD 10 9 8 7 6 5 4 3 2 1

To Barbara, for her love, her confidence, and her strength

Contents

Acknowledgments

Working Musicians owes its existence to the interest, assistance, and cooperation of many fine organizations and people. Chief among them is Cherry Lane Music Co., Inc., which graciously permitted me to use excerpts from many of the interviews I did during my tenure as editor-in-chief of *Guitar for the Practicing Musician,* as well as parts of articles that originally ran in *Guitar Extra* and *Playing Keyboards.* Erik Philbrook of the ASCAP magazine *Playback* performed an immense service on behalf of the book when he ran a short article informing the vast ASCAP membership of my search for stories from working musicians. Jonathan Daniels, Clyde Lieberman, Ron Solleveld, and Jennifer Press at BMG Publishing and Rob Santos at Buddha Records allowed me unlimited access to their massive Rolodexes. Independent publicists Randy Mahon and Lance Cowan translated their excitement about the book to their astounding client lists. Of course, none of this would have been possible if not for the vision of my agent, Jim Fitzgerald, who saw the potential of this project right from the beginning, or my editor, Tom Dupree, whose initial enthusiasm never flagged. Finally, the biggest thank-you has to be to the musicians themselves, whose voices and stories comprise the heart and soul of this book. See you all at the top of the charts.

Special Thanks

Because *Working Musicians* is, in a certain sense, a summation of my career thus far as a music journalist as well as a testament to the idea of creative community, I would like to take this opportunity to thank some people whose recognition and encouragement helped me a lot along the way. It is a table of contents I find at least as impressive as the one that adorns this book:

T. Mike Walker, Jimmy Curtiss, Jimmy Ienner, Ann Petrie, Richard Goldstein, Irwin Stark, Frederick Tuten, Jay Garon, Anatole Broyard, Roger Angell, Daniel Menaker, Jane Rotrosen, Melanie Kroupa, Martha Bradford, Hy Cohen, Walter Wager, Bruce Carrick, Sy Peck, Sue Donohue, Michelle Hush, Peter Knobler, Ben Fong Torres, Chet Flippo, Henry Beard, Susan Blond, Don Kirshner, Joe Dera, Cameron Crowe, Norman Shreiber, Rick Mitz, Robert Cornfield, Susan Elliott, Joan Raines, John Wagman, Billy Altman, Don Hutter, Pete Fornatale, Rita Rosenkranz, Art Cooper, Ellie Kossack, Roger Director, Ernie Baxter, Stephanie Brush, John Rezek, Roland Gelatt, Hollis Alpert, Peter Young, Richard Curtis, Dan Weiss, David Hajdu, Chris Browne, Lisa Faye Kaplan, Hugh Wachter, Alan Oren, Joan Bierman, Elizabeth Geiser, Larry Baker, Milt Okun, Lorain Levy, Lauren Keiser, John Stix, Mark Phillips, Peter Primont, Tom Mount, David Harp, Robert Axelrod, Richard Carlin, Jon

Weiner, Marybeth Payne, Bill Flanagan, Ethlie Ann Vare, Joel Gallen, Hank Bordowitz, Ted Myers, Gary Klein, Hank Hoffman, Ed Osborne, Felicia Gearhart, Robin Manning, Bob George, Charlie Conrad, Lauren Pollack-Gellert, Michelle Lerner, Matt Baxt, Sebastian Bach.

If anyone feels his or her name is missing from this list in error, please notify me in care of popmuze@netzero.net and I will gladly add it in the next printing of this book, or my memoirs, whichever comes first.

WORKING
MUSICIANS

■

Introduction

It all started the day I saw Jerry Garcia in a laundromat in Santa Fe, New Mexico. Dead for several years by then, this apparition inspired me to begin work on a new novel, which I called *Channeling Dead Rock Stars*. I abandoned the novel a few months later, when I realized I was far more interested in writing the book I'd invented for the main character as his singular claim to fame. That book was *Working Musicians*.

In it, as I had been doing for the past thirty years, I would be talking to live rock stars, as well as total unknowns, itinerant sidemen, studio drummers and plenty of songwriters, maybe a jazz musician or two, someone on the classical side, a country journeyman, a wedding-band guy, lots of struggling bar-band and acoustic-café-circuit types, headliners, one-shots, opening acts.

From these working musicians I would gather war stories and stories of the home front, between tours, studio stories, stories of huge success and utter humiliation, bad managers and chance encounters with fans and superstars and the ghost of Elvis Presley. And from these stories, told in their own voices, I hoped would emerge a larger canvas of memories and epiphanies that make up the everyday circumstances and aspirations of thousands of disparate artists, all united in their common quest to play and to be heard and to make a living doing it.

As the discerning reader will note upon scanning the varied and awesome table of contents of *Working Musicians*, the resulting book has some dead rock stars in it as well. These stories have not been the result of channeling. Having been, as I said, in this career for nearly thirty years, and being famous for never throwing out any newspaper or magazine article with my byline on it, manuscript, tape, floppy disc, notebook, stray piece of paper, etc., I was not about to give up the chance to memorialize my encounters with some of the major musical figures of our time whom fate removed from us all too soon, like Phil Ochs, Laura Nyro, Frank Zappa, and Garcia himself. So you have Phil with the foreboding notion of his creative demise not long before his actual demise. "Both me and the country were deteriorating at the same time," he told me in 1975. "But to my dying day I'll always think about the next possible song." And earthy and ethereal Laura Nyro describing herself as "a goddess of creativity. You're taking care of everyday things, but you're living at the edge of a song," just before being diagnosed with breast cancer. I spoke to Garcia on the phone in 1986, when his philosophy of playing was clear and cogent: "An important part of music is the texture, the layers, and the talk. I'm into the conversation." While Frank Zappa, speaking from the shadows in a Brooklyn motel, some years earlier, held to a more contrary point of view: "The main thing wrong with writers is that they're dealing with something that is almost obsolete but they don't know it yet, which is language. They have a problem similar to people who write music. There's just bunches of problems in getting true meaning across. The only guy who's really got it made is a painter."

Carefully chiseling excerpts out of various other highlights from my copious archives, my object was not to reprint or collect or recall verbatim, but rather to crystallize moments when the superstar became one with the day worker, tilling the creative soil for insights, ramifications, happy accidents. Removed from the trappings of promotion and celebrity, and, foremost, the distracting ruminations of the critic, I left them with only their words to define them, which were, I was not surprised to find, often poignant, illuminating, and revealing.

My approach, ever since my first book, *In Their Own Words: Songs & Songwriters, 1955–1974,* and especially after starting the magazine *GUITAR for the Practicing Musician,* in 1983, has always been to let musicians speak about what they know best, and at some length. Rather than engage them in specious forays into politics, economics, or their fabled social lives, I have felt it to be my mission to get them talking about their craft, the thing they do all day long and often all night long. Here is where I feel they are by far more interesting and interested. At the same time, as a novelist and onetime obsessive lyricist, talking to guitar players, bass players, keyboard players, and the occasional singer, I was determined to avoid the dry how-to or overly technical approach. My feeling was that these words, when spoken from the heart of the subject matter, should transcend mechanics, and I wanted to shape them into something approaching a kind of poetry. In this way, and definitely in this book, I have been able to tap into the frequently frustrated desire of most artists, known and unknown alike, to talk about what they do, what it felt like, what it meant.

Except, perhaps, for the notable exception of Ace Frehley, who, when I asked him how his guitar style evolved, replied after a long, long pause, "It just evolved."

Far more verbal and passionate was his original partner in Kiss, Gene Simmons, who relished talking about the fine art of staging, when he almost burned himself to death the first time he breathed fire during the song "Nothing to Lose," opening for Teenage Lust, Iggy Pop, and Blue Öyster Cult at the Academy of Music in New York City on New Year's Eve, 1973. Or Kool Mo Dee, who waxed positively euphoric about first seeing Grandmaster Flash at the age of twelve and deciding there and then to become a rapper. Here you have Hüsker Dü founder Bob Mould noting, "To be a musician you've got to be callused all over." And 10,000 Maniacs' bass player Steven Gustafson describing their nascent lead singer Natalie Merchant as "probably the strangest person in Jamestown." Bruce Springsteen extols the virtues of playing Pittsburgh on a Thursday night: "The people come out of their gray little houses and for a while you feel like you won something." The Rolling Stones' stalwart Keith Richards sums up the simple joy of songwriting, saying, "Somehow [the songs] never sound as good as they do that first night when you're playing them on the living room couch." To which Rush's verbose drummer Neil Peart had the perfect counterpoint: "To me, the joy of creation is extremely overrated."

One of the most thrilling aspects of doing this book has been that it put me into contact with vast overlapping communities of musicians. Friends telling friends about it, doors opening up into back rooms, where the jam sessions went on all night. It was not dissimilar to the feeling Dan Zanes spoke of in the early days of the Del Fuegos. "You get accepted by these people and you find out that they all associate with each other and you think someday I could be part of this scene where everyone's into music." A write-up in the ASCAP magazine *Playback* resulted in a steady stream of e-mails for several months, which produced at least a half-dozen pieces for the book, some done by interview and others delivered entirely through back-and-forth sessions on this wonderful (and at times instant) modern-day tool. Here was itinerant folkie James Durst with a never-before-published tale straight out of the heady L.A. sixties, of a stolen guitar and lost love. Then there was, appearing on my computer screen one night out of the blue, an almost pitch-perfect piece by Dan Lipton, as current as the moment, about his landing a new job as pit pianist for a show about to open on Broadway, *The Full Monty*. I corresponded in this way with a music professor from Ohio, a Beatlesque duo from Holland, a French chanteuse, a Chinese novelist/composer, an original Bride of Funkenstein, and a woman who channeled Elvis Presley.

Over eggs and coffee at a local luncheonette, my wedding-band maven, Milt Jacoby, gave me about two dozen more stories than I could use. At the renowned Polish Tea Room of the Edison Hotel in New York City, the nearly forgotten anti-folk alt-rock innovator Brenda Kahn touched me deeply with "As an artist you just put the best work out that you can, and it will be meaningful for the people who need to find it. Those people will find it. And it will change people's lives." To which the Canadian poet and songwriter Leonard Cohen affixed a typically mysterious addendum: "Over the years I have somehow fallen into some lives that my songs have led me into, and some of these lives have ended—rather violently, rather sadly."

It is the same kind of musicians' community, in this case Nashville, that embraced Cindy Bullens when she lost her daughter to cancer and helped her to create the compelling *Between Heaven and Earth*. "She obviously provided the inspiration for the songs," she said, speaking of her daughter. "This may sound funny, but there's no question in my mind that after her death, she also kept kicking me in the butt, saying, Get out there, Mom, this is what you need to do." In Austin, the entire community turned up on Ian Moore's guest list when he opened for the Rolling Stones: "Here I am in this maelstrom of energy and everybody's partying and going crazy and having sex with each other, living the rock-and-roll dream, and I'm the one who brought these people into this thing, and I'm just sort of sitting there watching it happen, super-aware of not wanting to piss anybody off." In Boston, in the late 1980s and early 1990s, the scene was at Fort Apache studios, although Sebadoh's Lou Barlow might not agree. "It wasn't like, Juliana Hatfield's recording, so I'll just pop in. It was just a very friendly place for me. It was a place where I knew I could set up time and walk in there cold."

Eschewing the personality profile, the instant biography, the *Behind the Music* ebbs and flows of triumph and disaster that make a musician's life so outsized and ultimately fictional, I strove instead for the defining moments, the nuggets of insight that could shed light on an entire body of work. You could see the notoriously self-effacing Paul Simon wince when someone in the garage where he parked his car asked him if he was famous. "Yeah," he replied, "you know, somewhat, to a degree, I'm famous." T-Bone Wolk, bass player for Hall and Oates, only truly began to know what fame was when he joined the *Saturday Night Live* band. "Whether you've won on *Millionaire* or you just go on *Jerry Springer*, anybody who's on TV, their life changes." For Robby Krieger, life changed when his band, the Doors, fell apart. "If you listen to what I played, it was good for the Doors, but when I tried to put that into another situation, it was totally wrong. After the Doors broke up, when I'd go to a jam session, I'd be out in left field." When Cheryl James broke up Salt-N-Pepa, the group was still capable of making millions, but that was no longer a priority to her. "It was all hype and glamour and glitz and people on their knees tying your shoes and Grammies and stylists and hair and makeup and drama. It got to be exhausting. I felt like I was being pulled in ten different directions. I didn't have control of my life and that's a bad bad feeling." Fame was like a cruel mirror to Peter Tork of the Monkees, showing him a face he didn't like at all. "I think I was a sort of Gatsby. I was isolated and did not have a continuing sense of community. At the same time, by giving my money away I thought I was returning something to the community. I didn't see myself as apologizing, which is how I see myself now."

In constructing the book, the most important thing to me was the sequence; like a mix tape, the pieces needed to be in thematic blocks, with interesting segues, points, counterpoints, corroboration, elaboration, revelation—and then the startling change of pace, bringing it all up a notch, lifting it to the next level. Within this concept, where context is everything, the leadoff slot is especially central. In it should be all the elements that will be touched upon and filled in by the hundred or so voices to follow. Johnny Bee Badanjek, the once and hopefully future drummer for Mitch Ryder, lately taken to oil painting to fend off fallow times, perfectly epitomized the working musician I sought. His eloquent harangue on the state of the art of freelance drumming set a high standard for the stories to follow: "It's a real rough life, especially the older you get. I can't remember half the stuff I was on. Even the biggest guys are always hustling, looking for work. It doesn't matter if you're playing with Madonna. Madonna goes out for a month and then, boom, you're back looking again. Everybody becomes an oldies act at some point. A lot of guys say I'll never do that, but all of a sudden here they are." Later on in the book there are some substantive musical motivations on naked display. "We had to settle on one thing," said Aerosmith's Steven Tyler, "and that was that we were going to give up the drugs and play like we owned the world and we want it back again." "The next time I went to L.A. it was to headline at the Troubadour," Neil Sedaka recalls of his 1976 comeback. "I took over the town. I wanted it with a vengeance. My old manager said I'd never make it again; that drove me. The critics in L.A. couldn't believe that anybody could write and sing with such enthusiasm, with such spirit, and with this vengeance." As a veteran hip-hop songwriter and producer, Darren Lighty knows you have to prove yourself every time out. "As much as you're successful in this business, there are people who don't want you to succeed for whatever reason. Eddie F and myself have been in this business for over ten years, and that's a hard thing to do. So much so that we're honest with ourselves in thinking that okay it's redemption time every time we get in the studio." Roger McGuinn caught onto something truly cosmic—perhaps unintentionally—in his memories of meeting the Beatles: "I think what initially attracted me to the Beatles was the fact that they were using folk changes. I thought they were doing their version of the fifties rock-and-roll/rockabilly sound and the folk thing combined. When I got to meet them I found out they didn't know they were doing that. They didn't know how to fingerpick and they didn't play banjos or mandolins and they weren't coming from where I thought they were coming from at all, which I'd given them credit for. I thought they knew all that stuff and were just being real slick about it. But it was just an accident. It was a great accident." In concluding the book, sideman to the stars Emil Richards was a little bit more effusive when describing his time on the stage with Frank Sinatra: "I used to get goose bumps and think what a thrill to be with somebody so good he could make you feel like that. I wish all my loved ones could have heard it. I used to stand right next to Frank when he sang, and those are the moments I remember."

It is the hope that these moments, taken individually, will prove to be inspirational, entertaining, thought-provoking—or all of the above—and as a whole will provide fascinating, informative, and rarely glimpsed slices of life that any musician or anyone who wants to be a musician or once wanted to be a musician or who wants to know about musicians will read with empathy and identification. But jazz drummer and Miles Davis protégé Lenny White is well within his rights to fret about the future. "What happened is, since the 1980s, you no longer have to be a musician to make music. Kids that were studying to be musicians now say, wait a minute, I'm studying, knocking myself out here, sacrificing, trying to learn my instrument, and I could just get a program and put it together and make five times more money than if I was going to school. That's what it's become. It's a whole other working situation. A whole other dynamic"—so is Television guitarist Richard Lloyd, who prefers to put his money on the continuation—despite changing styles and shrinking playlists and venues, and in the face of or aided and abetted by technology—of what he describes as "an untouchable urge," this desire to play music, formed early and often openly in defiance of reality. "That's well protected," says Lloyd. "If you don't have that in the beginning then you might as well hang it up right away."

As for me? In these matters I tend to side with Garcia: I'm into the conversation.

STARTING OUT 1

Johnny Bee Badanjek
You Need the Work

Drummer, Mitch Ryder and the Detroit Wheels

A friend down the street had an old snare drum he wasn't playing anymore. So he gave it to me for twenty-five dollars and I started playing. I was in two band classes in school, orchestra and band. Then my parents got me private lessons. I got pretty good at what I was doing. Somehow I got in a wedding band and started making money on the weekends at twelve years old—a hundred or two hundred dollars. My brother had a paper route and I was making way more than him. Then the girls started coming into play. There it is. All right, I think I'll be a drummer.

My parents had a real big house in the northern section of Detroit. When my brother and I got a little older my dad stopped renting the upstairs out and we moved up there. I had one whole room that was covered on all four walls with 45 record sleeves just taped together floor to ceiling and my first drum set was in there and a big stereo. So I'd just blast out, learning how to play drums by playing to everybody else's records. When we first started that's where Mitch Ryder and the Detroit Wheels practiced.

We were known as Billy Lee and the Rivieras and we were very successful for about a year or two playing all these big ballrooms in Detroit, sold out dances with Smokey Robinson and the Miracles, Martha Reeves and the Vandellas, Stevie Wonder.

We were the house band on *1270*, which was a Dave Prince show on channel 7. We'd always be on TV. In my basement we made this tape for Dave Prince to send to the producer Bob Crewe in New York. Bob loved the tape and wanted to bring the band to New York. We didn't realize that he didn't care so much for the band, he just loved the sound of Mitch's voice.

So we all took a train from Detroit to New York. I was sixteen. Bob Crewe's office, Genius Incorporated, was at Sixty-first and Broadway. Bob was on the sixth floor, Atlantic Records was on the second. His office was about the size of a bathroom. We set up and played "Shake a Tail Feather" or something. Charlie Callelo was there. He drags Crewe in. "Bob, you gotta keep this band. They're phenomenal." Then again, Bob does the first record with this big orchestra of session players with just Jim McCarty on guitar. The song was called "I Need Help." Then the Beatles' "Help" came out, so that sank like a rock. Then he put out a record with the band that harnessed our energy, which was "Jenny Take a Ride." That came out in '64 and broke in Philadelphia.

We all lived in one room at the Coliseum Hotel on Seventy-first and Broadway for a couple of years playing six days a week for $105 a man—Trude Hellers, the 8th Wonder, the Metropole, with Gene Krupa, Dizzy Gillespie. Four sets a night with Jimmy Castor. We were living the Manhattan life, waking up at five in the afternoon, going to the gig. When we went out to promote the hit single, everywhere we'd go we'd buy records. We'd buy the most obscure R&B songs and we'd learn from that. We were in awe of James Brown and I talked to all the drummers James had. The early guys who constantly got fired, who you'd find in Atlanta playing the Whiskey Au Go Go with a local band. There were some phenomenal drummers. They would take us out to the Blind Pig in Atlanta and we'd be the only white guys there.

It's a real rough life, especially the older you get. I can't remember half the stuff I was on. Bob Ezrin once asked me to tour with Alice Cooper. I said I wanna go home, put my own band together, and write songs, which was such a nice brilliant statement at that time. McCarty was down south just leaving Cactus in Memphis. I said get your ass up here and we'll put a band together. So he came up to Detroit, brought a keyboard player with him, and we started the Rockets and proceeded to play every night between Ann Arbor, Toledo, Detroit trying to get a record deal. John Sinclair managed the band. I was the singer. I did that until I collapsed a lung. They had to blow it back up in the hospital. In '75 we got so tired we broke up for a year.

I probably could have pursued studio work more and I should have, by moving to L.A. or New York or Nashville, 'cause that's where the work is. I did a commercial in '89 and they said, "Hey where are you from? There ain't a drummer in L.A. who plays with such fire." I'm in Detroit! All you gotta do is pick up the phone and I'm here. They never called me. The crew in L.A. told me I could do every commercial in this town, they're all yours. I should have moved out there. But I was never really one to constantly want to sit and play jingles. Now, though, when you're starving in Detroit, jingles would be fine.

Even the biggest guys are always hustling, looking for work. It doesn't matter if you're playing with Madonna. Madonna goes out for a month. It's not like she's on a ten-year tour. And then boom, you're back looking around again. I was out playing with the Romantics. Last thing we did was opening at the Football Hall of Fame in Canton, outside, for a hundred thousand people. Good gig. Then those guys decided not to work this summer; they decided to work on their record. Last year I was painting, doing pastels and oils, because the work was so slow. Mitch and I got into a huge fight and I haven't talked to him since. I played with him for twenty years on and off.

Everybody becomes an oldies act at some point. A lot of guys say, "I'll never do that. I hate it." But all of a sudden here they are. Fireworks is always a good headliner. Nobody can compete with fireworks. They'll have these free shows where you can draw eighty thousand people in the middle of Illinois. Hey, Mitch Ryder's on the show; we can hear "Devil with a Blue Dress On." But the fireworks will be the main draw. It's like one big circle back around. Sometimes on these shows there'll be ten acts, just like in the early sixties when we played the Brooklyn Fox on a Murray the K show and there was one set of drums and you'd just have to run out there and throw your snare drum up. It's the same today, except you don't carry gear anymore. You carry drumsticks on the plane. You get there and they got a rent-a-kit and that's what everybody's using.

Right now I'm covering for a friend of mine who's on the road with Robert Bradley's Blackwater Surprise. Since June I've been playing every night, three sets a night, with this bar band, for a hundred bucks. No money, a lot of carting gear, no road crew, and all these young girls with forty-two piercings everywhere you can think of, the young alternative college crowd. But it's packed every night. We had the Chili Peppers a few weeks ago sit in with us. We've had Nazareth, Night Ranger, Kid Rock. In the meantime, I've been writing songs, which I always do. I've got three hundred songs here. I need a publishing deal, so I've been talking to Bug Music. I just sat with these guys the other day and we're thinking of going and recording.

There are two things that make a person complete, love and work. Freud used to say you need the love and the work. Most of the time musicians are creating something, they're in the house writing, but you have to be out there on the road, playing and getting paid for it. You need that work too.

Harry Connick Jr.

If I Wanted to Have Fun
I'd Be Out Fishing

Keyboard Player

It wasn't until I was about sixteen or seventeen that I started listening to Erroll Garner and Thelonious Monk. It wasn't until I was nineteen or twenty that I started really listening to Duke Ellington, Frank Sinatra, Louis Armstrong, and people like that. As I got older I realized that the greatest musical challenge lay in jazz by far, and that was the kind of music that I chose to play and to dedicate my life to, and it also provided me the most enjoyment.

I don't spend any time at all thinking about people who are less than genius, 'cause it's a waste of time. If you're gonna be a baseball player, you're gonna look at Joe DiMaggio's batting technique. You're not gonna look at some third-string guy. If you look at the cumulative works of Cole Porter, Harold Arlen, George Gershwin, Hoagy Carmichael, and Irving Berlin, among many others, those songs, not only lyrically, but melodically and musically, are at such an incredibly high level that it's very difficult to match. It's very intimidating, but on the other hand, it's inspiring and challenging to see if I can try to match that level of musicianship. If I hear something that Duke Ellington plays that interests me—which is everything he does—I try to figure it out. If I hear something that Frank

Sinatra sings, I'll try to do that—technically. As far as emotionally, it's kind of hard to capture what those people are capturing, because I haven't lived long enough. But on a technical level, I try to get a big sound like Monk out of the piano. I don't practice scales. That's nonsense, really. I mean, I played so much classical music when I was young that, as for virtuosity, that's something I have no problem with. But as far as playing, as far as real technique, that's what I'm trying to practice.

I play so much, and I'm so busy, that when I relax among friends, I try not to resort to playing piano too much. I mean, I don't play for fun. When I'm doing an album, I'm doing it to try to further jazz music, as opposed to doing something I think is fun. If I wanted to have fun, I'd be out fishing. Music is something that's extremely demanding and depressing and requires all of my thought and it's very difficult to accomplish anything in the idiom of music that I play, so I don't really have a tremendous amount of fun. Most of it is agonizing over the complexities of it all, but once in a while, we hit a groove and we have a good time.

Early in my career, when I went on the road with *When Harry Met Sally*, that was a very difficult show to do, 'cause there were thirty-five people on the stage, as opposed to me and a bass player. It was a whole orchestra. And the reason it was so difficult is probably twofold. One was that we were dealing with a different orchestra in every city. We weren't bringing the same band with us, so I had to rehearse and then do the show at night, which was demanding physically and mentally, just 'cause it's hard to sing all that much. The other reason was because it's difficult to do the same show night after night. Being a jazz musician, you like to improvise, and this show didn't lend itself to a lot of improvisation. When I'm with my trio, then we are creating music. On that particular tour, I couldn't create, 'cause everybody was playing an arrangement. But I did it because I've always wanted to be in that position and I'd never want to be back where I was. Now I have the opportunity to broadcast my music to literally millions of people through movies and through albums and through television appearances and I would not trade that any day for sitting at home playing to myself.

Richard Lloyd

(richard@richardlloyd.com)

An Untouchable Urge

Guitarist, Television

When I was younger I made a lot of mistakes. I once went to one of those New Music Seminars. They had a panel called "A Million Dollars' Worth of Mistakes." These lawyers and A&R people were going to discuss all of the things that could go wrong in an artist's career. So I go in there and it was jam-packed and people were asking questions and people were talking, and after everything they said could happen I said, Yeah, this happened to me. After about fifteen minutes I left the room completely depressed. What I'm saying is, I made some ridiculous and major mistakes. The first mistake I made was not being like Mick Jagger, who was a business major. I'm like one of those traditional artists who knew nothing about business and got completely screwed.

But that can't affect your feeling about music. That's an untouchable urge within. That's well protected. If you don't have that in the beginning then you might as well hang it up right away. When I was a teenager and decided to be a musician, I knew a lot of people who were much better musicians than I was, whose parents were wealthy and they had all the instruments they wanted. And none of them went anywhere. They didn't have that internal demand—you don't know where it comes from—that you have to play music. You have to have it as a kind of faith and walk the plank with it. There's no job security. Zero. Less than none. There's minus job security. How many musicians get wealthy from this, compared to the amount of people who go into it? It's exceedingly slim. You end up in debt to your patron, the record company. It can be a nightmare and if you're lucky they'll offer you a limousine ride to the poorhouse.

I was always able to get by playing music, but you have to understand that to be able to get by playing music you need the ability to accept complete and utter poverty for long stretches at a time. Every once in a while I used to pawn my instrument. It was safer in the pawnshop than it was with me for a certain time. If you had a gig you had to go get an advance to get your instrument out. There was one pawnshop that had both Johnny Thunders's and my guitars. I remember one guy, because Johnny and I did some co-bills, and the guy was like, "I gotta see the pawn tickets, man. I'm not givin' ya a dime more than the pawn amount."

After Television disbanded, I did some solo albums and I played on some records, not as much as I would have liked. I'd get a lot of guys saying, "I would have loved to have you on my record," and I'm like well, why didn't you call me? "Well, I thought you'd turn me down" or "I was sure you were busy." This is the dilemma of having a certain amount of fame but not enough to thumb your nose at work.

Playing with John Doe was a fun experience for me. We did forty cities in a Winnebago. Usually you're in a tour van or a tour bus. If you're lucky, you get out of the van and into a bus. I don't know where John got it into his head that it would be fun to get into a goddamned mobile home! Remember a band called the Golden Palominos? They had a steady guitar player who quit one day, leaving them with two or three shows left on the tour. Anton

Fier called and said, "Listen, can you learn fifteen songs in two rehearsals?" I said, "No, Anton, I can't learn fifteen songs in two rehearsals. But I can look like I have. I won't know them, but nobody else will know that. You tell me the keys and I'll listen through once." It worked out fine. That's how I met Matthew Sweet. Matthew was in that band and we played a couple of his songs. We really got along and that's where that relationship was formed. I ended up going on the road with him quite a bit doing the lead guitar. That was great for me because, whereas in Television there's a kind of flipflop of rhythm and lead and there's interlocking guitar parts—and in my own work I have to come up with basically all the parts—but with Matthew all I had to do was play leads all the time.

I have a new CD coming out soon. I'm very excited about it. Because of the Internet, I have fans all over the world in small pockets. We'll see if I can make a success out of this lower level of sales base. I do some producing and some playing on some stuff now and again. I've been teaching guitar and vocal studies for a year or two. That's good. It's made me a lot stronger. I have a rehearsal studio and give lessons. I probably play more physical hours on the instrument and think more about music at the moment than I ever have. I'm constantly practicing. Lately I've been playing with the band from the record every Wednesday at Manitoba's [in New York City].

I love playing. It's not the playing the tours that gets you. It's having it stop. That's what really knocks you for a loop. You're in this momentum. People are taking care of you. It's like people who learn to live in a hospital—being institutionalized. In a way, tours are just like that. You're guaranteed your meals, a bed and fresh sheets. People are applauding at you, paying attention to you. Camaraderie develops between you and the crew. And then all of a sudden, it's over. They drop you in front of your house. All of your friends have forgotten you because you've been away for so long. You're estranged from your family. It's like coming home from war. There's no more stimulus. What are you going to do, twiddle your thumbs? A lot of people go off of the deep end on account of it. They can't handle having the stimuli stop. I love touring. It's a real tough thing when you have one gig a month or one gig every six weeks. You need to play every day to build your strength and your chops. If you have a bad gig you tend to beat yourself up internally. I mean, everything is riding on this one gig. If you're out touring ninety or 130 dates one gig doesn't mean as much because you have tomorrow. That's really important. That's the only way a musician is going to get that tough skin.

We've also got this Television reunion show coming up, which is basically a one-off. There may or may not be other gigs behind it. But right now a festival in England has made a pretty good offer and there are some other bands on the bill that we like, Yo La Tengo being one of them. We like to think of ourselves now as like one of those old jazz quartets; you know, they get together and make a record and then they do other things and then they return ten or twelve years later, and maybe do more years after that.

I remember an audition we did for Atlantic Records. It was January 3 or something like that and there had been a blizzard and we had to go up from the Lower East Side to Sixtieth and Broadway, to the Atlantic studios. So we got there and Keith Richards and Ron Wood are in the big room mixing "Crazy Mama" from the *Black and Blue* album. So we have to set up our paltry equipment in the actual studio itself. After a while, Keith says hello and good-bye and he leaves and all the Atlantic people come in. There were seven of them. They had come from a Sarah Vaughan session—that's why they were late. That's some co-bill, Sarah Vaughan and Television.

The plan had been to put something on tape first but because Keith was there we couldn't do it. The engineer said, "There's no speakers in the studio, so I can't do any vocals in there." So he put the vocals in the control room. The music was in the big room. So the seven of them from the record company would go back and forth listening to the song—just the music—and then go running back to hear the vocals. Finally, Ahmet Ertegun turns to Jerry Wexler and says, "Jerry, I can't sign this band. This is not earth music."

And that was it. They passed. But that was one of the most endearing things I had ever heard. It wasn't like, "Jerry, I can't sign them. They suck." It was, "Jerry, this is not earth music."

In a way it was true. You needed to be a different kind of visionary to sign us.

Tracy Nelson

Self-Indulgence

Singer, Mother Earth

At first we were all so serious and intense about what we were doing. We were making music with a capital M. In San Francisco, we'd rehearse for hours and hours 'cause it was so much fun playing. The first time we performed as a unit after all this endless rehearsing we were so tanked up that we were terrible. But they absolutely loved us and we got the gig at the Straight Theater. Within six months we were signed by Mercury Records. I went from earning thirty-five dollars a week to earning sixty-five thousand dollars a year. And of course we gave it all away. We were all so democratic and everybody got their cut and we lived high off the hog on the road. The money was just there and was always going to be there. It made me think I could do whatever the hell I wanted to and get away with it. I needed discipline when I was first starting out, and I had total freedom. Now, I don't think I would have accepted any discipline if it had been given to me, but I wasn't at all sure of what I was doing. And to be pandered to like we were is not very valuable for anybody. There was total self-indulgence for a long period and it was nearly the ruination of me.

The first few years I was pretty hard on my voice. I was hoarse a lot and even when I wasn't hoarse I sang too hard. I would frequently be agitated or annoyed or just jacked up from adrenaline or drunk. So I would oversing. Every time I got up to sing I was just trying to get everything out all at once. If I let myself I could still just push as hard as I could and let everything out every second. But that's not really the best way to make music.

But I was contending with a lot of hassles. Dealing with the musicians, trying to keep them from each other's throats, trying to keep everybody from getting drunk all the time on the gigs, dealing with promoters who treated me like garbage when I thought they should be treating me with respect—I was a great musician, after all. I tend to take charge in situations, or try to, and therefore I have always taken on these responsibilities, and I've been pretty weighed down by them. It took me a long time to recognize the things you need to worry about and the things you don't need to worry about. It's my biggest fault, always having to have a say in everything and not being able to let somebody else handle something that's important in my life. Also, I had no recognition at the time of the kind of conflict that goes on when you work with male musicians. I didn't understand where it was coming from. They would get defensive and snotty and I wouldn't understand why they would come down on me so hard for doing what I thought I had to do. My work suffered and my performing suffered, because by the time the show came around I'd be so tense my throat would go, or I'd just be physically exhausted.

It's difficult to prepare for an album when you're hustling on the road trying to keep your living together. I've always felt rushed when I've gone into the studio. People always recognize my potential, but each time I make a record they go, uh-oh, Tracy's made another of her self-indulgent albums. I don't think so, but they do. They think my taste in music is too eclectic to be salable and I've never been able to prove them wrong. And it's been the same with every record company. But my goal, and I swear to God I'll still do it, is to one day have a song on the pop charts, a song on the R&B charts, and a song on the country charts.

Lita Ford

One of the Guys

Guitarist

Guitar playing to me is like riding a bicycle. You never forget how to do it. You might get a little sore if you haven't done it in a while. When I was younger I traveled a lot; my parents were always living in different areas: Boston, Dallas, L.A., London. I was kind of all over the place and I never really got close to anybody, so I spent a lot of time playing guitar. My first guitar was a chocolate-colored Gibson SG. I got a job working in a hospital and I saved up $450 and I went out and bought it. Later I sold it to one of my old roadies. I wish I still had it. I could play it good; I mean, I didn't think I could play it good, but when I think back at what I was playing, it was good. I used to sit there with records and learn all this stuff. I could play all these Black Sabbath riffs, Grand Funk, and people would come up to me and go, "Hey, you can play that?" Well, yeah, can't you? It was just sort of second nature.

I used to love Johnny Winter. That guy sings and plays at the same time and doesn't even watch his hands. He's looking off into left field while he's singing and playing. I thought I'd like to do that, so I just worked at it. I worked at not looking at my hands when I play. I don't even have inlays on my neck when I play. There are inlays, but they're not in the right places.

Like it'll say "Lita Ford" instead of a dot on the third fret, a dot on the fifth fret, a dot on the seventh fret. So sometimes when people come in and pick up my guitar, they're like, "What fret is this?"

Before the Runaways I played bass with this band in Long Beach with some guys I went to high school with, which is how Kim Fowley found me. The Runaways were looking for a bass player and a guitar player. Fowley called up thinking I was a bass player. I said, "I'm not a bass player, I'm a guitar player."

It's very flattering when people say to me, "Is that a girl doing that? Is that you? It sounds like a guy." To me that's very flattering because it says to me that it's strong and it's powerful, 'cause girls are supposed to be weak, right? When I was auditioning players for my band, sometimes a drummer would come in or a keyboard player or something, and I'd say, "Get rid of him, he plays like a girl." I would say that. So when a guy tells me I play like a guy, that's a compliment. I love it.

With my new band the guys have jam sessions before I get there. When I get there we work on new stuff. We rehearse two weeks, take two weeks off, then rehearse two more weeks and that's what we do until we go out on the road. I don't think a band gets completely tight until they've done a good two hundred shows. You can sit home and play till your fingers bleed, but you're not going to get it out like you do live.

I just feel like I'm in my own field here, like it's all mine. I don't think being a woman really has that much to do with it. If you're good you're good. In the Runaways it was a problem; there weren't a lot of female musicians and people didn't take us seriously. But I think now there's a lot of women musicians out there and the guys just seem to take them as one of the guys if they're good.

Dan Zanes
A Professional Attitude

Guitarist, the Del Fuegos

We started out playing cheap guitars. I didn't even change strings for the first four months I was in the band. Nobody told me you had to change them, let alone tune them. That was our thing. We thought it would be a great statement playing cheap guitars. The band would be really huge but still only play Danelectros.

When we went to make our first record and we met our producer, Mitchell Froom, we played for him and he checked out the tunes. Then he looked at all our gear and he said, there's some potential here, but I'm not going into the studio with those guys until they shape up their gear. He came over to our house and he talked to us about groove and attitude. He said, listen to some old Stones records, listen to the stuff you dig, like Tom Petty. It's all got groove and it's all got an attitude. It's the attitude of wanting to be a professional musician. Not where it takes your edge away, and not where it takes your energy, or where you don't rock as hard. But the whole concept of taking it seriously has made us rock a lot harder and put on a better show.

The biggest thing to dawn on us was that if you practice a lot you get better a lot faster. I didn't realize that maybe there was a big difference between an hour and four hours of practice a day. At the time we didn't have the concept of a backbeat. A backbeat was just something that you pulled out from the whole jungle of beats. Somewhere in there was a backbeat. It didn't take us long to realize that, wow, if this feels so good, I wonder what else is going to feel really good. It just starts a whole chain of events where you know there's so much ahead of you to learn.

We went through a transitional stage from being proud to be a garage band to really seeing the limitations and wanting to take it one step further. We realized that none of the bands we really dug were garage bands. We were listening to professional bands. And we wanted to be accepted by other professionals. For instance, Tom Petty was supposed to come to one of our shows at the Roxy. After the second night he hadn't shown up and we were totally bummed out. So we were in the hotel room at 3 A.M. and the phone rings and it was Tom Petty apologizing that he couldn't make the scene. We talked for about twenty minutes then he said, "Hey, give me a call tomorrow and you guys can come out to the house." We were so nervous. It was really living out one of our biggest fantasies. Tom told us how he met Phil Everly. He said he was so blown away he couldn't even look him in the eye. He said, "I couldn't believe I was talking to Phil Everly. Next thing I know I'm in London and I get a call and it's Phil and he wants to know if I want to drive to the reunion concert with him at the Royal Albert Hall." So it was just him and Phil Everly in a cab going to the show.

Those are the kind of things that keep you going, besides just working on your own and digging music. You get accepted by these people and you find out that they all associate with each other and you think someday I could be part of this scene where everyone's into music. These guys meant a lot to us when we were a garage band. We always dug these people and it would be great if someday people dug us in that way. It's really something to strive for.

Max Cavalera
Total Sex Pistols

Guitarist, Sepultura

We first got into music not as musicians but as fans. When I was about twelve, we took a bus to see a concert about six hours from where I live [in Brazil]. It was this thrash band from Rio that was heavily influenced by Voivod. They were the ones that made me want to play music. They played with so much power and adrenaline that after the show I went home with my mind completely set that I'm gonna learn to play the guitar. I'm gonna be a musician.

I ended up buying a really cheap guitar. But it was the only thing I could afford. I took lessons for one week and I got in a fight with my teacher. He was trying to teach me original Brazilian bossa nova stuff. I was talking about Motörhead and he's talking to me about Antonio Carlos Jobim. So we didn't get along very good. I played the stuff I liked for him and he was like, "This is all noise, man." I said, "But this is what I want to play." He said, "You don't need a teacher to play this kind of music." So I said, "Well, fine, then I don't need your lessons either."

I learned a lot from a couple of people from my neighborhood who were more like rock musicians. There was this guy who was a big Led Zeppelin fan who showed me some of the riffs that helped me to actually start to play other people's music. At that time I was really into heavy stuff, but for some reason I thought Led Zeppelin were cool. They didn't bother me like they did some of my friends at that time.

I think poverty and lack of access to instruments and places to play gave Sepultura an aspect of frustration that fueled us to play with fire and an attitude of anger and power. The fact that we were struggling came through our music. When we started to play nobody would book us. So we wound up playing at a lot of Battle of the Bands competitions. We actually got signed to a record deal at one of them. This one had a jury judging the band. We were like really cussing on stage, and this old lady who was one of the judges was right in front of me. She got mad at us for cussing, so she cut my mike off and told us to get off the stage. So I went right in front of her as the music kept playing and I just collected a ball of spit inside my mouth and I looked right at her and just delivered it to her face. It was total punk rock! We got thrown off the stage by security, and the lady was screaming that she'd get us killed. It was total Sex Pistols!

This one dude who was watching the whole thing came up to us after the show. He was from a record store and they had decided they wanted to start a label. He said, "Man, I don't like your music, but I love the whole riot scene. I'll sign you guys just for that." So their first investment was an EP that was us on one side and this more established band, Overdose, on the other side.

Many people all the time ask me in Brazil, "How come you guys made it big and nobody else did?" I say, it's not an easy road. You have to really want it hard. I did things other people wouldn't do. The biggest thing was in 1987, after we did an album in Brazil called *Schizophrenia*. I was determined to get it released in the States. So I managed to get a free airline ticket from a friend of mine in Brazil who worked at Pan Am. The deal was I had to look normal. I had to pull all my hair back. I had to wear a tie. So I said okay, I'll make that sacrifice in order to get my band signed. I went to ten different record labels in New York with this album. I just went like a complete newcomer. I had no idea whether I was going to see anybody. I didn't know the presidents of any of the labels. I just met the receptionists and said, "Can you pass this album to your A&R guy?" I came back to Brazil two days later the same way, with the tie, hair back. In two months we got a call from Roadrunner that they were going to sign us.

Everybody refers to our first gig in the States as the one where we opened at the Ritz for King Diamond. We got a really killer reaction and from then on people started taking us very seriously and things opened up. But actually our first gig was the night before at a place called Zone D.K. The funny thing about that place was that it turned into an S&M club after we played. So we're walking around the venue after our show and there are these naked guys on the floor with chains and chicks in leather. We're going like, "What's going on here? This is crazy." Not that they don't have things like that in Brazil, but I guess we were always too young to be allowed in to see it. That was quite a first gig. Unfortunately, we never played another gig like it. It was a one of a kind.

Kool Mo Dee

Raising the Bar

Rapper

What changed my life from being a fan to becoming an artist was one night in November 1978 when I was up at the Autoban in Manhattan. Basically I went to see Love Bug Starsky, who was on from twelve to two and then again from four to six. That particular night Grandmaster Flash turned the music down on Love Bug Starsky, who got off very reluctantly, because he was in a good space and everybody was dancin'. Now there's dead silence. But the crowd still wants to dance; a DJ's supposed to keep them up as long as he can. Never let them sit down. We didn't know that Flash was doing that intentionally. He didn't really care if you danced. I mean he wanted you to dance, but he mainly wanted you to pay attention to him. So he brought the music to a dead stop and the spotlight came on. It wasn't really a spotlight; a light came on and one of his DJs, Kid Creole, basically gave the crowd in echo form a big, long, elaborate introduction:

"Ladies and gentlemen, welcome to the greatest show on earth. Never before have you seen anything like this. . . ."

And I'm like, an introduction for a DJ? I've never seen anything like this before. He's using the echo chamber and it's like he's saying who he is and it's like, "Kid Creooooooole.

Solid . . . solid . . . solid. Gold . . . gold . . . gold." This is something new. I'm not as skeptical as before. Shortly after that he said, "Are you ready?" And simultaneously he cued Flash and he came on and got another MC who was called Cowboy, who I'd never seen before either.

Soon as Kid Creole and Flash hit the music, Cowboy started rhyming. I'm blown away this point. I'd heard an echo chamber, I'd seen a DJ cut on cue with another MC coming in at the same time. Cowboy's rhyming and saying, "What's my name?" and the crowd is responding back and he's saying the most colorful things I have ever heard. A guy who's spelling his name out seems very simplistic now, but back then I was like, "What the hell was that? Say what's my name? Champagne! Say what's my name?"

He had all of these sayings that everybody knew and we suddenly felt like we were behind in something. These Bronx people knew what was happening. We were like, "Who are these kids from the Bronx coming down here with these crowds who already know what to say?" We had to learn what to say real quick if we wanted to particpate. You didn't want to be left out of hip-hop at that time.

After he finished, he passed the mike. Which we'd never heard of either and you heard: "One, two, three, four, Melle Mel what ya waiting for?" Melle Mel gets on and he proceeds to do metaphors. This is the changing point for me from being a fan to this is what I want to do for the rest of my life. He goes, "I make Alaska hot, I make Africa cold." That was ingenious to me. He went on this long rhyme and he said, "From Melle Mel from the top of the World Trade to the depths of hell." And I was like, That's it. That's the formula. How many incredible things can you do? How many can be put into rhyme form to wow the crowd?

Shortly after that, Grandmaster Flash started scratching,

which we also now take very very much for granted. He's doing this record called "Apache" and everybody went berserk. And while he's playing the record, he's scratching it back and forth and it's like warp speed and we can't comprehend what's happening. I'm watching it with my mouth wide open like a little kid. I just couldn't believe it. Shortly after that, Kid Creole stops the music again and says the "Never before have you seen this greatest show on earth" thing again. Grandmaster Flash is now doing what's commonly known as backspinning. That was it. I was literally not thinking about dancing anymore. All I'm thinking about is how I was going to be onstage doing what I just saw. I was blown away and that was the moment that changed my life.

I'd wanted to do it before, but now I had a passion for it. I was just starting high school and I began writing rhymes secretly. My legacy is that I was going around to all of these parties, following Grandmaster Flash. But anywhere anybody had parties, I would go to them. Sometimes three or four a night. And I was always like Mr. T, standing at the front of the ropes with my arms folded, and I would look at the MC that was rhyming and shake my head and give him the thumbs-down. Very slowly, very wrestling-like. So I was already known before I even said a rhyme. Who the hell is the little pipsqueak always standing in the front of the crowd shaking his head as we rhyme? So I just went around from party to party, standing in front, usually in something all white or all red, from Kangol to sneaker.

Finally I decided to test my stuff. I got on the mike as we sat at the café on lunch break in school. We were one of the first schools to play music and I remember everybody danced to records like "Good Times." I did the same thing that Flash did, in reverse, from an MC's standpoint. Don't play anything that they can dance to cause I wanna rhyme. I wanted them to hear my rhyme. My DJ at the time was a guy named Dano B. and he basically cut the record to a very slowed-down beat and I started rhyming but I rhymed double time. I wanted a slow beat and to rhyme fast. I knew that would blow the crowd away. I became kinda popular overnight. I started raising the bar early on.

When I was young I planned on being a boxer. I was always an Ali, Bruce Lee, and Sugar Ray Leonard fan. The one thing that they all had in common was flash. I was like, Okay, I have to be flashy, but with substance. I couldn't just come in dressed like Liberace and rhyme. I was planning rhymes before I knew what hip-hop was. I would have rhymes for each of my opponents. It worked out differently, but at least I didn't have to get punched. Basically that's when I started to figure out that I needed an angle to separate me. I had to stand out.

One thing I never respected was off-the-top-of-the-head rhymes. I get it now, but I never respected off-the-top-of-the-head before, even though there's an art to that. For me it's absolutely about putting thought into rhymes. After putting thought into it, then you go to the styles and how you're going to say it. You have to be passionate about it. I think nothing on the planet can be done without passion. A lot of people take it for granted. Some of it is a God-given talent. But a lot more of it is hours of practice.

In 1980 we made our first record, *New Rap Language*, which was all of the fast rhymes. Being our first record, we knew nothing about production or sound. The technology wasn't what it is today. We were in a situation where we thought we had to get it right in one take. We didn't know we could do it over. The bass player, the guitar player, and the keyboard guy were all in the same room. The stuff was bleeding over. As a matter of fact, we might have even recorded it in mono.

This was the early days of rap, when people were skeptical, and we were ahead of the curve. We were on tour with the Bar-Kays. The crowd was going berserk for us and the Bar-Kays would have to go on after us. That's where some of the backlash in hip-hop started coming from. To those guys, we were not musicans. They would say, "They don't play instruments. They cover other peoples' songs and basically they just rhyme over records. Where's the band? The DJ's scratchin' and he's rhyming and the kids like this? It's not real." Shortly after that, we started getting our own tours.

Eventually, I wound up going solo, which was a learning process in itself, in terms of signing with a record label. I used to talk every day to a guy who was working as a box boy in that company. I kinda felt sorry for him because he had all this knowledge and ambition and he was just a box boy and nobody paid him any attention. So he was like, "I know a guy named Teddy Riley who plays music. You're one of the best guys over here. You should hook up with him." So he hooked me up. He introduced me to Teddy Riley and we made a record together, *Go See the Doctor*. The rest is history.

Kevin Kadish

Show Me the Money

Singer-Songwriter

I'd have to say that the hardest things to deal with in the music business are all the false promises. People like to hype you up using words like *genius* and *smash*, but frankly these words get to be so overused that after a while they don't really mean anything.

I had a development deal to do some demos with Republic Records, a label distributed through Universal. Very few artists get signed off of development deals, but some do. So, I did some demos for them. Two weeks after I finished recording, there was a big buyout involving Seagrams, the parent company of Universal. When I talked to the people over at Republic about my demos they said that they had to make decisions concerning artists who were already signed to full record deals and they weren't going know anything about my situation for at least five months. I didn't want to wait around that long.

I hired a manager who told me, "Look, I'm going to talk to them and if they can't make a decision this month, we're going to take those demos and get you another record deal out of it." I guess they decided to pass, because I never heard from my A&R guy again. I did, however, get a call from a business affairs person at Universal, who said they needed my Social Security number because they wanted to send me a W-2, "for the twelve thousand dollars we gave you for the two songs you recorded for us." I never saw a penny of that money. They paid the musicians directly. They paid the producer directly. So I never gave them the Social Security number.

I moved back to Baltimore. My manager told me that he could get me a deal if I put together a "made-for-radio" modern-rock band. That wasn't necessarily what I am, but I understood why I was doing it. My friend Mitch had just gotten a record deal with SR-71, and people were kind of sniffing around because they knew I had co-written some songs with him. There were actually a lot of labels and management companies interested in the band, Stereolife. We successfully created a "buzz." We had a little blurb in *Hits* magazine. We got written up in *Demo Diaries*, which is an Internet hot list of unsigned bands. We did some showcases in New York and Andy Martin from Deep South Entertainment put us on one of his Deep South Showcases.

Meanwhile, my band hated my manager. Once all the labels got interested they were like, get rid of him or we quit. Logic seemed to tell me, what good is a manager if you have no band to sell? However, a lot of industry people were also coming up to me after seeing the band and saying, "The songs are great, we think you're great, but your band's not cutting it." There was one management company that actually said, "We want you to dissolve the band. We'll move you to L.A. and put studio players behind you." I felt like every opportunity had a condition. Lose your band. Lose your manager. So, I did the only sensible thing. I got rid of both!

I told all the labels that were interested that I'm gonna come back with a new lineup and I'll see you in a few months. At that point, the two people in this management company who were going to move me to L.A. and co-manage me had a little tiff. They couldn't work out who was going to take on what tasks. I got kind of scared that they were having problems even before I signed the contract. I mean, I just disbanded my band and you guys are fighting over this? I'm not going to do this. So I wound up kind of left out in the cold. I had no band. I had no manager. I had these songs recorded, but I couldn't play them out live.

Over the next few months, I put together another band that was musically more interesting. We showcased in New York a couple of times and people seemed to like it. One day I got a call from Melisma Records, which is Matt Serletic's label through Arista Records (based in Atlanta). They had come out and seen every incarnation of the band. They said they liked the songs and wanted me to come down to Atlanta. Matt's an amazing producer and songwriter, but I'd been through all this before. I ended up going down there for a meeting with Matt and his brother Dean, who is the general manager for the label. I sat in the conference room and played some songs on acoustic guitar and Matt said, "I really think you're talented. I gotta figure out what I wanna do, but I definitely want to do something with you."

A few days later I got a phone call and Matt says, "I'm not interested in signing you to a recording deal." I was like, "Well, thanks for calling. I appreciate it." That's when he asked me if I'd be interested in moving to Atlanta to join his team of songwriters and producers.

I knew this was an amazing opportunity. This was the guy who just produced Santana's "Smooth." This was the guy who did both Matchbox Twenty records, Edwin McCain, Celine Dion, Collective Soul. But I'd spent the last fifteen years of my life trying to be an artist, trying to be a performer, and he's saying, "You wouldn't be able to do the touring thing and you

wouldn't be able to pursue a record deal while you're with me."
So I needed to think about it. I'd spent the last four years of my
life basically not working so that I could focus on writing songs
and honing my craft. Total dedication is what I've given to this
career. I don't remember the last time I bought something extravagant or went on a vacation. Total dedication is what it takes to
make it as a working musician. At the same time, I definitely
knew my main priority at this point had to be to get out of debt.

I agreed to go down to Atlanta again. This time it was to
record six songs at their studio, with Mark Dobson (Matt's Pro
Tools guy). It was basically drum loops with me playing guitar,
keyboards, and singing. The demos came out really well and
around 9:00 P.M. the next night everyone came over to the studio to hear what we had done. When we were done listening,
Matt asked everyone to leave the control room except me. He
sat down and said, "The stuff is great. I think three of these six
songs could be hits, and I would really like to move forward
with this relationship. You've got a unique songwriting style.
You have pop sensibility and your lyrics are unique. We think
that we can really do something with it."

It took four more months, but we finally signed a deal.
There's a song I have called "Go" that everyone thinks is a
smash. I'm so jaded by that word that I'm like, "Okay, that's
great, it's a smash. Just show me the money."

FIRST GIGS II

Gene Simmons

Breathing Fire

Bass Player, Kiss

Our first gig was at the Academy of Music in New York City, New Year's Eve, 1973. We opened for Teenage Lust, Iggy Pop, and Blue Öyster Cult. We didn't have a record out yet. Our record came out a month and a half later, on Valentine's Day. Somebody put us on that bill as a favor. At that point, nobody knew anything about the band, but we already had a show. We had the levitating drum set and the fireballs. We came out in makeup and high heels and played really aggressive songs, as opposed to just a lot of riffing. Our opening song was "Nothing to Lose." It was real simple, straight-ahead stuff. So the combination of simple song structure and high-energy performance, plus the effects and everything, just left people with their jaws hanging open.

I breathed fire for the first time in that show, on a song called "Fire House," and caught myself on fire. People thought it was part of the act, of course. Here I was, seconds away from dying, and everyone went bonkers. At that point, nobody put their name up on big signs like us. You were supposed to be very subtle about that. So we were roundly criticized by everybody. What is this stuff—the bombs, the fireworks, our name in big letters?

When we played Canada, opening for Manfred Mann and Savoy Brown, for the first number or two there was dead silence, and then there was complete mayhem. We got an encore on the very first show. At the second show we were told we were not allowed to do an encore. That's when you know you're good. Those were the days when you had to fight for everything. At the second show we did an encore anyway. The road manager of the other band wasn't around to put the lights on, so we just did the encore. Later they found him locked in an Anvil case.

Our road crew back then were killers. They were the dregs of the earth, scum who couldn't find work anywhere else. And we were paying nothing. But after a while we all had a sense that it was a crusade. Our crew got so dedicated to us that, all by themselves, they went and designed an outfit. Everybody wore jeans, big studded belts, and leather jackets. Every one of them wore shades. You strike fear into the hearts of other bands when your road crew walks in dressed like that.

Ozzy Osbourne admitted to me about a year ago that he knew his days with Black Sabbath were numbered right after a time in Boston when we blew them off the stage. Geezer Butler ran over to him before the show, telling him that this seven-foot bass player had come up to him and said he was going to chew him up and spit him out. And Ozzy was shrieking, "So what? That's what he's supposed to do. They're supposed to try and bluff you." But Ozzy knew his days were numbered because Geezer was affected by it. That's when we knew we were going to make it, when we could push the other bands around, 'cause that means you really are a threat.

Steven Gustafson

Star Quality

Bass Player, 10,000 Maniacs

I met Natalie [Merchant] at the college radio station when she was sixteen and I just thought she was probably the strangest person in Jamestown. In those days, I was booking Rob [Buck]'s band for our little new wave coffeehouse. I'd just read Tom Wolfe's *Electric Kool-Aid Acid Test* and we were all trying to be as strange as possible. We'd rented this warehouse, this cool-looking place no one knew about. We had plants hanging from the ceiling and movies and we'd throw parties to pay the rent. I said, "Natalie, we're just going to have a little party and play and make some noise. Why don't you come down and sing?" She had a magnetism then and she didn't even know it. She'd have to sneak out of her house at night 'cause her mother didn't want her hanging out with the likes of us. Then we started booking ourselves gigs at the local dives and Natalie would come down and sing and there'd be a couple hundred people there, slam-dancing and stuff, and her mother would come in and drag her out.

We started out as Still Life. Our first gig was at a place in Pennsylvania, in the winter of 1981. Rob, Dennis [Drew], Natalie, and I practiced for about three weeks. We wrote about five or six songs, all about twelve minutes long—no beginning, no ending; a lot of feedback. After the set, our drummer was sitting at a table and there wasn't any ashtray so he flipped his cigarette out onto the dance floor and the owner, this big greasy-haired man, came over and started yelling about that. And then Rob's wife, who was in the band, stood up and tried to reason with the guy and he yelled at her. Dennis stood up and yelled back and the guy eventually chased Dennis out the front door with a big leather blackjack. We threw our equipment out the back door and as we drove off I smashed Dennis's car into this marble bench. We were all laughing. It was like the Sex Pistols would have been proud of us.

The first gig we played as 10,000 Maniacs was the Christmas Dance at Fredonia State. We'd play a set and when we were done they all got up and played Christmas music, Bing Crosby, and big-band stuff, and the kids would dance. The guys were in their tuxes and the girls were in their gowns in the big cafeteria, and boy, they hated us.

In the beginning, we almost made up our own kind of plan, even though it changed every inch of the way and we changed with it. We had friends in Atlanta who said they could get us a lot of bookings, so we went there for a few months. Some friends rented a little house and we slept on the floors and played a handful of gigs and it was miserable and we went right home. We knew there was no way we could move to New York City and live without having to get jobs. So we said, "We're just going to have to tour." We had a couple of independent records that we made at the university for five hundred dollars—we pressed up one thousand copies each and stuck them in the back of the van and hit the road, booked all the dates ourselves, slept on people's floors. On one tour we took a big seven-man tent with us and used that. We were like a band of migrant musicians going where the weather suits our clothes. We got some financial backing from our families and went to England and played three shows in London and got pretty good reviews.

In those days we were always looking for the ultimate set. The set would change all the time and we were always arguing about playing setless. In our songs there was no structure either; it was just sort of a couple of chords. Natalie had a verse/chorus sort of thing and Rob could definitely go nuts. When we came back from England, Elektra offered us the contract.

Dawn Silva

The Key Is to Blend

Backup Singer, Sly and the Family Stone, Funkadelic

At the age of seventeen I formed an all-female band called Windsong. We were lucky enough to land a gig at one of San Francisco's hottest nightclubs, the Orphanage. The nine-piece band consisted of keyboards, bass, percussion, a drummer, rhythm guitar, violinist, and my sisters and me on vocals. As a unit we weren't very good and we lasted only two sets before the club owner decided enough was enough. The only good thing about that gig was that Cynthia Robinson, trumpet player for Sly and the Family Stone, was in the club that night. She approached me, saying, "Sly is looking for background singers, if you're interested give me a call." She gave me her number and then sat in with the band that was playing. Whipping out her golden trumpet, Cynthia was exceptional. She created her own environment of screaming, howling precision and clarity—cutting through the externals, going straight to the core of excellence.

I phoned Cynthia and one week later I drove ninety miles west of Sacramento, crossing the famous Golden Gate Bridge, past Mill Valley into a small tourist town called Sausalito. I pulled up to a recording studio with a sign that read: *The Record Plant.* I approached the large double handcrafted wooden doors and pushed the doorbell twice, then a third time. There was a distorted giggle and someone saying, "State your business." The buzzer sounded and I pushed open the heavy doors. I was directed to walk down an oval wooden hallway that twisted and turned and told to make a right. Going through another heavy door I almost tripped over something and someone caught me and said, "Sit down there."

The recording studio was made into a deep circular pit, similar to a gladiator arena. A large board was located at the bottom of the pit with multicolored lights blinking off and on like a flat Christmas tree. The room was dark and when my eyes adjusted I saw three girls centered around a microphone. I heard the sound of a massive tape recorder rewinding backward and a voice in the darkness saying, "Let's try it again."

The song blasted loudly from speakers hanging from the ceiling. A voice came from the darkness again: "Okay, that's cool. Put up the next track. Cynthia, where's that new girl?" Cynthia pointed and the silhouette of heads sitting or standing turned in my direction. I couldn't see his face but I knew the voice in the darkness was Sly Stone's. "Okay, so what are you waiting for?"

"Who, me?"

"Yeah, you!"

I looked down into the pit and saw the engineer wiping sweat from his brow. I stood on wobbly legs and envisioned myself crashing to the bottom. I smiled, swallowed, and climbed the four steps to the top of the arena. One heavyset girl was glaring at me. I ignored her and managed out a squeaky hello. I didn't have a clue on what I was suppose to do. Someone said, "Get her a headset." Another said, "Honey, you'll have to stand closer to the mike than that. My name is Vet. I'm Sly's sister. Can you sing the tops?" I nodded my head. "Do you talk?"

"Yes, I can talk, what's the part?"

"Have you ever sung in a studio before?"

I looked at the girl, whose glare now transformed into plain old-fashioned pissed off, and said, "No."

Vet sang the vocal part down once, and I said, "That's it?" She shrugged and said, "That's it." All of a sudden I wasn't petrified any longer. Wow, I had much more difficult parts in my high school choir. This was a piece of cake. The heavyset female glanced at her watch, glared at me again and said, "Are there any plans for us to do this today?" The engineer was instructed to roll the tape and when my part came up I sang it as though my life depended on it. I heard laughter and the music stopped. My heart began to race. The heavyset female smiled at me and said, "Maybe you need to back up after all."

She extended her hand and said, "My name is Tiny. A few words of advice. If you hear yourself louder than everyone in your section, that's because you are. The key to a great background singer is to blend, to sound like one voice. To stay on pitch, push one of your headset speakers behind the back of your ear."

Sly stood and said, "Now that we got that out of the way, let's get this done now!" Twenty minutes later we were finished. The lights were suddenly turned up and the room returned to normal, almost shrinking. Someone said, "Cash or union?" Not knowing what she meant I said, "Cash will be fine." She handed me three hundred dollars. I couldn't believe this was happening. Three hundred dollars for singing twenty minutes? I watched the people leaving one at a time nodding, smiling, touching my arms as they filed past me. I sat in a daze listening to the engineer play the song over and over again. I had never heard my voice on a song before, and even though it was mixed in with a group I could distinctly hear my note. I was beaming. Someone touched my face, instantly snapping me back to reality. "Sly wants to see you. He's in his private room."

I followed her to a sliding glass door. She knocked and walked away. I heard a voice say, "Come in, it's open." The first thing I noticed was an enormous bed that took up the entire room. It was shaped like a mouth. Large lips with huge white teeth framed the bed. I thought my eyes were playing tricks on me, for the mattress looked like a swollen tongue. There, lying in the center of the tongue, was Sly, surrounded by four women. He smiled that same ridiculous smile as the manmade bed. He was wearing a large afro wig. His glasses were thick, and large glistening diamonds and glittering gold nuggets spelled out the name *Sly Stone* across his eyebrows. His long thin fingers bore massive diamond rings that seemed to weigh his hands down. The animation of the real-life character before me was something straight out of *The Twilight Zone*. I didn't know whether to sit down or run.

As if reading my thoughts, Sly offered me a seat and said with a childish giggle, "You sounded good." He introduced me to the four women. All of them looked me over suspiciously except for Cynthia, who said, "Welcome." Sly walked to the sliding glass door, opened it, smiled, and said, "Congratulations. You are now an official member of Sly and the Family Stone."

Larry Dunn

I Made Them Proud

Keyboard Player, Earth, Wind and Fire

My mom used to say, "We never had to make Larry practice; we had to make him stop." By the time I was fifteen, me and Philip Bailey had a group called Friends and Love that played really serious fusion stuff. One night we opened the show at the Hilton Hotel in Denver for the original Earth, Wind and Fire, from when Maurice [White] had the older guys from Chicago with all the dashikis and stuff. Later Maurice and Verdine [White] came down to this little nightclub where we were playing and they said they really liked what they saw. So Philip moved out to L.A. after that and ended up with Maurice when the first group all quit. That was like 1969–71, when it was Verdine and Maurice in a hotel room by themselves.

Later Philip came back to Denver just to hang out, and he came to Manuel High School where his wife had attended. War was going to appear there. The little bar group that I was playing with, the Sammy Mayfield band, opened the show and I took about a five-minute Hammond B3 solo. Philip said he went right to the phone and called Maurice. "I think I got us the guy. He's young and doesn't have a lot of experience, but he can really play and he's a good guy." Maurice took him at his word. So I learned the tunes on both of the two Earth, Wind and Fire albums on

Warner Bros., packed up and flew out to L.A. When I got there I took out my Fender Rhodes, Verdine took out the bass, and we just started playing a little bit of Herbie Hancock's "Maiden Voyage." I took a little jazz solo and Maurice was like yeah, and that was that.

Maurice was a smart cookie when it came to rehearsals. He wouldn't take a lot of the gigs around town. He said if we played a couple of nightclubs those same people are not going to be willing to spend fifteen dollars to see us at the Forum. So we just rehearsed and rehearsed and rehearsed. He paid us enough for me and Philip to have a little apartment. We had an old Wurlitzer and I would rehearse on that every day and do scales and listen to jazz. Finally one day we had this little showcase in New York for Clive Davis. I'll never forget it. He came in wearing these white shoes and he heard about a thirty-minute set and he walked out and the next thing we were getting signed to Columbia.

We literally went up and down the United States, to every nook and cranny, from '72–'73 all the way until I left in '83. We were on the road like 290 days out of 365. When you're young and hyped up like that it's great. Our first big gig was at the Spectrum in Philly. Earth, Wind and Fire was just the opening act for Gladys Knight and the Pips, but when we walked out on stage and heard twenty thousand people screaming their heads off for us, I was like, WOW! Not only did they know who we were, but they knew our music. I remember opening for ZZ Top in '74 or '75. We were just kicking booty every night and it got to the point where after we came on and then they came on, about five songs into their set, almost all of our fans were gone and a good portion of theirs. Leonard Smith was our road manager at that time. He was a big buff guy, who used to play football with Jim Brown. I'll never forget the time he said, "Look, baby, I got bad news and good news. The bad news is they kicked us off the tour, because we were kicking their ass! But the good news is, we're all going home tomorrow!"

One of the most memorable moments occurred at this college concert we played in Atlanta somewhere around 1976, '77. It was our first big gig with the Phoenix Horns. We had rehearsed up the yin-yang, as always. Then we did some warm-up gigs and now we were playing this big sold-out college date in Atlanta. We went into a live rendition of "Reasons," where after we went through the main part of the song, we broke it down and Don Myrick stepped up to the mike and started playing a real nice smooth jazzy solo and the people just lost it. Then there was another portion of the show where I did a big keyboard solo. That night was outrageous, like we had moved to another level.

I remember a night at the Capitol Center in Washington, D.C. This was when technology was just starting to bloom. One day there was nothing and the next day you'd go into a big beautiful room like that and there was a huge screen in the middle of the arena so people could see your big face. And so every show we did over the years they'd give me these spots to solo, where I could play anything from jazz to weird bass sounds, bombs crashing and mini-Moogs, to melodic stuff. And I don't know where but I picked up this little plastic flower that was battery operated and it lit up. It was a rose that lit up a beautiful red and I put that in my teeth like those flamenco dancers. So I was playing the mini-Moog and would always do this thing at the end where I'd raise that note till it was just piercing. So that night I got it to the highest point and the camera went to my face, and I dropped the rose out of my mouth. All the girls went crazy. It was unbelievable.

When you've got a great show like we did you're always

pumped up. When the show was over you'd head off to some local little club to see what the people were doing and sit in. We just loved playing music. It was a great thing to know you had a big following. You knew the record company was going to get the stuff out there, so you knew when you were in the studio it was going to be heard. You could concentrate on coming up with the greatest product and that's what we did. We took our time and we would write individually and together. Every couple of years we'd go up to Carmel with Maurice and we'd write and come back to L.A. and put the latest tracks down step by step.

I always liked recording. I started producing very early. I started my first production at twenty-one with Caldera. From there I never looked back. I did three albums with Lenny White, I did Stanley Turrentine, Ramsey Lewis, Level 42. I would always ask Maurice, "Are you sure you're done with me?" "No, no, Larry, you did great." "I could give you more." "No, you did fine." And I'd just go and do my productions, 'cause I loved being in the studio. Maurice didn't mind. He would always say, "We like this guy. He doesn't do all of this talkin' and negotiating. He just goes in and does his work." I think I made them proud because every production I did is still being played today, just like Earth, Wind and Fire.

Brian Q. Torff

Breaking the Code

Bassist, Jazz Educator, Fairfield University

In 1974 I was a wide-eyed music student at the Manhattan School of Music in New York City. I had just returned from a summer at the Aspen Music School when my close friend, drummer Warren Odze, suggested I meet the great bassist Milt Hinton. "He likes to help young musicians," Warren explained. I soon went downtown to Michael's Pub and met the man who would become my mentor, and as it turned out, my lucky star. Milt suggested, as he had to many aspiring musicians before me, "Come out to the house for dinner and we will hear you play."

Milt Hinton had been a star with Cab Calloway during the swing era and went on to play with a who's who of jazz greats, including Count Basie, Duke Ellington, and Billie Holiday. He was one of the first African-American musicians to break the color barrier in the New York recording studios and appeared on over one thousand records. As both an in-demand musician and as a photographer whose images of jazz musicians had been exhibited at the Smithsonian, Milt Hinton's lens had just about seen it all.

When I arrived at his home in St. Albans, Queens, Milt welcomed me with his characteristic wide grin and open arms—that was his way. He heard me play bass, and then we read a few classical duets together as he put me through the paces. "Remember," Milt warned, "you got to play some time. You got to be the bottom of the music." I guess he liked what he heard, because at the end of the night he stunned me by casually inquiring, "How would you like to go on the road with Cleo Laine and her husband, Johnny Dankworth?"

At the time I didn't know who they were, but it didn't really matter. Just hearing the phrase "go on the road" was enough to make me levitate. Now before this I had played plenty of blues and rock from my days growing up in the Chicago suburbs, but jazz represented a vast and daring frontier that seemed to promise a lifetime of challenges. I yearned for something more than rock could convey and in jazz, I felt like I was growing into an adult music, the real thing.

The next day I rushed out and bought some of Cleo's records, and though I was still apprehensive about this sudden turn of events I felt I could do it. The first rehearsal was held in a Manhattan brownstone in the East Sixties and I knew as I arrived that Milt had taken me this far, but now I had to prove myself. The other musicians in the band included Rudy Collins, a drummer known for his work with Dizzy Gillespie, and Paul Hart, a gifted pianist and composer who was born on the same day as me, March 16, 1954. We were both twenty and about to embark on our first big tour. During the three-hour rehearsal with Laine and Dankworth, I was delighted and relieved to find that I could understand and even play the music they put in front of me. When I reported this to my friend Warren, he laughed and said, "Did you think the music would be written in Egyptian hieroglyphics?" I must have figured I was James Bond who had just broken the code to the world of professional music.

I have to admit I was uneasy about dropping out of college to go on tour, but everyone, including my mother, my fellow schoolmates, and my bass teacher, Orin O'Brien, felt that this was a big break and that I should take it. I will always remember

Orin reminding me that "before you become an artist you must learn to be a professional."

To add more butterflies to my already frenetic nervous system, our first gig of the tour, just ten days away, would be at Carnegie Hall! I'll never forget the feeling of walking out on that Carnegie Hall stage for the first time, as the immensity of the place towered over me like a giant. I realized that here on this stage once stood immortals like Caruso, Ellington, Sinatra, Dylan, and the Beatles. It was enough to make you faint in your tracks. But the night went well. I didn't miss any notes, Cleo gave her usual stellar performance, the audience threw roses on the stage, and there was an encore. I can't recall an after-party; I just sort of glided back to my Riverside Drive apartment in a daze.

From this point on, Milt Hinton was my lifelong friend, a confidant who would dispense advice to me when we were on the same bill at jazz festivals across the country. He and his wife, Mona, gave my daughter a toy xylophone for her fourth birthday. I tried to repay my enormous debt by having him sub for me on a date with jazz violinist Stephane Grappelli (he loved that), and I brought him to Fairfield University in the mid-nineties to perform with my students. I had the honor of presenting him with an honorary doctorate, and I wrote a paper on his life that was presented at the International Association of Jazz Educators convention in the year 2000. I wish I could have done more.

Everyone in life needs a break. We also need a friend, a mentor, someone who believes in us a bit more than we might believe in ourselves. Though many years and gigs have passed, I can still remember the feeling of standing on that stage and looking out past the footlights into the audience that looked like a thousand stars. And then I remember it was Milt who put me there.

Milt Hinton passed away in December 2000, at the age of ninety.

Raquel Bitton

Dreaming Big

Chanteuse

Singing has always been my way of expressing my passionate self. Actually this gift was good and bad, growing up. Being so close to my brothers, and growing up with loving parents, who had no direction themselves in life, life's lessons were hard and scary for all of us. Holding on to this little girl's dream that began in Marrakech when I was five years old was the hardest thing I had to do, because each year brought me a new lesson. But I never doubted my talent. It's not always that a person sings and makes people cry even if they don't understand the words. I grew to recognize the power of my delivery; my voice was the instrument that channeled what's in my heart. There's a lot in my heart. Sometimes I feel like I die a little when I sing, just because I give it all. It's hard to find those songs that make you feel that way, but I find them, because I am always looking.

My father always told me to pay attention to the songs I was choosing to perform. He told me that my voice was too rich to sing insignificant lyrics, that my voice had to tell a story, and an important one that could be found only by digging into a repertoire that was older than I was. I got the message loud and clear and became an avid collector of songs of the heart. I would listen to so many records, dig out lots of sheet music, and read about the composers and the reason why they wrote that song in particular. This is how I discovered the repertoire of Edith Piaf. When I dug into her repertoire I learned that she had recorded hundreds of songs. It became obvious to me that her life was in her songs, and my passion for the music grew deeper with every tune.

A movie I loved was *Les Enfants du Paradis* (*Children of Paradise*). I had seen it at the Castro Theater (in San Francisco) many times. In Piaf's repertoire I heard a song that depicted the first scene in the movie, "Boulevard du Crime." In the movie, Jean-Louis Barrault, who played Baptiste, witnessed someone stealing a watch. I thought, wow, Piaf liked that movie so much that she had a song written about it. I dug more into books and sheet music and came up with thirteen of her songs that were telling perfectly the story of *Les Enfants du Paradis*.

With lots of confidence, after spending several months writing the scenario and the concept, I took a bus to the San Francisco Ballet. I asked the receptionist to let me speak to the person in charge of the ballet. She was amused and polite but turned me down, so I sat there watching the door, hoping to catch the eye of some official. I guess I was staring intensely and this gentleman smiled at me. I stood up. He was embarrassed. He only meant to smile, but I was on a mission. I said *"Bonjour,"* hoping to charm him. He replied *"Bonjour, vous êtes Française?"* He was French. He happened to be the San Francisco Ballet musical conductor, Jean-Louis LeRoux, and I hurriedly told him that I had this incredible concept for a ballet based on the classic film *Children of Paradise*, sung to obscure songs of Edith Piaf. He said he loved Edith Piaf and the movie. He offered to show my script to Michael Smuin, who was then the ballet director. I handed it to him, my eyes filled with excitement. That same afternoon Michael Smuin called me at home and invited me to his office. I spent a whole year going to his home where I would tell the stories and sing the songs, and in turn he was choreographing.

When *Le Ballet des Coeurs* (*Hearts*) opened at the San Francisco Opera House, I stood in the pit amongst a hundred musicians (me who had known only a piano, a violin, and an accordion as accompaniment) and Jean-Louis LeRoux was conducting. People thought it was a recording they were hearing. After the show, they'd hang on the walls of the orchestra pit staring in disbelief and pointing at me.

Bob Holloway orchestrated and arranged the music for *Hearts*. With the exception of the pianist, no one had a chart. So when I stood in front of the San Francisco Ballet orchestra and for the first time heard the magnificence of Bob Holloway's orchestrations, I thought I was at the gates of heaven. I tracked him down after the run, spoke to him in a shaky voice and asked him if he would give me a chance to sing those songs outside of the ballet setting. Not only did he give me his blessing; he made sure I had more songs orchestrated. There is no doubt in my mind that he is the very reason why my career propelled from tiny cabarets to grand theaters. Since then Bob Holloway and I have collaborated on four CDs and several live concerts.

Some people take their show around for a while and then end at Carnegie Hall. I did it the other way; I began at Carnegie Hall. That afternoon, at the orchestra rehearsal, when I stood, big as a minute, trembling at the site of such magnitude, a viola player came up to me and said, "Miss Bitton, please allow me. I have played this hall for the past twenty years. It's a warm place, a loving place. Don't be scared, just let the place come to you, don't go to it." I think about this viola player with lots of gratitude as well.

Indeed dreams do come true, with time, hope, and vision. The hardest thing to do, I found out, is to stay focused on a dream. Life's lessons can drift you away, but when I stop and remember the reason why I chose my dream, then I get teary eyed and feel connected again to the hope of dreaming big.

Dan Lipton
(danlipton@danlipton.com)

Into the Pit

Pit Pianist, The Full Monty

I moved to New York City after four years of college at Northwestern University in Chicago, where I enrolled as a piano major but graduated with a degree in composition. Originally from New Jersey, I decided to come back east and begin working as a musician for the theater. I had worked a good deal in college. It was a steady diet of jazz bands, solo gigs, vocal accompanying, music-directing student productions—by senior year, downtown jobs began to rival my commitments on campus. In New York City, I already had a slew of contacts in the business. So I felt pretty confident that I would be getting paid to play piano in no time.

One of the first people I got in touch with was Joe Church, a music director I had assisted—er, gotten coffee for—at the Goodman Theater in Chicago, on Randy Newman's musical *Faust.* He was about to start previews for a little show called *The Lion King.* Joe and his associate conductor, Ted Baker, decided to give me a shot at subbing on Ted's Keyboard 1 book.

Ted Baker is one of the best keyboard players I've ever seen. Aside from working (under Joe) with Pete Townshend to bring The Who's *Tommy* to the Broadway stage, this guy records with Philip Glass. He tours with Steely Dan. I admire him immensely, and I felt pretty damn lucky that he would give me, a twenty-two-year old kid, this chance. He hadn't taken a single show off during *Lion King*'s Minneapolis tryout or during the preview period in New York. Every Broadway pit musician needs a list of subs they can call when they get sick, take a day off, or go off on another gig. At that point, I was the only potential sub learning Ted's book for this most-coveted freelance gig.

I started coming to the pit to watch and tape the show, then copied the book in order to practice at home. From day one, I could tell Disney had manufactured an amazing and lucrative spectacle. As the show sailed through its previews and opened with hoopla usually reserved for national elections, I felt the pressure mount. A lot of what Ted plays is not scored out. His fingers deliver a nuanced and improvised extension of the written music, so I was forced to learn the part largely by ear. I was trying to absorb his playing style from a tape, working day and night in my tiny Hell's Kitchen sublet. Meanwhile, we set a date for me to play my first show. I came into the pit on off-hours to practice on his synth. That's in addition to the handful of times I watched the show. I didn't want to come and watch too much, though. Musicians (myself included) are rather egocentric, and there's an air of quiet competition among a group of working musicians. The weapons: consistency, accuracy, and deceptively easy execution. Some of the best musicians in the city were in this pit, and it was one of the more intimidating baptism-by-fire experiences of my career. I was obviously the youngest person there, so I felt the need to prove myself.

To sync the orchestra up with the stage action, Joe Church decided to put a few numbers on a click track, which I had never dealt with before. I didn't even have that much experience following a conductor at that point, much less playing to an automated click piped through the headphones! Plus, the foot-pedal choreography on Ted's book was ridiculous: half a beat to switch to the next sound or adjust to a new volume. The obstacles to my first Broadway paycheck were mounting.

Joe offered to come in early one day and conduct me through some of the major numbers. He worked fast and made it clear that he didn't have any time to waste on mediocre playing. I did not follow him, messed up a bunch of quick pedal changes, and played sloppily. I still had work to do and we both knew it, but he gave me the benefit of the doubt. My show date came sooner than I wanted it to. Probably sensing my insecurity, Joe suggested that I "ghost" Ted, splitting the book instead of playing the entire show. So, I took the plunge on a no-pressure Sunday matinee. I played "Circle of Life," "Hakuna Matata," and most of the first act. It took me a while to get over the fact that I was playing on Broadway, not to mention the elephants and hyenas stomping over my head. My nerves calmed down a few numbers in, at which point I tried to focus on the music.

I did okay . . .

. . . but not great. Afterward, the awkward phone conversations I had with both Ted and Joe confirmed my worst suspicion: they would not be asking me back to *The Lion King*. I saw it coming, but that didn't make the situation any easier to swallow.

I decided to take a little break to reevaluate my launch into the New York City working-musician scene. I needed to work my way up the ladder instead of trying to jump in on top. That meant starting with dance classes, and posting flyers to advertise my services as an accompanist. Work was infrequent and did not pay much, but it got my name into the pipeline. Slowly, the volume of calls and the caliber of work increased. Soon, I was doing rehearsal piano on a musical at Lincoln Center Theater. I subbed on easier keyboard books both on and off-Broadway. I began music-directing readings. Before I knew it, I was leaving town as the pianist on a five-month national tour. I developed my reputation and some great working relationships, parlaying one job into the next.

Now, three years later, things have somehow come full circle. I am the regular pit pianist for *The Full Monty*. The show just opened to hoopla usually reserved for national elections. Some of the best musicians in the city are in this pit and—unfortunately for my subs—a lot of what I play is not written down. I am still the youngest person here, but I don't have to prove myself. I proved myself by getting here.

And it looks like I may have a job for a while.

Johnny Douglas

Doing What You Love

Drummer, Keyboard Player

One of the most profoundly influential moments of my young life occurred as I entered my first high school dance as a ninth-grader. I distinctly remember walking into the gym where a four-piece band of older boys called the Black Bishops were playing. They were dressed in black stovepipe pants and wore black turtlenecks. At the foot of the stage were two lights, one at either corner, one blue and one green, aimed at the four dark figures. They were playing a Stones song. They were loud and raw and beautiful, the way rock and roll is supposed to look and sound. This was too much to absorb. Four guys whom I saw on occasion in the hallways at school—not that they would have deigned to acknowledge my lowly presence—were somehow doing this monumental thing. They had figured out how to play rock and roll. They had opened some Pandora's box and were now in on the secret. Seeing the Black Bishops caused me to make the quantum leap from experiencing rock and roll at a distance to the realization that this could be actualized in the here and now. And that, maybe, just maybe, I could be a part of this wondrous thing. I stood transfixed and drank in their essence. This was simply too good to be true. The girls and the dancers and the teachers lurking around the edges all disappeared. It was just the Bishops and me. Alone, together in a trance only we understood. The spell was cast.

What drew me to the drums is difficult to pinpoint with any degree of accuracy or certainty. Perhaps, after a number of years playing piano with an eye to precision and nuance, the notion of pounding out the primal rhythms of rock and roll at full tilt and with complete abandon seemed liberating. As much as anything I am tempted to think that it was the way they looked—so clean and primed for attack, commanding center stage, cymbals glistening in the lights. Maybe it was something about being at the bottom of this huge sound that is a rock-and-roll band, driving it from the back, powering it from verse to chorus, solo to bridge. It is a wonderful vantage point on the world, sitting behind a set of Ludwigs, sticks in hand. Especially when people are dancing. To be the beat to which they are moving is a fabulous responsibility. They are dancing to me! In this tremendous tribal ritual, we are all part of the heaving mass of humanity, caught up and lost in and carried away by the beat—the beat which I am establishing, coaxing, defining. In short it was just too much fun not to want to do it as much, as long, and as loudly as possible.

My first gig as a member of my own band was playing drums at an after-football-game sock hop known as a "tea dance." The group, aside from myself, was a well-seasoned outfit, having played a grand total of one engagement with their former drummer. On the day of the dance, we wheeled, carried, and generally lugged our equipment down the hill to the high school we all attended. The football game was in full swing while we set up on the stage at one end of the gym. We tuned up as best we could and ran through "Mustang Sally." The sound in the gym was cavernous. The roar of our amplifiers and the boom-crash-thwack of the drums swirled around in a strange, indistinct muddle of reverberation in which no single instrument or voice could really be termed discernible. The sound careened off hardwood floors, concrete walls, and bleachers, colliding back into itself. The word *cacophony* springs to mind. Bedlam might also be appropriate. In short, it was perfect!

We could hear that the game was over and people would soon be pouring into the gym. We worked up a certain collective courage. This, combined with our best attempt at John Lennon–inspired bravado, was all we had to sustain us as our clearly skeptical or at least highly curious classmates, erstwhile friends and potential if not probable detractors, straggled into the gym. The lights went down. As drummer, I counted off the first song and away we went. I think it was "Gimme Some Lovin'," although it could just as easily have been "Midnight Hour" or "The Last Time." Then an amazing thing happened. Nothing. No one threw anything. No one yelled disparaging comments related to anyone's ancestry, sexual proclivities, or mother. We played. They danced. It seemed to be working! And it was fun. Wildly fun, as a matter of fact. "Wipeout." "Eight Days a Week." "Hang on Sloopy." All these and more sped by in a blur of ringing guitars, thumping bass, and splashing cymbals. This was clearly very, very good. Not necessarily good in terms of musicianship. Probably horrendously out of tune. Undoubtedly somewhat shaky in its overall execution. And yet absolutely right. Whatever else happened, whatever repercussions might be encountered, whatever the consequences of having put ourselves out there for all to see and hear, we did it. Like thousands of other rock and roll kids, unknown to us, were doing it. Not out of ambition. Or aspiration. Or issuing from some White Anglo-Saxon Protestant work-ethic-induced drive for success. Not for parents or teachers or anyone else. This we did for love.

In time we played virtually every conceivable gig our little town had to offer. We rented the Masonic Temple and promoted our own dances, where we engaged our friends to sell cases of Coke and Orange Crush that my father helped us get wholesale. We would pay a cop ten dollars to hang around the door for security. And we'd play three sets of ever-improving rock and roll. We played every talent show that would have us. We played a wedding reception at Fisherman's Paradise, where we all got stinking drunk and rode back into town in someone's pickup truck, bouncing around with all our equipment, holding on for dear life as we careened down dusty gravel roads at 3 A.M. We played high school dances, basement parties, and a Boy Scout father-and-son banquet where we did "Toad" by Cream, featuring a ten-minute drum solo, never dreaming that this might not be appropriate to the setting and occasion. We played the just-built local arena, a phantasmagoric mess of crashing reverb and noise that made the high school gym sound like Abbey Road Studio Two. We played the Riviera, a seedy restaurant/resort motel that had seen better days, on the edge of town, with our new matching paisley shirts, bought for us by our new manager, who lasted approximately three weeks. We played the Bicentennial Celebration parade, blasting merrily away on a flatbed pulled by a tractor for thousands of revelers. We played a summer resort called Bewdley, where American girls that we were sure were "doing it" came to vacation with their families. The venue in question was in a church presided over by a seven-foot-tall pastor with enormous teeth. The teen club in which we played was in the church basement. At night it would be packed with kids and we rocked them silly. Then, when the last of our audience had gone off to their cabins, we moved some of the tables and slept on the floor.

In short, we played everywhere. And I loved every ragged

minute of it. We had, by this time, supplanted the Black Bish-ops as the happening band about town. In fact, their singer sat in with us on occasion and we would sometimes go to his house to listen to Paul Butterfield albums. I don't recall an incident of my choosing to be a musician. I simply stopped the other activities that were interfering with my playing music. Years later, the lesson learned is that life is less about choices and decisions than it is about doing what you love because you love it.

Peter Tork

Mistaking the Finger for the Moon

Bass Player, the Monkees

What I remember most are the screams. That was annoying. But what the hell, the audience didn't come to listen to music. They came to vent their oppression. Before we went on our first tour, I saw the Beatles at Dodger Stadium in 1966. I couldn't believe the kids were not listening to them. Here was the greatest single musical operation of all time and they wouldn't listen. It was all just screaming. The Beatles did about twenty minutes and I don't blame them. When we toured England, Jimi Hendrix was our opening act. Once Jimi came along everybody said, "Gee, if I turn up my amps, everybody will go berserk." But what they were really going berserk for was Jimi Hendrix's pioneering musicianship and his art. No matter what kind of inspirational thing happens, somebody will latch onto the external details and call it that. It's called mistaking the finger for the moon. You point to the moon and somebody looks at your finger. It's inevitable.

The Monkees left the air early in 1968. We toured the Far East, made the movie *Head* and a TV special. We didn't go into the public eye in America at all. That's one of the reasons the movie didn't go, the special didn't go, and nothing ever happened to the Monkees again. But one of my points of pride is that as a musical operation, the Monkees did amazingly well, not World Cup, but national class, without a doubt. Even when we first made our pilot, the four of us got onstage and we were supposed to be doing a dance set. Mike had his guitar. I had my bass. Mickey knew two beats on the drums. During breaks in the filming we asked the stage crew to fire up the amps, and, never having played together before on the same stage, we knocked out a song and the audience liked us. Everybody danced. When it was over they applauded. Some people from Capitol Records, who had heard us, said they would have signed us even if we hadn't had a TV show.

At the outset the background instrumentals were almost entirely studio musicians, but the lead vocals were always one of us. On "Pleasant Valley Sunday" I played piano, we had a studio drummer, the producer played bass, and Mike [Nesmith] played guitar. Essentially we created that record ourselves. At recording sessions, Davy [Jones] played nothing but tambourine. So he had his part down after the second take, and we would sometimes do fifty takes to get our basic track down. Davy's arm got tired. He got sick of banging the tambourine all day long. And Mickey [Dolenz] lost faith in himself. He never did believe he was a decent drummer, so he didn't want to do it anymore. Mike wanted to produce his own records. He wanted to have total control. I was the only one who believed in the group per se. So there I was, all by myself, wanting a group, with no one to be a group with.

I've heard that Mickey later said that we weren't the Monkees any more than Lorne Greene was a Cartwright, which is true. At the same time, we were the Monkees. It was a unique phenomenon, to be a member of a group that wasn't really a group and yet was a group. If we'd been a group, we would have fought to be a group or we would have broken up as a group. But we were a project, a TV show, a record-making machine.

The thing that made the Monkees so successful was the incredibly adept commercial push that was behind the phenomenon, and a lot of people resented that, particularly people who wanted some of it, and I was in sympathy with them. But there I was, you know, racked with self-doubt. Do I really deserve to be here? And then, being a member of a synthetic group, I suffered from the criticisms, while in the meantime I wasn't able to make the music I thought needed to be made. From the producers you'd run up against a lot of "You guys are not the Lovin' Spoonful, so shut up."

I think I was a sort of Gatsby. I was isolated and did not have a continuing sense of community. I didn't know who my friends were and anytime somebody asked me for a favor, I wrote them off as a hanger-on. And I wasn't able to ask people for favors because I was supposed to have all that it took to keep myself together because I had the money. At the same time, by giving the money away, I thought I was returning something to the community. I didn't see myself as apologizing, which is how I see myself now. But I had all this money and I tried to make amends to the world by throwing it at people, and essentially what that did was to isolate me all the more. I didn't have the sense, as the money ran out, that I had to hold on to it, because nobody was going to save it for me.

FIRST ALBUM

Cindy Bullens

It Was the
Rock-and-Roll Dream

Backup Singer, Elton John, Bob Dylan

It was the end of July 1975; I was living in Los Angeles and my friend Bob Neuwirth called me up and said, I'm sending you a ticket. You have to come in to New York for a week and do this thing at the Other End. Dylan's going to be there. Mick Ronson and Ramblin' Jack Elliot are coming down. T-Bone Burnett and Steven Soles are going to be there; David Mansfield wandered in—he's still one of my closest friends to this day. I was basically part of the backup band and we all sang songs together for a week. And out of that came the seeds for the Rolling Thunder tour.

I went back to L.A. and all of August they were pulling it together, so I assumed that's what I was going to be doing. Then in September I crashed this party and met Elton John and was literally asked that night to go on the road with him. It was a Wednesday night; rehearsals started Friday. So I had Thursday to make up my mind. I had no manager. I had a few people who were in the music business who I may have asked at the time, but to be honest with you, I had to make the decision in a day. It was Oh my God, should I go on the road with Bob Dylan as a band member and be able to do one of my own songs? Or should I go on the road as a backup singer with Elton John, who was one of my idols?

Money didn't even cross my mind. I don't even know if there was any money involved in the Rolling Thunder tour. There certainly wasn't a lot of money at that time with Elton John. But there was nobody bigger than Elton in 1975, in terms of being an entertainer. Dylan was in kind of a lull in 1975 and this was part of what was bringing him back. It was two totally different ideologies. And at that point, much to the chagrin of Bob Neuwirth and some of my friends, who thought that songwriting was the most important aspect of what I did, I felt that my performing capabilities, or my wanting to be a rock-and-roll performer, was a more compelling pull to me.

I never felt I made the wrong decision, I just have felt over the years regretful that I couldn't have done both. I ended up doing three concerts with Rolling Thunder. But I would have loved to have been involved in the whole subculture on a daily basis. I did have some moments backstage, in the hotel rooms, in the bus with Allen Ginsberg. But I wasn't involved in the daily aspect of it.

Elton John was a whole different ball game, let me tell you. He had his own jet. We were traveling around in private jets and limousines. It was the rock-and-roll dream come true. I went from having done a few backup vocal sessions on record to actually being out there playing in front of thousands and thousands of people. We did Dodger Stadium, seven nights at Madison Square Garden. I had to get used to being in the limelight. I got a lot of attention, a lot of press, because I was the only girl, I was young, I had a tiny bit of history with the Bob Dylan thing; I had done backup vocals on Gene Clark's record, a couple of Bob Crewe records. Elton made sure that I got attention, which was very gracious of him. I learned a lot from Elton in terms of working with a band, working an audience—a huge amount about working an audience. We rehearsed for a week and once we got through the rehearsal part of it Elton pretty much delegated what he needed to say to other people, at least with the background vocals. His guitarist, Davey Johnstone, was more of the director of the background vocals.

Obviously that put me on the map. I was on the road in '75 and '76; in '77 I mostly wrote, and in '78 I got a record deal with United Artists and *Desire Wire* came out in '79. The album got incredible reviews. I was called the next big thing in rock and roll. People called me the female Bruce Springsteen. They said I had the energy of Springsteen, the look of Jagger, and played guitar like Keith. The single "Survivor" was going up the charts. It was number fifty-six after three weeks. And then it disappeared, because the record company folded. That was devastating to me because I knew I had made a great record.

A year later my second album came out on Casablanca—and that label folded too.

In 1982, we moved back to New York from L.A. and I had my first daughter and then moved directly to rural Connecticut. So I was really isolated. In two years I went from being a rock-and-roll star in L.A. to being in rural Connecticut with a baby. As anyone who's had kids will tell you, it's kind of tempting to just shut yourself off, and I did that. I shut myself off for a number of years. I lost touch with a lot of people. I think at that point my dreams of being a rock star were starting to fade; I always did think of myself as a musician and a songwriter, but I had no idea how to get back into the business while having this child.

Then in 1984 I got pregnant again, and it was really when I was pregnant again and gave birth to my second daughter that

I came to a resolve that somehow I was going to have to find a way to do my music. So we moved closer to New York and I started writing again. I would go into the city and co-write, which I had never done. I'd take Jessie with me in a little basket. That's how I started kind of easing my way back in. I put a band together of local musicians and started playing once a month at the Red Rock Café in Westport, Connecticut.

In 1988 I got another record deal, with Al Teller at MCA. Al had originally wanted to sign me back in the 1970s. I was Al Teller's first signing when he became president of MCA. And then he immediately went to CEO, so he wasn't even involved in the record, and the record never got heard. It wasn't even panned; it was just not heard. That was a heartbreaker. That was even more of a heartbreaker than the first two records not being heard. Because I really thought I had a shot this time and nothing happened. I felt that was kind of the last straw. I've had three major record deals. I'm in my thirties and have two kids. But then I said okay, I've got to figure something out, because I have to do music.

So in 1990, at the suggestion of some friends and acquaintances like Emmylou Harris and Bonnie Raitt, I took a trip to Nashville. I got an incredibly positive reception there. People knew who I was. They thought my writing could be a breath of fresh air. It took me a couple of years to figure out what country music was. Roots music and country music are not the same thing. Country has very strict standards on lyrics, direction, even though it was breaking open at that time. But I met with some wonderful people. I wrote with Al Anderson, Matraca Berg, Mary Ann Kennedy, Kye Fleming. Radney Foster and I had a couple of hits. I could have made a really good living there, but my family didn't want to live in Nashville, so it was a compromise. I'd go down there for about a week a month, but at least I got my foot in the door again. I was doing something I loved. And I re-created myself as a Nashville songwriter.

A lot of these people helped me put together *Somewhere Between Heaven and Earth*, when my daughter Jessie died after a long battle with cancer in 1996. She obviously provided the inspiration for the songs. But, this may sound funny, there's no question in my mind that after her death, she also kept kicking me in the butt, saying, get out there, Mom; this is what you need to do. In the last year and a half I have played every type of venue you can possibly imagine. I do a lot of benefits. I played at the Experience Music project in Seattle. The other extreme was playing in an office building in Washington, D.C., for a bunch of executives who just wanted to hear me sing. I've literally played everywhere from Maine to Alaska.

My next record won't be *Somewhere Between Heaven and Earth*. I can never do that again. I don't want to do that again. I won't top it. It's an entity into itself. There will be shreds of the same sentiment, but there will also be a lot of rock and roll. A year and a half ago I could do nothing except the songs from *Somewhere Between Heaven and Earth*. That's all I wanted to do. That's all I cared about doing. And it's all that people wanted to hear. Those songs are still the bulk of my set, but in the last six months, I've been doing some songs I've written since then that are going to be on the new CD. I also do a few of the old songs, things people might know, like "Survivor" and "High School History." As an encore I always do a rocker that people absolutely love. It's just a flat out rock-and-roll song. I know now that I have the capacity to go out and play solo, with just my guitar, or I can rock you out with a band. I'm performing mostly with my drummer, who plays a full set of drums, so we sound like a band. I've only played maybe three or four gigs with a full band this year, which I absolutely love to do, but it's not cost-effective. I've always loved performing. Since I was six years old I've loved to get up in front of an audience and sweat. The only thing is, I don't jump off any pianos anymore. I already had a knee operation that probably was the result of jumping off one too many pianos.

I have no idea what my future is. I could be dropped by this record label in two seconds. I used to want to be famous. Now I couldn't care less if I'm famous. That doesn't make my life complete. The music makes my life complete.

Essra Mohawk

I'm Starting to Remember Why I Forgot

Backup Singer, the Mothers of Invention

I remember friends of my parents saying, "Watch her, she's going to grow up to be a beatnik." They were right. By the time I was fourteen I had a piano and a guitar, and I was filling up books with my songs and playing in coffeehouses. Music always got me over. Whenever I sang, everyone liked me. For that moment everything was cool.

Frank Zappa invited me to join the Mothers the first time he heard me play. The first time I heard the Mothers live, Jeremy Steig was opening that night. It was the first concert I ever saw on acid, and I ended up being in both bands. Frank liked to use names that meant the opposite of the character they represented. That was part of his humor. Suzie Creamcheese, for instance, was a tough little cookie, not soft and friendly like you'd expect from the name. I was really young and innocent, so Frank called me Uncle Meat, a name the Mothers' lead vocalist, Ray Collins, made up. I didn't mind being Uncle Meat as a member of Frank's band, but I didn't want that to be my name for my own music. After a couple of months of it I said, "Hey, I really don't want to be Uncle Meat." And Frank said, "I'm sorry, but I must insist that you are." I didn't quite agree. A few days went by and he said, "Okay, you don't have to be

Uncle Meat. If you don't want to make money out of the name, I will." "Fine," I said, "More power to ya." Later he came out with the album *Uncle Meat*, just to prove his point.

For my first album, Frank took me into the studio with the Mothers of Invention backing me up while I sang my own songs. We started with "Archgodliness of Purpleful Magic," since everyone knew the song from my performing it every night in his show. Frank had added it to the repertoire soon after he inducted me into his band. The guys proceeded to lay down a great track, except it didn't really cook until Billy Mundi, the drummer, let loose in the ride-out where the chart ended. You see, Zappa, whose process was to chart everything, had notated every drumbeat. I felt that although that might work very well for his music, my music was more organic and Billy's natural feel served it better than the patterns Frank had written out on Billy's charts. I had all the respect in the world for Frank Zappa, but this was my music. I respectfully asked him if Billy could play like he did in the ride-out from the top, so that the song could cook from beginning to end.

"Who's producing this album anyway?" said Frank, with that voice that made me want to fall in a hole as I turned every color.

"I guess you're not!" I blurted out, and walked out of the studio.

For once I didn't need my manager or anyone else to blow it for me. I blew it for myself. I kept walking. No one followed. I was still a teenager, so I guess I can forgive myself. The unfinished album of mostly naked piano vocals that was eventually released on Verve as my first album was the result of Frank making the point to me, "You want natural, I'll give you natural!"

With that incident in mind, I would like to bring up the ideas of Gurdjieff. One idea in particular, "recurrence," describes a kind of reincarnation where the deceased, instead of continuing forward along linear time to a new life, goes right back to the exact moment of birth of the same life she has just lived. It's like we keep going through this same time loop over and over until we get it right. Just like Bill Murray in *Groundhog Day*, only the movie used a day to convey the concept instead of a whole life. According to Gurdjieff, each time we live the same life a little differently until we get the whole thing right, at which point we're finally born into a new and different incarnation, that is, we finally reincarnate.

When I first read about this, I felt infinitely relieved, having been given fresh hope that I just might get another shot at all these things that had been bungled in my past, thanks to myself and others. Now, applying this concept to the scene in the studio, I have begun rehearsing my new answer to Frank. When he asks me again, "Who's producing this album, anyway?" I will answer, "You are. That's why I'm asking you this question." I have rehearsed this now many times so that I will be ready when we meet again in 1967.

There are a lot of things I don't remember about those years. Little by little I'm starting to remember. With some of the stuff, I'm starting to remember why I forgot. I was supposed to perform at Woodstock in '69, but we got stuck in traffic and arrived in time to hear the end of the last song of Joan Baez's closing performance that Friday night. I remember thinking, "We made it!" Then the stage went dark and stayed that way until the next morning. Saturday was Band Day, no solos allowed, so I couldn't do my set, even though those were my people out there. I was one with them. You had others who flew in, did their act, and left. They wouldn't even dirty their boots. But I really felt it was right for me to sing to those people. I begged to at least be allowed to sit in with someone. I was as effective as Moses asking Pharaoh, "Let my people go." Saturday afternoon I came down with sunstroke and left that night in a helicopter with Crosby, Stills, Nash, and Young.

I lived with my then husband, Frazier Mohawk, in Laurel Canyon, across the street from Paul Rothschild, who was producing Janis Joplin's first solo album, *Pearl*, and looking for material. My stuff was perfect for her. But we were a little tardy getting the songs to them, and, I'll tell you, she died before we delivered that tape.

To tell you the truth, I had no idea it would take this long for my music to be heard. But to me making music is natural like a waterfall. Nothing can stop its flow. I keep writing and singing. I'm working on my next album now. I'm always working on the next one.

to sell ten million records, but they looked like they were doing something right with that band at that time. The employees would play my demo tape to cabbies around NYC in an effort to spread the word and they asked me about my family and we went to fun dinners and all the other bands on the label were happy. They were the perfect label at that time—there was no threat of them selling or merging. They were totally independent and the CEO and directors had wives and kids and, you know, they were normal. So I moved to NYC and made my debut record, *Figure 8*.

Making the album was a really strange time. I remember getting so stressed out in my hotel room, pacing back and forth, tears streaming down my face, and having to make these choices and thinking to myself, "I'm now an adult." I wanted to make an album that didn't sound like anyone else, which is a record company's worst nightmare! My producer was all for it. When it was finished, the CEO, the A&R people, and the director of my company came to the studio and sat in those swivel chairs and my producer pressed the play button. We were all very nervous. I'm sure my producer had the music up ten times louder than we had EVER listened to it. The record people twitched and grimaced and I went outside and paced again. That was the turning point; that's when everything got hard. That's when we realized that the independent label I signed with actually had big label ideas for me. It was a weird tension. We were all on the wrong page. It was a case of both the label and myself having to compromise. They wanted a single; I wanted an album. It should have been easy, but it's easier said than done.

One day I was in the offices of Wind-Up's CEO having Chinese food for lunch and they were all discussing how bad they thought my record was. I was nearly in tears. I loved my record. Sure it wasn't *TRL* or MTV or K-Rock, or anything re-

Julia Darling

(www.rockerUSA.com/EssraMohawk)

Nobody's Jewel

Singer-Songwriter

My first U.S. gig was at Largo in L.A. I was working with Glen Ballard and looking to sign with his label. I was so dressed up it was ridiculous. In general, showcases suck. No one really knows what they're listening to, they're talking on the phone and schmoozing and boozing and your life is in that thirty minutes! Lots of good things came out of that gig, though. Having Glen Ballard in the audience sent everyone into a frenzy. He should have been onstage, not me.

Auditioning later for these labels, I found that some were interested in me only because another company was. Some saw Jewel when I played for them. Some saw Alanis Morissette. You can tell the labels that see you as another artist. It's as clear as day. They don't really look you in the eye. While I was auditioning I didn't allow myself to get excited about all the limos and hotels and the best dinners I've ever had. I was willing to trade every dinner and every limo for someone to tell me that I didn't sound like someone else and that they were going to sign me 'cause they loved me.

I decided to sign with Wind-Up 'cause they were the only label that didn't hear anyone else when I played. They had a small roster of bands and I didn't know that Creed would go on motely commercial, but damn it was good. They told me that they supported my unusual songwriting and would always be on my side and they only wanted what's best for me.

"Were not in it for the money, Julia, we are in it for the long term and we'll always be supportive. We've all made mistakes with this album and we promise it won't happen again, but we need you to help yourself, be a little more universal with your lyrics and a little more simplistic with your melodies, and we can get this off the ground."

Then I took out my cookie, cracked it in half, and read the message inside. It said: "You are surrounded by fortune-hunters."

So now Wind-Up has heard twenty new songs for my next album and still can't hear a hit. And I can't start rehearsing or touring or making a record until they hear one. So I have sat every day for the past two months and tried to write something that's disposable, and I can't do it. It's probably been the most frustrating period of my life.

But I got an album out of it, the album I'd heard in my head for years. And when I'm eighty years old and playing it to my grandkids and they're giggling at my old-fashioned lyrics, I'll be proud. That's the main thing.

Speech

In My Room

Leader, Arrested Development

Most of my first album I did in my bedroom. My father owned a nightclub in Milwaukee and he let me start DJ-ing when I was thirteen. Because I didn't know any instruments, my first instrument was a little sampler and a drum machine. Now I have my studio out in back of my house. I have an Ensonic EPS sampler/keyboard/sequencer and an HR16 drum machine. I produce and compose on a twenty-four track Neve board.

I tried piano lessons when I was younger, and I tried them again with my son. He was four at the time and I quit before he did. Now I think I've gotten too spoiled. I know how to get my songs out from sequencing and having other musicians help me. And I just don't want to take the time to learn a new instrument.

Arrested Development started in Atlanta. First we were called DLR (Disciples of a Lyrical Rebellion), then we were called Secret Society, then we came up with the name Arrested Development. At the time it was just me; my best friend, Headliner; and a white guy named Poppa John. But as I started learning more about black issues, Poppa John didn't really feel like that related to him, so he left the group. We basically created a lot of it in our bedrooms and then we would do some shows in clubs— open mikes and battle-of-the-bands types of thing, where we didn't have live instrumentation but we would come in with our sampler and a soundman. We would bring people with us on-stage to hold signs up with the lyrics or dance for us. At first we were doing more of a gangster style hip-hop. But that turned out not to really be our style. I wrote a song called "Sour Love" and it was sort of a poem and that gave me my first clue that I could really develop a style of my own musically.

"Tennessee" was the last song I wrote before we got signed. We already had songs like "Mr. Wendell" and "People Every-day." We shopped for a label deal for over three years with no success. Then Chrysalis wanted to do a single deal with "Mr. Wendell" on the A side and a song called "Natural" on side B. Right about that time my brother and my grandmother died within a week of each other. The last place I saw both of them was in the state of Tennessee. So I wrote the song "Tennessee," dedicated to my brother and grandmother. The label was ready to release "Mr. Wendell," but I said, "This is something I just wrote and I really feel emotionally attached to the song and want to put it out first." Luckily they liked it too. We also did a video for it. At the time EMI bought Chrysalis and they were dropping a lot of their groups, but the video for "Tennessee" is what made EMI decide to sign us to an album deal.

By that time we had six members. In putting the group together, I was looking more for image and vibes than musician-ship. But it wasn't an audition-type thing. It totally happened by accident. We were at a show once where I met Dionne Ferris and her fiancé at the time was Rasa Don. We got booed that night and they happened to be backstage encouraging us and I looked at his dreads and I looked at her vibe and I was like, "Man, why don't you join us?" And they said they would.

We did a tour of black colleges and no one would come to see us. We would be in these huge auditoriums. We would be onstage and the curtain would open and there would be five people in the place, so we would invite them onstage with us. We would let them perform with us.

Those early shows definitely helped to refine me as a musician and refine what I like to do and why I like to do it. If you don't get booed a whole lot in the beginning you might do it for the wrong reasons. I do it because I love music.

At first, we were a little nervous because many of the fans were older black people. We really wanted to be a hip fresh new band. We didn't want to be known as an older type thing. I mean, we were only eighteen or nineteen ourselves. But we had all these older fans and they started coming out to our shows and even when our first single was released, most of the first buyers of it were older people. So we were worried because we just felt like the hip-hop community wasn't going to embrace this. But we were wrong. They definitely wound up embracing us. I didn't realize this until one night in Charlotte. We'd been touring the south in a twelve-seat van with a U-haul on the back. When we pulled up to the club I saw there was a line around the block. I asked my road manager, who was also the driver, "Who else is performing tonight?" She said it's just us. I said, "Wow." That's when it hit me, when I realized that line was for us.

Being successful definitely put on a whole lot of pressure because the band was so communally oriented. People joined the band just 'cause of the vibe of the music. What happened once the money and fame got involved was that everyone wanted their own manager. Everyone felt that they weren't being represented and partially that was true. We were all naive as to how the business should go, so there were a lot of contracts that were done in mistake and a lot of agreements that weren't the best for myself and everyone else included. So everyone got management, everyone got lawyers, and everything got very complicated.

Tim Rice

A Good Idea at the Time

Lyricist, Jesus Christ Superstar, The Lion King, Aida

I always followed the theater quite a lot for the average bloke, compared with the other people at school, but I don't have a fanatical interest in it. Andrew [Lloyd Webber] was the one with the burning ambition to write for the theater. I just did it because it seemed like a good idea at the time.

We met in 1965. I'd been trying to make it as a singer and Andrew as a pop composer. He said, "I've got backing for a musical if I can come up with a lyricist," and I said I'd have a go. Although the musical came to nothing, we discovered that we could work well as a team. We were then asked by a schoolmaster friend of ours to write anything we liked, just a fifteen-or twenty-minute piece, for his kids at school, the end-of-the-term concert. It was a great comedown, because we had all these visions of a fantastic show on Broadway and in the West End of London, and now we were writing something for eight-to ten-year-olds. There was no money in it, but we thought we'd do it. The schoolmaster said that if it went well he might get a publishing company interested and perhaps it would become something that schools would use.

It was called *Joseph and the Amazing Technicolor Dreamcoat*. We purposely chose a Bible story because we wanted something that would appeal to teachers, so that they might buy it for their kids. And we made it funny because we wanted the kids to be amused. So it was a big success at this school and the publishers who'd been asked along by the school said they loved it and would like to publish it. So we made it into a half-hour piece, and they printed it up in a book and we each made fifty pounds. Of course, since *Superstar,* we've expanded *Joseph* to ninety minutes and it has now been quite a big hit as a professional show.

For a long time I'd had a great interest in Judas Iscariot, whom I thought was a fascinating character. Even before I met Andrew I thought it would be great to write a play about Judas in which Jesus is only a minor character. Or tell the story with Jesus as a major character but tell it from Judas' point of view. If you study the Bible, which I have as a result of writing *Superstar,* you'll find that the character of Judas doesn't really have any motives. He doesn't say anything, and he's only mentioned a couple of times. The Gospels were written some time later and it was convenient and easy to make Judas 100 percent bad. It was obviously helpful to the story to have it blamed on one guy. But I couldn't believe that this was plausible. After the success of *Joseph* one realized that one could mix modern music and the Bible, so we thought, let's have a go at writing a play on Judas.

I had worked at EMI, so we had some connections in the record world. It was for economic reasons that we were forced to get somebody to back the project as a record first, when we really wanted to write a show. But one little success in the schools wasn't going to make people fork out fifty thousand pounds to produce a show with us. After being turned down by several people, we got MCA Records in London interested, but they said it would be too expensive to do the whole album. They said they'd put out a single first. And if that did well, it would prove there was a market for it, and justify spending all that money for an album.

This was late summer of '69. We just had an outline, the framework, which was a lot of work, but there were only a few tunes and a few ideas. We went away and polished up the song "Superstar" and took it back to MCA. As soon as the single was finished, even though we didn't know whether it was going to be a hit or not, we went away and began writing the rest of the album. The way we worked was that first we would both discuss the framework, the plot. We'd say, for example, this song is going to be a violent song. It's got to say A, B, and C, therefore, we need a certain kind of tune. Andrew would then write a melody knowing what sort of tune we needed and then I'd put words to it after that. In about three or four months we'd done 80 percent of it.

Meanwhile, the single by Murray Head began taking off. It was a small hit in the U.S. and a big hit in Brazil and Belgium and Australia. On English sales alone the project would have been killed, but the worldwide sales were big enough for MCA to say go ahead. By February 1970 we'd written most of the work and then we had the colossal job of actually getting people to sing on the album. That almost took longer than writing it. It was like a military operation.

In October it was released in England and America and it sank in England. It was an immediate total flop. It got very good reviews, but it didn't get any airplay. But we had been booked to come to the States, because MCA liked what it had been given. So we thought, at least we'll get a trip out of it. But when we got here, we were met at the airport by a great army of people, press and everything, and we suddenly realized it was going to be a big hit here.

Ironically, the whole thing was not what we'd aimed for, because we were still really trying to write for the theater, and this album was a kind of demonstration record.

Of course, since *Superstar* our output has declined colossally, largely because we've been so busy running around the world doing an awful lot of work connected with it—but not actually creative work. Which I don't think matters. First, it takes a long time to get over the shell shock of something like *Superstar*, and second, we don't really want to hurry into something else. Take Lionel Bart, who wrote *Oliver!* He's a great writer, but he did come out with a lot of stuff very quickly after *Oliver!* and each one didn't do quite so well as the one before. I don't know how he worked, but I often think if he'd waited three or four years and put all his best things into one, it might have worked out better. So we can afford to wait, but I do think that about now is the time to do something else.

Ravi Raman
A Case of Vanity

Leader, Stradavatt

Financing the first Stradavatt album was quite a feat. Seeing that we had ten songs to record and only one thousand dollars for recording and mixing (at fifty dollars an hour), we spent six weeks—three nights a week—practicing the songs before setting foot in the studio. Leaving nothing to chance, we rehearsed to the point of overkill and mapped out virtually every note and every fill. We put down all the basic live tracks and all the drum tracks in one nine-hour marathon session. The lead vocals were also (miraculously) recorded in one eight-hour session. Due to everyone's work schedules and studio availability, the four of us were in the studio together only on the first day, the day we did background vocals, and for the very final mix. Given that we were going for a somewhat slick, well-produced sound, with so little money, I'm still amazed that we were able to pull it off so well.

Another major pressure we had while recording was our self-imposed deadline. On a whim I had written to the New Jersey Arts Center and explained who we were and asked if there was any possibility of us playing there. A few months later, they replied saying that Levi's sponsors a second stage for some of the shows held at the Arts Center and that after hearing our demo, they wanted us to open for Duran Duran! The show was on August 10, 1999. We wanted to release the album in time for our show so that we would have something to promote.

We first went into the studio on May 15 and we had to have the album released by August 8. While this seems like a lot of time, it actually wasn't because of the availability of band members (everyone has a day job) and the availability of studio time. Needless to say, there were quite a few sleepless nights in the studio and just as many bleary-eyed days at work. I did all the artwork and design, an old friend of ours handled the photography, and our guitarist did the layout on his computer. The duplication company received a Zip disc with all the artwork, and all they had to do was duplicate. Miraculously, we managed to meet the deadline, and the completed album was in our hands in time for the show.

(The label is our own creation as well. You always hear about artists getting their own "vanity" labels. Well, Vanity Records is literally our own vanity label.)

All the while, we were also doing everything we could to promote our big show. Flyers were put up weekly at Rutgers University. Everyone on our e-mail list was sent reminders every month about the show and updates about the progress in recording. Work-in-progress photos were also posted on our Web site. We also mass-mailed postcards promoting the show and the album. Our e-mail and snail-mail list included fans and local press and anyone even remotely involved in the music industry.

Rehearsal for the show was the easiest part of our entire summer. We had practiced so much for recording that we had become an extremely well oiled machine, performancewise.

The actual day of the show/release party was almost picture

perfect. The weather was ideal. Duran Duran had an almost sold-out show. Ironically, friends and relatives who never attended our shows actually showed up to this one, in spite of the fact that they paid nearly thirty dollars per ticket and braved rush-hour New Jersey traffic on a Thursday night.

Playing in front of a few thousand people at such a venue was nothing short of thrilling. It was everything I dreamed it would be. The people at the Arts Center also went out of their way to make us feel like we were in the "big time." We had our own sound men, air-conditioned trailer, and deli platter and drinks. Duran Duran's fans seemed to be very receptive to our music. After playing in hole-in-the-wall clubs for so long through "vintage" (old and beaten-up) equipment, it was amazing to play on a large stage with state-of-the-art sound equipment. We finally heard what we really sound like.

Kenny Withrow
The Smell of Success

Guitarist, Edie Brickell and New Bohemians

The worst part was definitely right after we got signed. We had a lot of producers who fell through, so it turned out to be about ten months of waiting to record, getting discouraged month after month. We had five going-away gigs in Dallas. It's so funny, that mentality—you're signed and leaving. You're going off and they'll never see you again. You don't realize that life goes on after you've been signed.

Making our first album was one of the hardest things I ever had to go through. We came from an improv background, so playing in the studio was very foreign to us. On top of that, we recorded in Wales. It was just us and the producer, slugging it out. They tell you not to bring any equipment over, that you can rent whatever you need. Of course, it didn't work that way. I went through just about every amp you could name, trying to get a good sound, and it still wasn't happening. I didn't realize how much my equipment had to do with my sound until I didn't have it. We had to switch to a studio drummer and that was another thing to deal with, because the old drummer and I were really tight, and a lot of our parts went really well together. Once we got this new drummer, a lot of my parts didn't make as much sense. The percussionist felt even worse than I did. We had keyboard on the album because of the producer, and that ended up taking a lot of the percussion rhythms, so our sound went out of the window and the record started sounding a whole lot more generic.

A lot of fans felt the band wasn't portrayed accurately on the album, which was true. Also, there was resentment toward Edie, because the name was changed to Edie Brickell and New Bohemians. She took a lot of flak that the record company was just trying to get her away from us.

Having a single going up the charts is an incredible bonding agent within a band. We all started getting along a lot better once we started touring. To me, the band part is no problem. Making the music is no problem. It's being a businessman and being part of a corporation that's the problem. All during the time "What I Am" was happening, we didn't have a manager. We were interviewing managers. We went through a string of them, and they were almost always close friends or dating somebody in the band. We should have had people helping us get singles out. "What I Am" got milked for everything it was worth. It was out too long, so people became, in my opinion, sick of us. We made four videos for our first album. Somebody could have been there to tell us not to make that video. The record company's always willing to let you spend as much money as you want. We were ill advised, and we wound up not making any money.

The weirdest thing, to tell you the truth, was that nobody tried to talk us out of breaking up.

Later, I played in this band called Billy Goat for a year and they finally have an album out. They were totally regional, on the road three years, losing money. For them, all the touring and all of the being together came to a head just around the time they got signed. At that point, they totally exploded and broke up. I've seen it happen again and again. Success destroys almost every band.

THE ROAD **IV**

Bruce Springsteen
A Sense of the Audience

Rock Performer

I always try to keep the big lights out of my eyes or else you can lose your sense of the audience, and that's the most important thing. There's so much going on in a big hall; there's a certain entertainment factor happening in the audience, and if you look past it, you're going to miss it. Unless you can win an audience you're in for a tough time. That's the most challenging thing, to play the kind of music you want to play, do the kind of shows that you want to do, and win people who will listen to you, win people's ears, all kinds of people. And then be able to sustain that relationship by being responsible about it.

Part of the idea of rock and roll is to go on the road. When you get on the road it feels like you've been there forever. After five shows you cannot recollect what it was like being home. I was always excited about traveling. I never had a real interest in staying home. I feel most at home onstage. I always have, since I was young. There's a very different feeling that happens when you get out there, really out there, where there's nothing for miles and miles around. Then you ride into a town and see all the houses. Like when we play Pittsburgh. That city, when the sun's out it looks like it's cloudy. It's great, because you see all the people in their gray little houses, and they come out and down to the show, and it's wild for a few hours. Then you go back to your room and you see that gray skyline and you feel like you whipped it, just for a night. For a little while you feel like you won something.

A lot of times I'm out there for me. I'm doing something at night that I have to do for myself. Nobody is going to demand that I play harder at night than I myself would want to play. When I come offstage I know how I played and I know how I feel. I get a feeling from playing I can never get from anything else. It's something inside. It's winning and losing on the inside all the time, never from the outside. It's a quiet, personal thing.

It's funny. I go back a certain amount of time with the same guys. We can think of nights when we were sixteen, playing in this teen club, and we get into all the stuff that's come down in between. It doesn't feel that much different. What happens inside is very much the same. I always felt free when I was young because I liked my job. I was playing in a band. I'd get up when I wanted to get up and go out and play at night. I was writing songs and just going out and playing to the people. As you become more successful the idea is to maintain that particular freedom, because you can lose it easily. When you get a little success it can confine you or it can give you more room. My ideal is just to do it better, just to keep going at it. I think that's where I'm most useful.

Joe Ely

You Never Know
What to Expect

Roots Rock Performer

I don't hit the road as hard as I used to. I do fifty to one hundred shows a year now, whereas I used to play two, three hundred shows a year. You can still get in a groove where the band starts playing tight and it's a lot of fun when everybody is really well oiled. It makes your confidence go up and when musicians play with a lot of confidence they play incredibly. They can do things that are so otherworldly you wonder where it came from. It's kind of ironic that it comes from going out there and beating your head against the road.

I picked Muddy Waters up one time at the airport in Lubbock, Texas. He pretty much summed up his whole life as twenty-two hours of misery and two hours of ecstasy. And I thought he hit the nail on the head. That's what keeps you going. Those two hours onstage where everybody's in complete sync and it's like the universe is perfect. There's no flaw in the universe, until the next morning. And then you can't find breakfast and you gotta travel twelve hours in a day.

Every once in a while there's just a period of time where the road becomes incredibly complicated or twisted. I remember this one amazing tour of Europe that was just disaster snapping at our heels. We were in this tour bus that didn't have a heater and it was the worst winter in Europe's history and we were trudging all across Germany in blankets. Then we went up to Norway and were touring around and we got up to the Arctic Circle. Every time we would leave someplace we'd read in the paper that the ferry we had been on the last day had just sunk. The hotel we had just stayed at before had burned to the ground.

So we were up at this university in Norway about 150 miles south of the Arctic Circle. We had been in Europe for about three weeks and I was completely losing it. I mean, at every single place we were trudging through the snow and ice. We were in this damn truck that was just slidin' over the two-lane highways. And in Norway they don't have guardrails, so you can just slide over the edge to fjords two thousand feet down. Doug Sahm lost a band one time in Norway on an icy road like that.

So we get to this place; we're playing at the student center. It's this huge round room and there isn't a soul in the room. The promoter says it's time to play. And I'm saying, "Wait a minute, there's nobody here." And he's going, "No, you must go out. Play, just play." We all kind of looked at each other and went, "Well, maybe the only way we can get paid is if we play a song." So we hit the first note of a song and around the edges of the room all these doors flew open. Thousands of Vikings came rushing to the stage. Within seconds there were two thousand people in this room and it actually had the effect of kind of slapping me in the face, and I was "All right, we got a gig!" At the end of it we were ecstatic!

It's funny; the road's like that. You never know what to expect. Especially when you're out of the country and you have all of these communication problems with what the show's all about and the equipment you use. You have transportation problems, and problems with the food and hotel reservations, and then you hit these places in the middle of nowhere and it turns into a memorable night. It doesn't matter if you have a record on the charts or if you don't, if you're in a huge hall or a nightclub. Going on the road there's always a conflict. I think that's the difference between new bands that are suddenly tossed out into it. They take everything personally. A young band will tend to make three or four albums then break up because they go out on tour and things aren't like they want them to be. Whereas us seasoned professionals, we know nothing's going to be right anyway. When you start going around to different countries, a lotta time you just have to completely fake it.

But it's amazing how music kind of finds its own level, how people discover your music and how passionate they are about it. The songs I'm singing, they're not about hoping the public will like them. They're about my life, my everyday existence, where I come from, and stories along the road. I'm really just out there telling stories. So you wonder, how did this guy in Norway hear it? Or there's somebody in Italy who doesn't speak a word of English singing along with it.

On that same tour, the next night we were playing in this biker club, kind of the Hell's Angels of Norway. It was a huge club that held about three hundred people. Because it was so cold, all of them had their motorcycles inside the club. Some of them were taking them apart. And they were all drinking this kind of 180 proof moonshine, or whatever they call it. Some of the guys had pistols in the front of their pants. So by the time we started playing, it was downright dangerous. There were these couches lined up along the sides of the stage and all throughout the whole place. And some people would have a couch and have their motorcycle in front of it. I noticed after about three songs that all of the people down in front of the stage had started making out with their girlfriends. By about the fourth song they were naked and making love right there, and we're looking at each other like "Where the hell are we and how did we get in this situation?" After the songs, nobody applauded; everybody was drunk and making love.

James Solberg
Ruining a Perfectly Good Hobby

Blues Singer, Sideman

A couple of weeks ago, on our way to Michigan, some crazed maniac decided to commit suicide in the front of my bus. That was a first. She was going ninety miles an hour and decided to take the front of my bus off. We've been going through transportation hell ever since.

We had to play a baseball stadium in Sioux Falls, South Dakota, at a Harley fund-raiser for the Make-A-Wish Foundation. The next day I headlined a blues festival in Quincy, Illinois. So I had to buy a new van and a trailer. I drove the trailer out to Sioux Falls to play Friday. Saturday morning, facing a thirteen-hour drive to Quincy under ideal conditions, it was obvious that the transmission on this little hippie-dippy minivan I bought wasn't going to pull a trailer and we weren't gonna make it. So I chartered an airplane from Sioux Falls to Quincy and back. In Quincy they decided it was necessary to charge me for equipment rental, even though it was probably gear from other bands on the festival. I already lost a thousand bucks hiring an airplane to get down there and back and now I had to lose more money to rent equipment. So then I flew back from Sioux Falls and tried to limp the van and trailer back here to Wisconsin. We made it sixty miles and then I gave up and bought a couple of hotel rooms for myself and the band and went to bed. I woke up yesterday, walked around, found this ratty old Suburban, bought it, and nailed my trailer on the ass end of it. On the way home last night, me and the organ player stopped at this casino; it had been such a disastrous weekend I decided I'd gamble whatever money I had left to try to meet payroll. So now we're penniless and I'm working on the stupid truck myself when I'd rather be out riding my motorcycle.

It's like I said once when I quit music for a while and went to work for Harley-Davidson: I ruined a perfectly good hobby by trying to turn it into a career.

But from a blues-band standpoint—from any standpoint— if you don't absolutely love what you're doing in life, you better not be doing it. I love the blues so deeply and have gained and lost so much from it, had so many incredible experiences and friends from it, that I wouldn't have it any other way. I try not to look at it like a business. I'd rather look at it on an enjoyment level rather than a career level. The only problem is, in this day and age, you can't afford to play the blues, no matter how bad you got them. But I'll get through this because I know things will get better. The summer is good if you pick up the festivals. For someone like me who has a band on salary whether they play or not, some of those gigs are rather lucrative, blues-wise, and you normally can get a chance to recoup in the summer what you lost from playing clubs all winter.

Assuming we get past our transportation problems, the whole next month we'll be playing almost every night. We leave tomorrow night for Norfolk, Nebraska, then to Wichita, Kansas, to Columbia, Missouri, and to Osage, Missouri. When things are going right I like to play sixty towns in sixty days or ninety towns in ninety days and then take a month off. To come back and forth every weekend like I have been is really strenuous. You get out of the road state of mind and get back in the home state of mind. And then a day later you have to turn around again. When you're on the road, you put the blinders on and you just go. You don't have to make any choices. You know what you gotta do. In a sense to me it's vacation. When I'm home it's crazy. When I'm home I've got to worry about all the things people worry about when they're home, like kids and bills and stuff.

Every gig has its own merits. I can't say there's any bad gigs out there unless you turn it into one. As long as there's one person in the crowd that came to see us, I'm gonna give them the same show I'd give to ten thousand people. When there's a really stone blind drunken idiot in the audience it's a challenge to get his attention away from what he's bound and determined to be distracted by and turn him into a fan. Sometimes you just can't do it. I used to play around Wisconsin in the sixties and the Packers were a big deal. I mean, don't even try tuning your guitar up on a Sunday when the Packer game is on. I don't get into too many of those situations anymore, but it still happens.

I played with Luther Allison on and off for over twenty-five years. There's a lot I learned from him as a human being and a musician and an entertainer. Like I always wondered what the hell he was up to, when we'd be up there for five hours and we haven't taken a break yet. It took me a long time to realize that what he was doing was connecting with each and every person in that audience. He didn't feel he was done performing until he was done making some sort of a connection, eye contact or whatever, with each individual person. I feel the same way, if we don't reach somebody in some shape or form, then we're not doing our job.

Dave Van Ronk

A Professional Performer

Folk Singer

The whole thing snowballed when the Dylan storm broke in 1963. Every guest set the man did, by the time he'd do the second song, the word was out on the street that Dylan was on-stage and his coterie would start pouring in. And while New York was kind of late on the scene as compared with Boston or Los Angeles, the typical New York attitude was, if anything is worth doing it's worth overdoing. There weren't three or five rooms to work in, there were fifteen or twenty.

We had five or six real fat years. Some people bought houses in the country, some people built recording studios—some people acquired expensive drug habits. And all of it was taken for granted. Every time you went out and had a couple of drinks with somebody you heard that someone had just landed some kind of bonanza, so-and-so just signed a contract with Columbia for mucho buckos and all of a sudden a town house is being ren-ovated on Commerce Street. And it was a kind of a situation where if you didn't have the money you could make a record or get another gig and then do what you wanted. There was an awful lot of money kicking around in 1965. My God, it was the big rock candy mountain. There was incredible prosperity for all of us.

Essentially, everybody was performing for everybody else. The community was the audience that counted. To get the approval of Joni Mitchell was infinitely better than a three-page write-up in the *Times*. And of course Joni herself was working for the same approval. We were all very conscious that something important was going on. I remember one time Phil Ochs came back from a recording session. I asked him how it went. "How did it go," he said. "We have just changed the entire course of Western civilization; that's how it went."

But the sixties as a paradigm allowed for a good deal of sloppiness of detail as well as form. A lot of the material you just couldn't get next to unless you were the person who had written it. I'm reminded of something Lenin said in 1920. The state publishing house had brought out a book of poetry, love poems from the poet to his wife, and Lenin said, "Don't they know there's a paper shortage? He should have printed two copies. One for him and one for his wife." Paris in the twenties comes to mind. There was an awful lot of smoke there, too, and not terribly much fire. Everybody was a genius on the Left Bank in 1922. In terms of staying power I think what was happening on Broadway in the thirties was more important.

I've always been a doomsayer. For years I'd been predicting grass growing on Macdougal Street, so I think it gave me some satisfaction when it finally happened. I probably felt like a Seventh-Day Adventist on the day the world really ended. I remember going somewhere on the train with Tom Paxton around 1970 and we were talking about the business end of the business. He said, "I saw this great cartoon in *The New Yorker* last week: one brontosaurus was talking to another, saying, 'I don't know about you, but frankly, this cold snap has me a little worried.'" A lot of things caused it. When political protest moved over to rock and roll, I think we lost a lot of our constituency. You had that business around St. Marks Place—the Fillmore East, the Electric Circus. I think the most important thing was the raising of the rents. Suddenly all those little dustbins on Bleecker and Macdougal started to look like gold mines to the landlords and they would jack up the rent literally every month. But in a club there's just so much you can charge for a cup of coffee, especially when the wave you're depending on is petering out anyway.

These days one gets very bad years, one gets phenomenally good years. You can't look at any twelve-month period and say this is a trend, because the trend is up and down and then up and then down. It's a living, which is probably more than I ever expected to get out of it. It's not a fortune, which at one time I did expect to get out of it. But that was a belief I only came to slowly and reluctantly. My attitude in the early sixties was, this is the way to make a decent living, it's not the road to the big rock candy mountain. I'm a professional performer; that's what I do for a living. The people who came into it after 1963—from between 1963 and 1968—their first exposure to the business was of visions of sugarplums dancing in their heads. For them the realization was a terrible shock.

Bob Malone

(www.bobmalone.com)

Another Kind of Musician

Keyboard Player, Solo Performer

As far as most people know, there are only two kinds of musicians. One kind plays weddings and bar mitzvahs, Top 40 covers, or strums an acoustic guitar at the local Beef & Brew. The other kind of musician is exceedingly rich and famous, whose latest hit gets played on the radio and who is invited to be a musical guest on *Saturday Night Live*. What most people don't know is that there is another kind of musician, who fits into neither of these categories. Like the famous musician, he makes recordings of his own songs, goes on the road and plays concerts all over the world, signs autographs, gets interviewed on the occasional radio station, and makes a living doing it. But also, like the other kind of musician working the dive bars and catering houses for chump change, most people have never heard of him.

I am this guy.

I do not have a contract with a major record label. I have, however, through years of busting my ass traveling around playing live, built up enough of an audience so that I can pay my rent playing my own music. It's a good life. I've never had to take a day job, and while there was a time when I had to play bar mitzvahs or wear a monkey suit and play wallpaper music in a hotel lounge, I've progressed to a place where I don't have to do that sort of work anymore. I do what I love to do, on my own terms.

Are major record labels actively seeking sarcastic thirty-five-year-old white guys who flail wildly at a piano and sing lyrics that will most assuredly go sailing right over the head of your average thirteen-year-old? Absolutely not. Is there a market for this sort of thing? You bet your ass! I have cultivated this market the old-fashioned, grassroots way: by playing thousands of live shows all over the world. In close to ten years of doing this I've played places that barely hold fifty people (and sometimes with far less than fifty people in them) and I've opened shows for crowds of anywhere from two thousand to ten thousand people. I've also played every kind of place in between. I sell CDs at the shows, and sometimes (especially in the early days) these sales would constitute my entire income for the evening.

Over the last five years, I've put out two CDs on my own record label, recorded with my own money. I have decent distribution, which gets my CDs into local record stores, which really helps. Each has sold slightly under ten thousand copies or so. Sales like this on a major label would be considered horrendous. And, with the mere buck or less per unit I would be making in a major-label deal, the debt a record and tour would put me in would have me back at the piano bar playing "Feelings" quicker than you could say "recoupable advance." On the other foot, as an indie artist who gets to keep essentially all of the money gained from his modest record sales, I'm damn near middle class!

These days, I play about two hundred dates a year on the road, I have a new record about to come out, as well as a book of road diaries, and my guarantee goes up a little more every year. I'm doing pretty well, and I'm doing what I love. Once in a while someone will even walk up to me on the street and say, "Hey! Aren't you Bob Malone?" and ask for an autograph.

However, my life is not for everybody. I have musician friends with comfortable steady gigs who often dream of striking out on the road to play the original music they have poured their heart and soul into. Then they have a good look at what I have to do to actually do that for a living, and they recoil in utter horror.

In the past year alone, I have driven cross-country and back four times. I have a minivan that is less than a year and a half old, and it already has ninety-five thousand miles on it. This February, I played my way from Los Angeles to Charleston, South Carolina, and back to L.A. again in just under three weeks. Along the way I barely missed getting blown away by a tornado in Arkansas (I sat in my van under an overpass while cows and house trailers swirled in the air around me). I drove seven hours through a snowstorm so bad that except for the big orange snowplows, and a few semis trying to make that Florida-to-Boston nonstop run in twenty-four hours, I was the only person crazy enough to be attempting to drive on the interstate. When I got to the venue, I found out only then that the show was canceled due to the weather. A deer came barreling out of total darkness and ran in front of my van on I-80 in western Nebraska; I clipped its back hoof. Luckily for both of us, it kept going. I was doing about eighty-five miles per hour at the time. If he'd run out there one second later, both me and that deer would have been roadkill.

Often, I am up at seven or eight in the morning to do a radio interview (morning drive time is the best time to be on). Sometimes, if it's a really good market for me, there will be two or three radio stations to go to in the course of a morning. This will often be followed in the afternoon by an in-store appearance at a record store, then sound check, then the show. Then, if you have a morning radio thing in the next town, you get in the truck after the show and drive all night. If you don't, you go back to the Motel 6, call your girlfriend, watch some TV, and get up the next morning and drive to the next town/state, set it up and do it again. Glamorous it is not.

The other important thing to note is that like so many of the other people who do what I do, I do it alone. I have no tour manager, no band, no personal assistants, no roadies. I have cultivated some excellent rhythm sections all over America, and when the money is particularly good, I will hire one of them to back me up. The rest of the time, I play solo. The hardest thing is the loneliness. It can really eat you up after a while. The best part is the hour onstage. That's what you put yourself through this for. On a good night, the hardships, no matter how absurd and soul crushing, are all worth it.

When I am not on the road, I am at home in the office eight hours a day: booking gigs, dealing with the radio people, the promoters, the distributors. Just me, the phone, and the laptop. Sometimes I even get a chance to write new songs.

I mostly play what is called the "listening room" circuit. Sometimes I headline; sometimes I open for someone who can pack the place, depending on how well known I am in the region I'm playing. These are small concert venues, set up with rows of chairs and a well-lit stage, like a small theater. Serious music aficionados come to these places and listen to you play. No one talks during your set, they laugh at your jokes, applaud appreciatively after your songs (and during, if you give 'em a particularly rippin' solo or social commentary), and, if you kick them in the ass with a good show, you get encores. When I first discovered this circuit, back when I was working the bars and didn't even know such rooms existed, it was a real revelation. I realized that I didn't have to wait for a big record deal that may or may not come so I could put on concerts and play my own music. I could do it *right now*. After being lucky enough to get an opening slot at a couple of these places, I decided I would either make a go of it playing original music and nothing else, or I would go back to school and get a real job. I went hungry for quite a while, but the decision eventually paid off. It was the best decision I ever made.

The third element of my job is the occasional gig opening for someone really famous. This is a whole different kind of thing entirely. Usually, as the support act, you will be facing anywhere between five thousand and ten thousand impatient fans, who have paid a lot of money and have waited a long time to see whoever it is that's headlining. Nobody wants to see the opening act. I have learned that in a situation such as this you have exactly the first half of the first song to make the crowd yours, or you are doomed to the longest forty-five minutes you have ever spent on a stage.

Do I want to be rich and famous? Most certainly. Do I want roadies, a band, a limo, and a suite at the Four Seasons when I am on the road? Of course. Do I want to be a musical guest on *Saturday Night Live*? Hell yeah! On the other hand, do I want a musically challenged record company A&R guy saying he "just doesn't hear a single"? Absolutely not.

Vast commercial success is perfectly fine. But I do believe that in the end you should do it for the sake of the music or probably not do it at all. If that means doing it on your own, we should all be thankful that we live in an age where we are able to do just that. I've got my Web site. I've got my record label. I can make a really great-sounding CD for around three thousand bucks. I take Visa, Mastercard, and American Express. Twenty years ago none of that was available to an artist. It was either suck up to the label, or it was back to doing four sets a night at the Beef & Brew. We have choices now. If the right deal comes along I'll take it. If the wrong deal comes along; I don't need it. That is the greatest joy of all of being independent.

Milt Jacoby
I Still Do the Same Job

Keyboard Player, Weddings and Bar Mitzvahs

The first guy I worked with was a trumpet player in Middletown, Connecticut, but his occupation was piano tuner. He would tune the piano for me and we would play at the Knights of Columbus, the Sons of Italy, the Italian-American club. We'd do a dance on a Saturday night or a Sunday afternoon and we'd get twelve dollars. New Year's Eve was good because sometimes we got paid fifty dollars. We played popular dance tunes, standards. Thirty, forty years later, I still do the same job. Some of the stuff is new, but most of it is still the same job. You do Gershwin, Cole Porter, Glenn Miller. We do a big-band set. We do a fifties set that always gets people up. We used to do Eagles, but we've been a little weak on the rock stuff over the years. At one time, when the line dances were big, we used to get people up with the Macarena and the Electric Slide.

When I came down to Fairfield, Connecticut, I started working for a band in the area, and then I found out I could do more on my own. I never worked with agents. I did all the booking myself. There were times I was doing a hundred, 120 jobs a year. We were doing every bar mitzvah, every wedding, and we kept that up for ten or fifteen years. But the problem was that DJs came along and we really couldn't compete with them, so that was the end of our run. But even when we were making fairly good money, you couldn't bring up a family on it because it wasn't steady. I've always worked other jobs. In addition to playing I taught English, I did sales. The worst part now is when I see a lot of very old looking people coming up to me, saying, you once played my bar mitzvah.

I usually had a five-piece band; one fella, who still works with me, played sax, clarinet, and flute; I had a drummer, a guitarist, the singer, and keyboards. We never had one rehearsal. We'd rehearse on the job, sometimes an hour before the job. I would go out and meet with the people before jobs and they would give me a list of the tunes they wanted. Usually we knew them. If we didn't we'd get the music and we'd figure it out. One time there was a wedding reception at the Three Door Restaurant in Bridgeport, and they were friends of the singer Peter Lemongello. They asked us to play at the reception and the first dance was a Peter Lemongello tune. I went to every music store, I went to every record shop, and couldn't find the song. So I went to the job and I'm a little nervous now, because they really want this tune because he's a friend—even though he wasn't going to be there. So were standing in the parking lot waiting for the guests to arrive from the ceremony and a guy pulls into the parking lot in a Corvette with the top down. I went over to him and I said, "Do you have any Peter Lemongello tapes in your car?" He said, "I've got all of them." So all the musicians got in the convertible and we learned the song off the tape deck. And we went in and played the first dance.

I used to rate the jobs on a scale of one to ten. I'd come home and my wife would say, "How was the job?" I'd say it was a twelve or it was a minus three. A high rating would be if you got everyone up dancing. We were always good at being somewhat aggressive. My son used to get angry with me, he'd say, "Dad, people want to talk, don't push them around." I'd say to him, "No, they hire me to push them around." I was very aggressive. I almost never had a job where people didn't get up and dance. Sometimes it got very difficult. I had a wedding at a beautiful home once where the bride's parents were on one side of the swimming pool and the groom's parents, who didn't speak English, were on the other side. I couldn't get these two families together, they had nothing in common, and they didn't like the idea of the kids getting married anyway. Nobody was there to have a good time. I thought they'd throw us in the pool.

You never knew what you were gonna do on a job, because there were so many factors. At one party they kept the baby carriage next to the piano and as I was playing the baby started to cry. They were all busy, so I reached out with my foot and instead of pumping the pedal of the piano I kept rocking the baby carriage. Another time I played for a very wealthy woman and they put a fella next to the piano who had had a stroke. And he started to lean over and fall and his wife was talking and didn't see him, so I kept pushing him back up. She stuck a hot dog, one of those pig in a blanket things, in his mouth, and she turned around again, and he started to spit it out, but I reached out and pushed it in. There was this one bar mitzvah where we could tell that everybody was sort of down. Then we found out by asking around that the grandfather had been found dead that morning and they were in no mood to party. So we packed up and went home. In bar and bat mitzvahs we did very little music. It was mostly games with the kids. One time we almost had to take the singer to the hospital, because some kid hit her with a limbo pole and she was bleeding on the floor. Luckily there was a doctor in the house who took care of her.

We had our little ways of doing things. Years ago at some of the country clubs you weren't allowed to fraternize with the guests. We played in Old Lyme, and they'd tell you, you go in this room, you go back and play, you go back in the room. And no drinks on the bandstand. There were a lot of rules. It used to be they wouldn't feed the musicians. But we negotiated that into a job once up in Middletown. The caterer had a reputation of being cheap, so he said to us during the job, which was strictly kosher, go in and get yourself some hors d'oeuvres. I said to him, we were supposed to get a meal. He said you don't need a meal, just get hors d'oeuvres. But I knew he had charged the people $7.50 for each of us. So I sent the guitar player out to McDonald's. At that time I was playing a Fender Rhodes piano with flat top. I told the guitar player, get the biggest bag you can get and put everything in it. He came back from McDonald's and I had him put the bag up on the piano. The caterer came running over. "Don't you know this is a kosher affair?" So I said, "Well, we gotta eat." He said, "Oh, put it away, I'll feed you."

Over the years I've had musicians who left the area. I had a singer who I talked into going into real estate. Then she wouldn't sing anymore because she was selling eight-hundred-thousand-dollar homes. A woman who sang with me became a cantor. Another guy went out to California. Another guy joined a show band in Las Vegas. I still do about thirty to fifty jobs a year. Most of the jobs I do now it's either a single or a trio. On solo shows I sing and I have a drum unit that actually sounds like a full band. Most of my jobs are corporate parties. I do the convalescent homes. People love the sing-along stuff there. This year I've got ten Christmas parties. Christmas and New Year's are the busiest part of the year. In my career I've only missed two New Year's Eves.

You always can tell how successful a job is by how many cards you get at the end of the night. I don't look for it anymore, but still I get calls. I got a call from a woman who was giving a party down in Westport. She said, "There used to be a musician named Milton Jacoby in the Hartford area; it must have been your father." Before I corrected her, I thanked her profusely.

Brenda Kahn

Almost Famous

Singer-Songwriter

My best gig was opening for Bob Dylan in front of six thousand people at the Zenith in Paris. It was the most exciting and proud night of my musical career. I was touring in France and my manager was trying to get me on the Dylan tour for months. I honestly never thought it was going to happen. But one night I was doing an interview and he walks in (which he never did) and says, "Just as soon as you're done come and talk to me." So I go into his office and he says, "I have good news and bad news. First the good news. I got you two dates on the Dylan tour." What's the bad news? "You can't play solo acoustic. They won't have any solo acoustic acts opening up for Dylan; that's the rule."

Well, the bass player that was on my record was playing with Boss Hog, and the drummer was the drummer in the last Replacements tour. I think he might have been out with them. So it was one of those things where I had to get a band together. I really didn't want to put a band together in France, because I didn't know anyone. Then I remembered meeting the guitar player from the Psychedelic Furs, John Ashton, when I opened up for Chris Whitley one night in Woodstock and John was running sound. He'd said, "If you ever need a guitar player let me know." So I call him up from France, and say, "Hey, John . . . you wanna play a show with me?" He's like, "Where are you?" And I said, "I'm in France and the show is opening up for Dylan in Paris." So he flew out. We threw this band together and it was totally amazing. The Dylan show in Paris was the apex of everything. I remember on my way over there listening to the radio and they had a Phil Collins song playing and then one of my songs. I'm being carted around in a Mercedes and my song is on the radio!

I opened up for Dylan a couple of dates; in Luxembourg they wouldn't let me out of the dressing room. It was bizarre. In Paris, I played one song solo acoustic, where the band dropped out, and after I got offstage Dylan's manager says Dylan wants to say hello to me. So I'm freaking out, excited, and shaking his hand. And he said, "Hey, I really liked that one song you sang solo," and I was scared to do it because they said no solo acts, so I said, "Well, it's not recorded, but as soon as it is I'll send you a copy." I didn't know what else to say. I was, like, "That is an awesome shirt you have on." We spoke for a few minutes and then I left.

I have to say the major-label experience was invaluable to me. Not only was it really fun touring around on someone else's dime, but I got do amazing things because of the Columbia hookup. I toured all over France to sold-out shows. I toured all over America even though I was never a big priority at the label. The record only sold fifty thousand copies, but I got so many people who E-mailed me after the fact and said, "I first got turned on to you by flipping through records and seeing the cover of your record and buying it because I thought it was so cool."

Unfortunately, my producer (and the head of A&R) had a big falling-out with the label and basically anything that was attached to him got canned. So, weeks before the scheduled re-lease, my next record was dropped by Columbia. Six months later I did a deal with Shanachie, just to get the record out. At the time they were trying to break into the original pop/rock-and-roll thing. But it wasn't a good idea for them. They weren't set up to do it and the record went nowhere.

It was a struggle when I first got dropped. I felt like a loser. You had to really be following my career to track me down at that point. As soon as my record was dropped, my manager stopped returning my phone calls. That was the most heart-breaking thing. By then I had obtained a certain level of profes-sionalism and I felt to go backward from that would somehow disappoint my fans and disappoint me. To all of a sudden be booking my own shows was really weird. I'd call up a club and they would be, like, "Oh, is this Brenda?" It was awkward. Like I had failed in some way. When really I had succeeded. I mean, I obtained such an amazing success in my music career and I'm just a kid from Jersey, right? I was touring for years and years and thousands of people bought my record and appreciated it and that's success, period. How many people dream of releasing a record? Opening up for Bob Dylan? When I opened up for David Byrne, at CBGB's, he stood on the side of the stage and watched me throughout the whole set, and when I walked off the stage he said, "Good songs." I was like, oh my God. It was my happiest moment. I'm totally cool.

It's really important to keep fame in perspective. For years I wanted to be famous and in a way I was and I never really knew it. Fame is like a drug; you can never be famous enough. But a record has an influence in the world way beyond yourself and your realm. As an artist, I think you just put the best work out that you can and it will be meaningful for the people who need to find it. Those people will find it. And it will change people's lives. That's the best thing you could hope for. It's the process, you know? It's the path. I finally realized after trying to push things through for so long that this is what you get. You get to perform. You get to play music for people. That's what you get. You don't get anything else. If you want to get money, then you have to be a businessperson. If you want to get famous, that's a whole industry networking game. But if you want to be a musician, you get to play music. That's what you get. You get that experience with the audience. That's the deal. It took me years and years and years to figure that out.

Bob Ayres

Who Was That Lady

Troubadour

After a ten-year period of having bands and playing with other bands, I set out on the road. One night, right after Christmas in '71, as I was playing to empty tables at a Holiday Inn bar in Oglala, Nebraska, a redheaded woman wearing sunglasses came and sat down at the nearest table. That night I gave a concert just to her.

At one point, she beckoned me to her table. She appeared fascinated with a song I had written called "Prisoner of the World" and asked me if I would sell it to her for five hundred dollars? I thought, if it's worth that much, it's probably worth a lot more. So I hedged on the deal.

Then she said "Frank has to hear this." I said, "Frank who?" "Sinatra," she replied. I thought it was a joke. But later she tried to call him or somebody connected with him, to no avail. I asked who she was, but she made it a guessing game. Said she was known for her dancing but she had made movies and had just purchased a home in the Malibu area. She told me how she studied for a part in a show about ladies of the evening. She told me of the Japanese custom of taking off their shoes before entering a room. She told me about doing a USO show at the Vietnam front lines.

The bar closed early that night and she and I spent a couple of hours on the town. At the end of the evening she was still a mystery to me. The next morning I checked the guest register of the hotel for a clue. The clerk said she was registered under the name of Parker and she had driven away in a car with Okinawa license plates. A few years later I found out that Parker was a name Shirley MacLaine used at that time.

Not long after that, the movie *Terms of Endearment* was made in Nebraska. Our then-governor (Bob Kerrey) began dating the co-star, Debra Winger. And I thought, Okay, but I dated the star of the movie one night—maybe. I've read most of her books since then, looking for a clue that says that night really happened. With all her talk about past lives, maybe that night was to work out some karma or make some more.

I met Bob Kerrey and wrote a rally song for him when he ran for the Senate. I was recently at his retirement party. Most of us think he should have run for president. But the point is, events and people seem to have common bonds, attractions, or threads that mold our destiny.

I sent an album of New Age music to Ms. MacLaine in 1985 and she wrote back that her secretary had filed it under "GREAT." In later years I sent a family-tree sketch to her and since I was big into interpreting names, I told her that her first name meant or came from a Scottish word "shire" which means a place of light in a grove or forest of trees. I don't know what I thought I might get by communicating. Maybe I could get that song off the ground. It's been in the closet for twenty-eight or twenty-nine years. She and the bartender might be the only ones who heard the tune.

I know I may never see you again
but I keep hoping that I'm wrong.
I know I may never see you again
but I'll keep your memory in this song.

I'll probably never know for sure who the woman was, but she sure fired my imagination. She inspired me to keep writing.

Richie Pollock

Playing the Metro

Guitarist, Love & Magic

We played the streets wherever we went: Greenwich Village in New York, Larimer Square in Denver, Mallory Square in Key West, Fisherman's Wharf in San Francisco, Hyde Park in London, Throlg in Copenhagen. In Old Montreal there were two main spots, Old Montreal and Prince Arthur Street, where there was no traffic so people could promenade up and down. From about 1987 to 1989, in Montreal we played the street in the summer and in the winter we played the Metro.

The Metro opened at a quarter to five. You had to sign up for your time slot and it was first come first served. Now, being the kind of people who had musician's hours meant we could never really go to sleep at eleven, which would have made sense; instead we'd go to sleep at one, get up at twenty after four, and jump into the car—which was our edge; everyone else had to wait for the Metro to open to get to the Verre Demondene station, which was one of the biggest stops, which meant there were a lot of ways to get in. But after hanging around and being part of the scene for a while, we found out where the guy unlocked the first door, and we parked where I could see the guy opening the door and be the first one through to sign up for a time slot—eight to ten, ten to twelve, twelve to two. We would take two to four at one part of the station and four to six at another part of the station. Of course, what most people didn't know was that you not only had to put your name on this list, but you had to lift up this certain garbage can and put your name on there too. If you didn't write your name down on the cardboard there, it meant that you were a pretender and you really didn't belong. If you really knew the ropes and were one of the regulars, you'd write your name on the cardboard of the garbage can, lift it up and put it back down.

At the Metro you could bring your sound system, and it echoed. Right in front of where you'd be standing is where the train pulled in, so that's where everyone was congregating. To the left is a huge escalator coming down and two big staircases coming down and we're at the bottom, against a wall. People are walking across, they're going all the way down the stairs, toward Longet, on the other side, which is where we went for our four-to-six slot. Overhead there's a balcony where people can also watch. It was a wonderful location. Our repertoire was mostly from the sixties and seventies: the Beatles, Simon and Garfunkel, Cat Stevens was very big. But one of the most amazing things happened when we finally decided to do Christmas songs. I mean almost every other person was throwing change. It was so overwhelming to me I almost couldn't take it, the outpouring that was going on. We made about two hundred dollars that day.

We saw a bunch of regulars, like the two little blond twins who would be dressed in identical little fur coats, with their mother, who would always give each one of them fifty cents or a dollar for us. Then there was the guy who was watching us and he comes over and he throws in a ten-dollar bill, but no smile, won't even make eye contact, and he walks away. Two minutes later he comes walking back in the other direction and he throws another ten-dollars. Then he stands around, and then he walks by again and he throws a twenty-dollar bill in. Then there was the guy who said, "Can you use this?" and he gives me a red short-sleeve shirt. I still have that shirt. One time we were playing and a lady who looked like Melina Mercouri comes over to the guitar case and throws a twenty-dollar bill in there. Linda's first impulse was to grab it, but then she figured she'd leave it. She asks us to sing "Leaving on a Jet Plane," and we do that song and, whoosh, she bends back down and she takes the twenty-dollar bill out of the case! And we go, "Oh, man, why didn't we take the money!" But then she reaches into her wallet and she pulls out a hundred-dollar bill and drops it in. Immediately Linda puts it in her pocket.

In 1989 we heard about the Buskers Festival. I thought, Oh, my God, I want to be part of this. I mean, we *are* the Buskers Festival. So there were 415 people from fifty different countries who applied and we were in the top ten, which meant they flew us to Fredrickton, New Brunswick, for five days, then flew us to Prince Edward Island for five days, and then eighteen days in Halifax. The whole town was taken over by buskers. We were billed as the folksingers. But we had to compete with professional circus acts. I mean, there were people up on stilts, swallowing fire, and riding unicycles, who had big sound systems blaring prerecorded music right down the block from us, yelling, "The show is here, the show is here!" Someone else was doing magic. It was intimidating. Everyone was making around two-hundred-dollars a day and if we could make eighty-dollars it was a lot.

And then we hit on what we were doing wrong. When we sang in the streets of Montreal and other places, we were used to going on and on and on, singing one song after another after another. Finally somebody said to us, "You've got to have a beginning, a middle, and an end, and then get rid of the crowd, get the next people to come. Hit them for your tips and then move them on." So we came up with the perfect solution. We sang around three songs together, in harmony, right up there, pumping, pumping. Then Linda would take the Big Gulp cup and I would sing "Mr. Tambourine Man" by myself and she would go up to all the people who had been sitting there watching us for those three songs and she would smile and wait in front of each person until they dug into their pocket and paid the piper. That's the day we made our two-hundred-dollars.

But the greatest secret we learned from the festival was Linda stepping out into the crowd. That became our trademark later on. And something else we picked up from watching these other buskers was that they would always take a volunteer from the crowd and have a bit revolve around them. That put us into the whole realization that the audience was something that needed to be interacted with, not just sung to, but interacted with. That was the main thing we took away from the festival, the realization of how to do it, how to go and dance with the lady in the back row. All of a sudden everyone's on your side, just from that one little isolated movement.

Amybeth Parravano

(amybeth_e@yahoo.com)

Elvis's Little Sister

Rockabilly Performer

My best gig was performing at the Peabody Hotel in Memphis, in 1997, for the fortieth-anniversary party for Jerry Lee Lewis. We performed in the Grand Ballroom. It is a full stage and seats five hundred to one thousand people. What made it special for me is that it was the first time I performed onstage not only with a known legend, but also with celebrity artist/actor Kris Kristofferson. The other celebrities I met that day were Sun Studio artists Billy Lee Riley, Malcolm Yelvington (grandfather of rockabilly), Alan Rich (Charlie Rich's son), and producer Sam Phillips and his sons. My producer, Joey Welz, from Bill Haley's Comets, was invited to play a "dueling piano" along with Jerry Lee and I got to sing backup vocals. I sang "Shake, Rattle and Roll," "Boppin' the Stroll," "Great Balls of Fire," Stagger Lee," and "Rock-a-Beatin' Boogie" with Jerry Lee. With Kris, the songs were "Me and Bobby McGee," "You Win Again," and "Born to Lose."

My transformation into Elvis's Lil Sista started when I began channeling Elvis while performing at a Sun Studio block party in Memphis during Elvis Tribute Week in 1996. During this week I also discovered that I am a sixth or seventh cousin to Elvis on the maternal side—the Smiths. The only surviving link would be Aunt Lorraine Smith, who is the woman that I refer to in my song "Roses on the Piano." When I went in the studio to record, I felt a "presence" come over me, as if I was being divinely touched by the Elvis aura.

I saw Elvis perform in concert in 1975 in Providence, Rhode Island, and almost rushed the stage. My unforeseen confrontation with his bodyguards sabotaged his receiving a copy of my first album, *Heaven.* So I wrote him a three-page letter about that day and included a copy of the album. He replied six months later with a signed autographed photo. Later I started communicating with Elvis in dreams. Then events occurred in reality that manifested what happened in the dreams. For example, he first appeared to me on an Opryland stage to an empty auditorium. In real life he had recurring dreams about being left alone in an empty auditorium with no fans! I discovered this fact long after I had the dream. Then I began singing to his recordings (and began to sound a lot like him).

Before becoming Elvis's Lil Sista, I performed country rock, Top 40, MOR, and gospel. Now I perform early Elvis cover songs and originals. I don't wear a costume but wear clothes similar to what he would have worn—V-neck shirts, flare-leg slacks, scarves, and sunglasses. My hair is in an up-do and sometimes a ponytail. I'd like to have a white-and-gold jeweled jumpsuit designed for me with a big collar! My band is mostly studio musicians, seasoned road players. Dave Fender (Leo Fender of Fender guitars' nephew) is lead guitar. Nick Gallup does some rhythm. I play most of my rhythm guitar live and on record. Players around Sun Studios are available when needed. Presently I perform a few times a month at concerts, fairs, and festivals.

My first gig as Elvis's Lil Sista was at the Sun Studio block party during the Memphis Crossroads Convention in 1997 at the Peabody Hotel. I sang "Hound Dog," "Blue Suede Shoes," "Heartbreak Hotel," and my original, "My Baby Thinks He's Elvis." The audience stood in awe of me.

Steve Fowler

The Night Bob Seger
Stopped My Show

Guitarist, the Fowler Brothers

My brother James and I formed our first serious band, Hobson's Choice, in the summer of 1978. Both of us had been guitar players in other bands and we had always worked with a lead singer. We were in the middle of a rehearsal when I heard the phone ringing. What luck! The owner of a club called Caribbean in southwest Houston was calling *me* to see if we could fill in a last-minute cancellation on Friday, which turned out to be the very next evening.

Normally I'd be elated, as I had been trying to book a gig at this club for some time, but there was a slight problem that kept me from being too excited. You see, we were in the middle of auditioning a new drummer. This may not sound like a major problem for a good drummer, but our old drummer was also the lead singer of the band. The drummer we were auditioning at the time had already stated that he did not and would not sing. So yes, this was a major problem. I told the club owner that I'd call right back.

We quickly had a band meeting. Though we'd only been rehearsing about two hours, the three of us agreed that we liked our new drummer. His ability and style on the drums were a level above what we had before and above all else his personality fit with ours. The feeling was mutual and he officially became our fourth member. After much discussion it was unanimously agreed that since this was the first time a club owner had called us, we should try and do the gig. After all, we'd be doing him a favor filling in at such short notice. It was also decided that since I had written most of the original songs we'd been practicing I would now be the lead singer. The bass player said he knew the words to a few of the covers and volunteered to handle those. We were in business!

As I was calling back the club owner to confirm the booking, this line went though my head, "When opportunity knocks you'd better answer the door."

Needless to say, we practiced long and hard that night trying to learn all the material. We kept scratching out songs from the set list that did not work well and highlighting those that worked. I also copied down the words to a few of the cover songs we decided to try.

We arrived early the next night. A sign by the door read: "LIVE MUSIC TONIGHT $4.00 COVER." As we loaded in, the bartender came over and said he had heard of us by way of Dallas, Texas. As we started setting up, the club owner came over and thanked us for helping him out. I thought, So far, so good.

Although only a few people were in the audience, we started our first song promptly at 9:00 P.M. Just as I began singing the second song, I noticed the club owner walk over to the sign by the door. He took out a magic marker from his pocket and slashed through "$4.00 cover" and wrote "$2.00."

If that wasn't demoralizing enough, it was soon to get worse. In the middle of the fifth song of the evening I started hearing a strange noise. I thought it was feedback at first. Then the stage lights went out and the strange sound grew louder and louder until none of us could continue and we had to stop playing. It was only then that I recognized the strange noise. It was Bob Seger turned all the way up on the club's sound system.

The audience was as confused as we were. After what seemed like an eternity but was actually only a few seconds, the club owner walked right up to the stage and gave us the heave-ho sign. As I pulled my guitar off and stepped down from the stage to see what the problem was, he said, "The music's okay, but you can't sing worth shit! Don't come back here unless you get a decent singer!"

We left quickly. I don't remember anything else about that night. But James and I decided that no one was going to tell us we couldn't sing. However, after a few weeks of humiliation, I knew that I would have to seriously begin working on my singing. I even went to a singing coach for a while. After a year or so and a few good reviews under our belt I decided it was time to return to Caribbean. I was determined to get back on the horse and redo the gig. But when I got there, I found out that it was closed down and boarded up. I guess that was a little bit of revenge.

Ian Moore

(www.ianmoore.com)

Mixed Emotions

Blues Rock Performer

We knew the Stones tour was coming up and we knew that it would be a great tour for us to do so we all kind of put our heads together and attacked them from every angle. We had a booking agent talk to them. We had a manager talking to them. We knew their production company. And at the same time we were also doing pretty good numbers in most of the towns where they were playing. We'd been working on it for a long time, but we still knew it was a long shot. So when it happened, you can imagine we were pretty excited. But I don't think we did anything special. I don't think we rehearsed or anything. At that point we were touring as much or more than any other band in the United States, so we were pretty confident.

We were there for a leg of the tour, six shows. The first show was El Paso. We had a good following there. That's part of why they took us. The Rolling Stones are a big business. They're definitely aware of the numbers. I mean, Mick's an accountant. He's the guy who makes most of the business decisions. What I've heard is that supposedly Mick was the one from the Stones camp who decided these guys would be great. So we met everybody in the band except for Mick. He was at the monitor board for almost every show, so he watched us almost every night, but he never introduced himself. Charlie came to the dressing room. I jammed with Keith and Ronnie a couple of times. I definitely bonded with the two them because I knew as much about the same music as they did. I had played with a lot of the same people, like Albert King, Albert Collins, a lot of the soul singers. We played some funky old soul stuff that 99 percent of the world doesn't know, bonded on that, and had a great time.

Everybody was really down to earth and the organization was really warm. When we got there they had people specifically set up to make sure we were all right. Our dressing room was really nice. They treated us with respect and I liked that because it showed me that you can be on that level and still have integrity. Because I found in my career, as small as it was in comparison, that as you brought more and more people in it got more and more difficult to keep your vision of a show. You can't control it. So you can only imagine what it's like when there's fifty or one hundred people talking for you. I was impressed by how well run it was.

We were the first band on. A lot of people came out to see us. It wasn't as packed as when the Stones went on, but at that point we had a really good thing going in Texas, so people came out early. Whenever you have something like that your ensemble of people around you increases tenfold. We have a pretty tight ship as far as my crew. Basically I have a couple of crew guys, and my manager will come out to the more important shows. Sometimes I'll have a tour manager. But for those shows we had people everywhere. It was really an occasion. I still have a bunch of people who let me stay at their house or take me out to lunch because I set them up with Stones tickets. Austin is a great rock-and-roll town, so everybody was out, and I felt like I was the eye of the hurricane. Here I am in this maelstrom of

energy and everybody's partying and going crazy and having sex
with each other, living the rock-and-roll dream, and I'm the one
who brought these people into this thing, and I'm just sort of
sitting there watching it happen, super-aware of not wanting to
piss anybody off.

The last show was Dallas, and that was definitely the best
show to me. All of a sudden it started raining and things got a lot
more electric and weird and that was really enjoyable 'cause I felt
like that was the closest to a classic Stones concert that I was
going to get. And on that show I had one of the biggest epiphanies of my career, in that I knew that there was going to be a really difficult couple of years after that for me, because I'd built up
to that point and that was a real peak, and there was a lot of mis-
understanding about where I was going in my career. So there I
was, at the height of the Dallas show, and instead of reveling in it,
I was realizing that, whoa, the next couple of years are going to be
tough. We had generated all this momentum and I realized that
there was a lot I could capitalize on but it wasn't necessarily the
direction I wanted to go in. So I kind of started changing. One of
the things I loved about the Stones was that at the height of their
career they were very, very unafraid to change. They were successful from the start, but they made some amazing turns in their
career musically and culturally, and that's something I feel very
few artists, especially artists who are big like they were, do anymore. And it's something that was a big influence on me. I had
my record deal, my publishing deal, but it was more a matter of
here is a music that had already pretty much had its day in a lot
of ways. The Rolling Stones and the Animals, and a few other
English bands, were at the forefront of creating this kind of rock
and roll and they had every right to keep doing it. But for a
young artist like myself it's really important to internalize all that
music and come up with something new. Imitating something

that's already happened and not really adding to it is a moot point. There's no reason to do it. If you were to come out and do that music now, then you're just held up to the people who did it better before you.

They weren't bad years, they were just tough years; in fact, they were probably some of the most rewarding years I'll ever have in my career, because I really had that feeling of doing my own thing against the odds. And I had little payoffs. I broke down my image of who I was, recreated it, and I'm still in the process of it. But as far as the tour, I was definitely glad to be involved in it. It made me feel good. It made me feel validated. When I was a kid listening to Stones records I never had an idea that anything like that would happen. When I first started playing my goal was to get onstage at Antone's. That was my goal. As far as I knew if I could get up and play on the same stage where a lot of the people that I really loved had played, that would be it for me. But I just had a sense of, here I am sitting on the stage at something other people will definitely look at as one of the pinnacles of my career, and realizing that there were a lot of other things I wanted to do.

When you play with arguably the greatest rock band of all time, it really puts your own music into focus and what you want to be in your career. I mean, these guys made a template for a whole sound. It gives you a lot of things to judge what you're doing. Of course, it also gives you bragging rights. I've never pulled that trump card, but I always have this fantasy of getting into an argument with some musician who's disrespecting what I'm doing, and going, "Dude, I opened for the Stones."

THE SET VI

Leo Kottke
In Concert

Guitar Player

I ran into a woman on a plane once who was a composer going to some sort of forum. She was writing something, and from what she was writing, it looked really serial and not very tonal. I asked her how she felt about tonality. She just lit into me as if I was tonality itself. She didn't want to hear the least bit of sentiment, romanticism, or melody. That was not what music was all about. She wanted to explore the math of it and she was dead set on it. I just don't know about that kind of stuff. I've heard some of it that I like, but I'm not convinced when it's really working that they've avoided sentiment, because I don't see how a listener can help but impose his own. Something I knew when I was starting out was that I wanted to play stuff that played itself. I wanted to write things that were not some tortured tour of theory, that could be played rather than overcome. There's a way to do complicated music so that it fits or it floats and that always has to happen. I don't care if it's Stravinsky.

Somewhere inside of me I never expected that I'd be doing this for this long. It seemed a little outside the realms of possibility. There's a picture in Dizzy Gillespie's autobiography that was taken of him sitting in a dressing room in the Lighthouse up in California. It's obviously one of those dressing rooms that just takes the heart out of you when you see it. There's a caption: "Sometimes I wonder . . ." And he's sitting there with his head hanging down. That's what gets hard to bear, as petty as that sounds; that really gets to be very draining, and if you don't get some confirmation of the fact that it's worth doing, and that it sustains a lot of people, not just you, I think it finally becomes unlivable.

The writing and the playing are what sustain you. That's what keeps you interested. For myself and for most people I know, playing in concerts is not what you're originally there for, but once you've had it for a couple of years, you could not give it up. It becomes, I think, the center of it all.

Early on, when I used to sneak a peek at the audience, it would just blow me out of the water, because I realized it was real and I'd forget everything that I thought I knew. Eventually I discovered that sense that I didn't have to think about what was going to happen. That's what I learned best. I usually know what tune I'm going to start the set with and what three or four tunes I will end the set with, and I go out there and I get the ball rolling, and I, just as much as the audience, follow my nose. I've come to enjoy going out and having to come up with something. It gives you another window, another way to see things, if you're willing to make terrible errors.

Arthur Rubenstein wrote about it in *The Cult of the Secret Current*. What "in concert" means is that you are together. You're not mind-reading. It's not doing what the audience wants or what you want, but there's a real communicated sense of where you're going next and you obey that because it's irresistible.

Phil Everly

Stand and Deliver

Singer, the Everly Brothers

A friend of mine had a father who ran a tent show. It was a real carny operation. Occasionally Bill Monroe would come on the tour. A couple of times we rode with him in his limo—thirteen of us. That's the way they toured in those days, in limos and station wagons. The station wagons were for equipment. Most of the time you rolled at night, what you call hit and run. You'd sleep in the car or else in a real dive. We hit some really seedy places where you wouldn't even want to use the toilet. And it was the best tour we'd been on! We'd only gotten it because our friend had talked her father into hiring us. We were making ninety dollars a week and thought it was hot stuff.

When we moved to Nashville in 1955, it was the first year anybody had heard of Elvis. The people knew there was something going on with him because he was stealing the show from everyone. He was on the Hank Snow tour, opening the show at first, but finally they had to put him on last, because all the stars were walking off the tour. Everybody with long hair was immediately thought to be in the same area, but the area wasn't big, it was just the one guy, they thought. They didn't know it was going on all over the country.

Nobody thought anything positive about what we were

doing. There was a thought process that permeated the fifties that you had to fight against. "They really don't know what they're doing. This isn't going to last because they're not really performers." But those short sets we did, the immediate aspects of it, helped create the foundation upon which this new stuff is built. In the fifties there were guys doing two-hour shows, but not on the Show of Stars, because the Show of Stars had fifteen acts and the whole show was two hours. Everybody only remembers the things in the big cities, but that's only sixty days and then you'd have the rest of the year to play. Eventually all of the acts got wise that they could do it themselves because all the time they weren't playing for Irvin Feld or Alan Freed they were making more money and drawing more people. It all depends on whether you can stand and deliver. If you stayed hot, you outgrew the big shows. By 1960 they were pretty much gone anyhow.

But we were at the forefront of every fight in rock and roll. It was a fight with your own tastes pitted against established, trained people. The whole world was anti–rock and roll. Nobody in authority knew what was going on. The only ones who knew what was happening were the acts. So the tendency was to leave you alone and let you do what you did. Afterward everybody would explain how you did it. We were fairly ignorant of its value and impact, which I think is why rock lasted. It's when you start analyzing rock and roll, which is what the industry started to do, to figure out what was going on and then to try to create it, that you get into trouble. The smarter older people were the ones who would let you do as much as you could and then guide you to a point where you were getting as much of yourself out as possible.

I knew at the time rock and roll wasn't something you could build a life on. But making music is something you can't help but do. You do it and you can't stop yourself, and you'll do it no matter what. I sing almost every day to somebody in this house, showing a song, doing something. And every time I sing, whether the audience is one, or whatever, it's the same thing. If you keep at it steady, eventually you'll turn out a lot of things. Once, after a three-year layoff, I played the Palomino. It was close by, and I didn't have to work too hard. I surprised myself. Before that show I just didn't want it badly enough to do something about it. But it was fun and I had a good time.

I'll do it again until it doesn't make me feel good anymore.

Bob Mould

Breaking Conventions

Guitarist, Hüsker Dü

We usually do a seventy-five-minute set. We work in blocks of three or four songs that fit well together, usually taken right off the records in that order. We'll jump from maybe half of side one of one album to side two of another album, and then interchange a lot of songs depending on the mood, depending on what the crowd's like, and depending on how we're feeling. If somebody blew their voice out, we try to avoid a song where there's a lot of high notes. We try to cover for each other. It's a matter of pacing, knowing your material, knowing how your material is going to affect people. You know how you run key changes together, how you run tempos together. We traditionally come out for about twenty-five or thirty minutes of solid blasting, where it's really loud and pretty up-tempo and aggressive. We'll take it down for about fifteen or twenty just to give people a little bit of a breather. We never used to give people a breather before. We used to play forty-five minutes straight just as fast as we could. Some nights my hands are so tired that I cannot bend a note a whole third. And some nights the acoustics in the room don't allow your playing to come across as well as it should. Those nights you fall back into your per-the-record playing. But the good nights are real good. Sometimes I think it's the best we ever played and people come up to us and go, "Wow, that was weird."

To get out there in your regular clothes and break convention and just play what you feel like playing is a big challenge. I think for a lot of people the accoutrements, whether it's the look or the whammy bar or whatever, are a confidence builder for them. The more clichés, the more trappings they can surround themselves with, the more comfortable they think they are because it's tried and true. We used to get a little nervous before we played, now we look forward to it. Every night is a challenge for us to get it across the way it's supposed to be. Not even worrying about breaking convention, just doing emotionally what's coming out of your hands and your head at that moment and hoping that you can get it across. People starting to accept your music helps. You get to the other side, where it becomes second nature. A lot of it is just winging it. Sometimes I'll get off on a tangent where I can't come back. I just go blank.

We spent about four months practicing and writing two sets of material, after that it took almost a year and a half before we played out of town because we were getting our chops together. Then we put a single out and then we hit the road, started touring, starting living on a wing and a prayer. We just got in a truck and went. We had some friends along the way who had some contacts with promoters and we tried to get on shows for ten dollars, twenty dollars, thirty dollars, anything we could do. We learned a lot about life. We were sleeping on people's floors, living on three dollars a day. It was not a lot of fun. Then the critics in the bigger papers started going, "Look, I don't like this kind of music, but these guys have an edge and an energy and a way with a crowd that nobody else has." And it just started filtering back and a buzz got started and once it gets started, then you can do real well. And then the buzz gets real big, and that's when they set you up for the backlash, which is inevitable. You've got to have a tough skin. If you're a musician you've got to be callused all over.

Peter Buck

Momentum

Guitarist, R.E.M.

When the band started I was Michael [Stipe]'s friend and I was going to be in the band, so it was like, "What are you going to do, Peter?" I didn't know, because Mike [Mills] could play guitar better than me at the time. He said, "Maybe you should play bass"; I said, "Please just don't let me play drums." There was talk about me getting an organ and just starting with two fingers and working from there. But I had a guitar lying around the house. Oh, I can play that. My younger brother is a classical musician, and I'd been too embarrassed up to that point to pick up the guitar. It was really hard for me to play Chuck Berry with him in the next room doing this stuff that sounds like five guitarists fighting at once.

We never play badly anymore. We used to be outrageously good or outrageously terrible and anywhere in between half the time. Now we're pretty much at the peak of our form virtually every night. That's because we've never made a step until we thought we were ready. We've played fairly large places and we don't really have a problem utilizing the space on the stage. It hasn't made us change, but I think you have to be a little bit more sure of yourself, because you can lose it easily in a big place. In a small club you can be bad for half the set and nobody notices 'cause it's hot and sweaty and people are dancing. In these big places the energy will disappear rapidly, so you've got to be a lot more focused. And you want to do that without resorting to stadium gestures or going overboard in any way.

If you let your concentration wander, things can start going wrong in a hurry. A lot of it is momentum. We've walked out and done four songs as great as we've ever done, and then fallen flat on our faces. We just didn't get it back. It's a real ebb and flow. It's difficult to keep the momentum high sometimes when you're doing a newer song that everyone in the audience hasn't already heard. We did a whole tour with twelve new songs in a seventeen-song set and the audience didn't really know what was going on. But we insist on challenging our audience. We don't want to do what they expect. We don't want to go up there and just play the hits—we want to do new material or rearrange some older stuff. We give our audience credit for intelligence.

Encores are the best part of the night. We'll do encores of three or four songs each. That's the most confident time. No matter what happens during the set we usually come up real good for the encores. It's a weird psychology. You leave the stage and then you come back and it gives you a second or third wind. You're dead tired and you can come back and feel refreshed. You can always play longer and harder than you think you can, but ideally, what we want to do is leave the stage feeling that that's it; there's no more; you can't top it. It's an old cliché that you like to end on a fast one; if we're having a real good night, we can end on a slow one. At any rate, you want to leave on a real high note. We change the set every night, so we change the encores, too, change the order, change the tunes. That keeps the concentration up.

In a lot of ways rock and roll is about illusion. There could be four guys onstage, but there's another twenty people making sure that it works well—even something as simple as the lights.

If the guy doesn't turn the right switch, you look like a dork. Part of working on the road is getting the cues straight. As a band we never really wanted to have an "act." When I read about myself or see tapes of us onstage and stuff, we tend to be a bit larger than life, but that's not an image we've created. I think that the kind of people we are onstage is pretty close to the people that we really are. I'm not a completely different person onstage, 'cause I don't want to have to maintain that. I'm too lazy.

David Lowery

Don't Worry About Having a Good Time

Lead Singer, Camper Van Beethoven, Cracker

We wanted a band that didn't have to worry about having the right style to get into the correct club, so we decided to just play parties. We played acoustic guitars that were plugged into amps. We had a friend who played violin. We went, "Great, just join our band; we'll figure it out later." Then another friend joined who was playing melodion and harmonica and all these odd instruments. I was playing drums and sometimes the drummer was singing. We were just switching off and playing these punk-rock covers like "Nervous Breakdown" by Black Flag, some great Fear stuff, Flipper, the Clash. We also made up a bunch of songs and we took a bunch of songs from other bands that we were in and played them in a different style. We started to get this real acoustic sort of cynical, harsh, but also kind of real innocent sound, half folk, half punk. And we liked it. We were developing into something good. We played San Francisco and we got fans there; we played L.A. and we got fans there, and we slowly built it up. Then we put out records and we discovered we could go on to other towns and we'd gain more fans every time we went to a town. When it comes down to it, I think records are sold by word of mouth. Touring develops a buzz about a band and that's where our appeal has come from.

Playing music is performance, so there's a certain amount of self-consciousness. Whenever you're singing, people are looking at you, so I feel that burden at times. You also have to deal with this kind of subconscious internal logic that you think you have to look like you're happy when you're playing and that's what the audience wants. It's not really true. In the last few years I learned to discard that. We've been told, "You guys didn't look like you were having very much fun last night." But worrying about it for the next six shows is much worse than just looking like you're not having a good time. Sometimes you look like you're having a great time and sometimes you don't. I tell everybody, "Don't worry about having a good time, just play the show. If you don't feel like saying anything between songs, don't say anything. If you don't feel like saying anything to the audience for the whole night, don't say anything." That doesn't always mean you're not having a good time. Sometimes talking just messes up your emotional state. You have to feel relaxed in front of the audience, not like you're under any pressure.

A good show has to do with the rhythm part, where everything is in the pocket, you're completely relaxed, and the whole show just seems natural. It's like you were born to do this and you play every song like it's incredibly fresh. I played this every night for two months, but this is just like when I first made it up. That's actually when you feel like the live show is transcendental. Sometimes this has nothing to do with what the audience thinks. But confidence with a band is like a roll of the dice. The first song you played, for some reason, you didn't get the tone settings right and you're thinking about it. Maybe you're playing really well but you're going, Oh man, this sounds like crap. And you walk back after that first song and get your sound right, but you never recover your confidence through the whole show. And you may play a really good show, but you didn't feel like it.

Nine out of ten gigs something happens that says, "This is why I'm doing it." You play a song and you're completely proud of your band, you're going, "We are playing really well and we've written a great song and people appreciate us." That happens for at least one song every show. Sometimes there's a whole set like that. Other times, some songs we thought were great six months later we realize the audience was right—we were just being weird. We were involved in the sound from some musician point of view rather than a fan point of view. The song is more fun to play than it is to listen to. I'll always give up songs like that.

Dee Dee Ramone
You Have to Keep Playing

Bass Player, the Ramones

I liked the bass originally because it was strong and I played in a violent style; it's a violent explosion of my feelings. I don't play a melodic style. I don't play fourths or fifths, scales, or anything like that in bass progressions. The bass line I play is the same line as the guitar plays. I just play the note of the chord and I stay on that. It's sort of a box pattern and I just hammer it out.

You have to stay in shape. You have to keep playing all the time. You've got to practice at home and get together with other musicians; it doesn't have to be the guys in your band. I do chromatic scales to stay in shape. First I do them slow. If I haven't been practicing 'cause I'm on the road and when I come home I'm rusty, I do them very neat. Then, when I get a lot of speed in them I turn the metronome up fast. If we take off for three weeks or so, then a couple of days before a tour starts we'll go into the studio and warm up. But there are times when we don't rehearse and we go up there after two or three weeks off and we still have it. It's just there. It's inbred in us now.

Our performances are rugged and fast and very hard core now. Everything has to become a physical thud, like an assault on the audience. We play everything fast no matter what the song was like on the record. It sounds like one long song. It's best to keep it at a natural level, and to do that you've actually got to get out there live; you can't just hide in the studio. You've got to keep in touch with your reality, and reality is live rock. The crowd excites us. They slam-dance and jump on the stage and dive off the stage and do those little things that they do. I like that. It keeps everything interesting.

It's hard to maintain what the group is all about, but Johnny and I have stayed the same on purpose because we don't want to sell out. Some people in the group may want to experiment, or get bored with the sound, but we feel like what we started out with is the best approach. The fans want to hear it like it sounded in the beginning. We're legends to them and they're aware of our first album, our history as a group, and it's fun to play those runs from "Sheena" and "Blitzkrieg Bop" off the first few albums.

I don't think after this band is over with I'm going to have another band. I might make some solo albums, but I wouldn't have a live band because I would hate to have to live up to the Ramones' reputation. I don't think I could live up to it. I need Johnny Ramone and Joey Ramone. All of us together are a unique happening.

Al Anderson

Our Fake Book
Is in the Head

Guitarist, NRBQ

We don't start with the same song, we don't finish with the same song—you never know what's going to happen. It's all spontaneous. There's certain songs we know we're going to be using, but we've been playing together for so long that you could just turn a certain way and you're going to know what's gonna happen. You can just feel it. In the beginning we were much less attentive to the audience than we are now. Back then we didn't care what the hell we played. If we wanted to be weird for the whole set and not relate to the audience, period, we would do that. Now we're much more aware of the vibe in the room. You have to keep working; if you take too much time off you lose your continuity. The bands that take off for three months every year, they're just perfecting one set that they're going to keep on doing over and over again. To keep our spontaneity we have to play a lot, to know what the other guy's going to play next, to get that feeling; if we stop much more than a month we won't be able to have that. If we were playing the same set for sixteen years, we wouldn't have lasted. I tell you right now, I'd be working in a pet shop.

It's an ideal life for a musician. I wouldn't want to change anything, just get more money. There's never enough zeroes. We don't even have to rehearse anymore, really. You could just be in a hotel room and Terry [Adams] could play the song. We all have pretty much perfect pitch, and we could actually play it that night without having played it on an instrument that day. Our fake book is in the head. Not too often does anyone have to stop anyone else to say, play this here. It's pretty much just go ahead. Longevity is the key to that, plus you have to have respect for the others so you don't have to wish under your breath that he was playing something else.

I wasn't that well educated musically when I joined the band in the sixties. The others have every record ever made. All my influences are guys from the fifties. One of the biggest things in my life was the James Burton solo on "Hello Mary Lou." Maybe the most influential solo ever played. I didn't know you could bend a note that far. I never knew you could buy strings you could bend. It took me until 1968 to find out you could buy light-gauge strings. I was a good guitar player for my age, probably the best around, not because I was so good, but because there was no one else in my town. My first bands were R&B trios. It was guitar, keyboards, and drums. We played a lot of black clubs. Three nights a week at the Red Ash in Hartford, and Sundays at the Rockabye, where there was always a big jam session from five to nine. It was a lot better to go over in front of black people than white people, 'cause you know that black people know you're laying something down. White people could just be there for the occasion. If you go over in a black club and you're white you feel like a million bucks.

It's just in the last three years that I've gotten my own style together. If I want to learn a little riff, I'll try to copy it. I'll seek out bits and stuff, but I don't go that far. It's more a matter of the confidence part. The feeling of I can pull this off, no problem. That's a good attitude to have. I used to do more what I was told. As soon as I did a solo album, I had a lot more power and confidence. Before, I didn't think my playing was right. Then, when I started getting confident, I actually got to be that good to myself. I can't remember when it happened, but I just remember it happening. No need for self-doubt. Just go in there and say you're the best and, by golly, you will be.

PLAYING VII

Liu Sola

Confucian Blues

Chinese Singer, Composer, Novelist

In 1987 I visited the United States for one month as a guest of the United States government. It was fun being treated like some kind of minister of culture. In the daytime, shaking hands with officials, smiling and feeling sleepy, looking forward to the night. At night, coming alive, enjoying the clubs, listening to rock and jazz. It was certainly different from my usual life as a Chinese writer and composer. I visited eight cities and heard, along with the music, the deafening sounds of America. I brought back with me to China a big package of American culture, which amused all my friends. But the one thing that could not be packaged, the one thing that could not be explained, was the experience of the blues.

I can still remember the night I first heard Junior Wells in Chicago. Seeing Junior Wells perform live unsettled me completely and made me ashamed of my own efforts. He went onstage with his harp, blew a note into it, and then a few more. It sounded like someone breathing. Then the band joined him. The harp began to sob, then silence, then sobbing once more. Suddenly Junior Wells hung his voice up high, then let it drift down in long melodic lines that wailed and cried. The voice reached up and came down, reached up only to come down. Sitting onstage, facing the darkness, his face a grimace, all his nerves, blood, muscles straining to burst from the marrow of his bones, he was not Junior Wells, but a blue-black tone. This kind of sadness cannot be described, you can't cry for it and you can't not cry for it. Even God will choke up if he listens to this music. It wraps itself around your throat, your soul, like a noose.

Two years later, I returned to the States to record one of my songs with a group of blues musicians I had met in Memphis. A few days before the session, we went to a big concert featuring Bobby Brown, held in a large sports stadium. The mostly black audience was all dressed up. Asians and African-Americans have at least this in common: they like to dress up. But the marriage of Confucius and the blues produces strange results: Confusion. I tried to join in with the crowd, to shout and dance with them, but in my mind I felt tired. Am I too old? Too Chinese? To be too Chinese means to be old. In China, to scream and shout with the music means you're mad.

On Sunday we went to church. In church, as the priest started preaching, the Bible became blues, the words circling up and down, slow rhythms balancing fast. God became flesh and bone, and religion got stronger as the congregation began to swing. When the preaching reached a certain point, the gospel choir started to sing. Black people can swing to everything, sacred or profane, and not even sweet Jesus can change their nature. When the Africans came to the States, they started using the instruments the white people gave to them, but what they played was not Bach, but blues, jazz, gospel. In China, the liveliest people are the "minority" people, who dance and sing wherever they can. It is only we Han people who treat dancing and singing as performances that we watch, without feeling a physical need to take part in them. Once, after a lecture I gave at a university in China, a nineteen-year-old student came to me and told me that the only emotional reaction he had ever had in his life was to knit his brows. Our culture encourages us to shut up, to control our enthusiasm, to look around first to see what other people think. We have learned the lesson of Confucius too well: "Think thrice before acting." In church while everybody was drowning in the music I was the only one thinking hard about what it all meant.

The next night I went to see Phineas Newborn, a well-known jazz pianist who was in his fifties and very ill, coughing all the time and hardly able to stand up. My friend and producer Dan [Greer] told him I came to Memphis to learn the blues and to record with blues musicians, and asked him if he wanted to join us. He didn't say yes or no, just slowly walked to the piano and started to play. As he played and sang, he even forgot to cough. The last song he played was a love song, with romantic lyrics and harmonies. His hands moved over the piano keys, then stopped as he looked at me. But he wasn't really looking at me; he was looking at an abstract idea of woman. Even when Phineas sang the love song to me, it wasn't for me. It was the idea of singing a love song to a Chinese woman that made him forget the pain. When he stopped playing, he started to cough again, but he said he would join our recording.

Dan and Phineas's brother Calvin came to pick me up for rehearsals. The rehearsal was at the bass player's house. It was a very hot day and there was no fan, no ventilation, just dust everywhere. An old piano, old instruments, an old sofa on an old carpet, some old photos . . . all covered in dust. The bass player had bandages round his neck and he was wearing some kind of apparatus under the bandages to help him breathe and clear the phlegm from his throat. The bass player taught me the blues bass line, and he kept trying to explain the blues to me.

The more he explained, the more confused I became. Here were three great musicians playing in this ramshackle and dusty house which stank of sweat. From the strange melody I gave them, they were making up their own key, their own sound, and their own harmony. But where was I?

The next morning Dan called and told me that Phineas had just died. I was too shocked to say anything. It was a cloudy day. Looked like a cyclone was approaching.

A week later we got to record my new song, "Reborn." It was another hot day in Memphis. The studio, on a dilapidated street, was very small and simple. There were Coca-Cola and coffee machines in an adjoining room, which looked like a truck stop on the highway. Musicians drifted in, started rehearsing. It was afternoon in America, morning in China. The streets of Beijing must have been very quiet. I started to sing: "You're my paradise."

My song has a melody based on Chinese opera, a blues rhythm, and English lyrics. It's not easy to sing. I felt my lips tensing up. I asked the engineer to stop. Dan asked me why. I said my singing was not good enough. "It's okay," he said. "You must relax and keep going. Don't stop in the middle. A spliced recording's not natural."

This is it then. I can't stop even if I make a mistake, so I can't make a mistake. What if I do make a mistake? I have to close my eyes and sing the whole song in one breath. Everything in one go, whether right or wrong. It was like playing with my life. My education tells me that self-control is virtuous and "thinking thrice before acting" is natural. But spontaneity and letting go are the bases for blues improvisation. If you hold on to balance and moderation, you don't have the blues.

I opened my mouth and started to run with the music:

You must be a child
You must, must, must
Be reborn . . .

Dan sang with me. I suddenly felt I could loosen up, I could scream, my screams began to have bone in them. Something was happening, something like the blues. I felt relaxed; I could feel my body. I could feel pain becoming something other than pain. This lasted only for a moment. Then the spirit of Confucius came back and I said to Dan, "I made a mistake." "What's the big deal about a mistake?" he retorted. "I like mistakes. They sound natural." He wouldn't let me do it over again.

When can I really sing the blues? Maybe only when I can run, stop, laugh, and cry at the same time, climb up and fall down at the same time, be beautiful and ugly at the same time, and control myself by letting myself go.

When will that time come?

Jerry Garcia

Zen and the Art of Notesmanship

Guitarist, the Grateful Dead

I'm into self-indulgence. There's definitely a certain amount of that. But I'm playing with a lot of guys who have very specific notions of what music is, which are very different from mine. In the Grateful Dead you can't play without listening to everyone. An important part of music is the texture, the layers, and the talk. I'm into the conversation. When I play a solo it's not really a solo as much as it is single lines. It's a solo only insofar as it's the only instrument producing that particular texture at that moment. But really there is talk going on. The way the keyboard player backs my playing has a tremendous effect on the dynamics and the structure and the intelligence of a solo.

Live music, for me, means being able to stretch out. I'm not so slick that I can pull off the perfect solo in one chorus. I don't have a prearranged solo. I need a minimum of three choruses, generally, and that's really restrained for me.

Playing live and recording are very different. Recording is like building a ship in a bottle. Playing live is like being in a rowboat in a storm. I find I'm much less emotionally suited to building ships in bottles. I get pissed off halfway through, or else I do a real sloppy job of it, saying, "That's good enough; they'll never look at it that closely." Patience is not something I come by real easy. What I do is kind of a Zen thing. It's Zen and the Art of Notesmanship. It really has to do with the moment and the live situation. That's where it's happening. It's what I do, and from my point of view, I'm still pursuing something. I don't think in terms of how long I've been doing it. I think in terms of what I'm trying to do. I get closer, but I've not gotten to the point where that thing is happening that I want to happen. I keep working at it. So I still feel like a person who's learning an instrument. I don't feel like someone who's gotten it down.

My relationship to the music I'm making onstage has to do with what my fingers are doing. The touch is everything for me. To change guitars is catastrophic. I'm not one of those guys who can have a million guitars and plug in any of them and just play. That isn't the way I work. I'm a one-guitar person. I rehearse with one guitar. I only take one guitar with me on the road. My chops are set for the guitars I play; my technique is at that edge. In terms of practice and my own technical studies on guitar, there are very definite things I go after. I work on something, but I don't try to stick it into the music. I'll be working on some group of harmonic relationships, or some esoteric fingerings, or what have you, and what happens is that a couple of years down the line they start to find their way into things, indirectly, in bits and pieces. They start to affect my playing in terms of making it so my vocabulary has a new punctuation and new expression available to it. Growth is a process rather than a goal. Things find their way in sort of sideways. I can't force them to happen. It's an ongoing thing. The farther I go in a direction, the greater that direction's capacity to lead me seems to become. It's something that's opening in front of me, rather than me conquering more and more of it.

Kirk Hammett

Feeling the Power

Guitarist, Metallica

When I hold a guitar in front of an amp that's cranked real loud and I can feel the power, I feel like a different person in that I know I have this power in my hands and I can guide it. I'm having a problem right now in that we're playing really loud and I can't wear earplugs because then I can't feel the power.

The guitar sound is different every place you go. You might have a place with a brick wall behind you or a steel roof or a place that's really ambient or really echoey. For me, almost always the best sound is right in front of my rig. My guitar tech knows exactly which guitars are being used for what songs. And the sound man knows the sound of the guitars, too, so he can make necessary adjustments. 'Cause I like a particular type of lead-guitar sound. I like a real warm MIDI sound for my lead and a real low-end MIDI sound for my rhythm. The sound I have is programmed into my setup. It's a MIDI-run setup, so the sound is pretty consistent most of the time. One time, the sound man and my guitar tech made some adjustments to my sound and it was just not there. I had to tweak knobs for an hour to get it back to where it was. One night, for some reason, there was too much low end. I freaked out. I was going to the monitor guy, "Hey man, there's too much low end." He took it out and everything was fine afterward. Within five seconds after he took it out, it was like, "Okay, cool, now I can start enjoying myself."

I don't go around saying this has to be a fast, ripping solo 'cause everyone else is doing it now. That's not my attitude. I won't do a guitar solo with the right-hand technique just because it's the "in" thing or I feel I have to compete with Eddie Van Halen or Jeff Watson. I'll do it because I find it fits the context of things and it's interesting. I just like to play things that interest me. It's the same thing with classical guitar. At this point, it's the most interesting thing I've been hearing. I listen to a lot of classical music and my wife plays cello, so when I'm at home, especially when I get in off the road, all we listen to is classical music. I'm heavily into classical guitar, but on the acoustic guitar, not electric. When you play classical guitar you're listening to these very intricate and at the same time very cool, almost beautiful, melodies. You're hooking into that leisurely frame of mind that comes along with playing classical guitar. I was actually thinking of maybe buying a violin or a viola. I just bought a dobro. I'm going to go out and buy a mandolin pretty soon. I like fingerpicking guitar and slide. It's helped my overall playing. The other night I had the slide and I played it through a Marshall on my Strat, heavily distorted, and it sounded cool. Two years from now I might be playing bluegrass, you never know.

Bernie Worrell

(www.bernieworrell.com)

It's Not Easy to Get the Feel

Keyboard Player, Funkadelic, Talking Heads

When I was four years old, my parents were told I was gifted. I think it was more that I had perfect pitch. I guess I started out with classical music because my mother was always teaching me scales. I used to go to the piano every day and play exactly as she showed me. Then she went through the process of trying to find me a teacher, which was hard because no one had ever taught someone three and a half years old before. I finally found a teacher and passed his eighth-grade students in six months. I had my first recital at the age of four, and at eight years old I wrote my first piano concerto. My parents and the teachers were aspiring for me to be a classical musician. I guess they knew something I didn't. I eventually rebelled against that stuff because the idea of highbrow music, blue-blood music, was a concept that I thought was bull crap. I was able to hear other music when I changed the radio dial and watched Ed Sullivan and watched the Beatles.

We moved to Plainfield, New Jersey, when I was eight. Soon word started spreading that there's this musical genius that just moved to town. But I wasn't known in the streets yet. I used to try get out; I mean, don't get me wrong, I could do some things, but everybody knew my mom. In grammar school I was raised kinda strict. I had to do my lessons before I could go out with the fellas. In high school I started to get away a little bit. I started to sneak down to the school or wherever they had dances.

I met George Clinton at the barbershop when I was a freshman in high school. At the time I wasn't doing too much with him, just getting my hair done down at the barbershop. One time he said, "When I can afford you, I want you in the group." That happened years later. He had Parliament. Funkadelic was just a young group of musicians from the projects hanging out in the barbershop jammin'.

In high school I had private lessons in harmony and theory from a Juilliard School of Music master keyboardist. But I was always confident about playing other types of music, whether it was playing in church, accompanying my mother's teas or fashion shows, or jammin' with somebody. I just did it. Also, I could sight-read really well. After you've been classically trained all those years, you have the technique; the other forms of music are simpler. But it's not easy to get the feel.

When I entered the New England Conservatory of Music in Boston they skipped me to the second year. At school I would play in the dorm lounge. In the evenings everybody would sit around and play Broadway stuff and all that. My teacher would ask me to play "Tea for Two." Half the time I'd show him up doing jazz or pop songs.

After college I went on the road with the famous R&B vocalist Maxine Brown as her bandleader. I was in Bermuda playing with her at the 40 Thieves—I think it's still there—when Judie (she wasn't my wife yet) got a call from George in Detroit. He said he was ready to make the move and he wanted to meet with her to talk business. She flew out and met him then called me in Bermuda and told me what was going on. I gave Maxine notice and flew to Detroit. It was finally my chance to go wild and do what I wanted to do, play what I wanted to play.

I was the musical director of the group, so I became the bandleader right off. If something was wrong, I'd tell George, "No, that's not right," and he'd listen. My word was say-so, and whatever I said they did. I would always open the show with classical stuff. Then I'd go to jazz to Latin or whatever came in my head before I segued to the first song of the set. When Maceo Parker joined us, we used to open along with the drummer.

Originally we had an underground following in the same vein as the MC5 and Ted Nugent. We did a lot of gigs with them and hung together. After the second or third Funkadelic album people started following us on the road to different cities. That was kind of the first hint that maybe something was gonna happen. I didn't necessarily think of how big we were getting. What made me know we were there is the first time we sold out the L.A. Forum. We were in a limousine going back for sound check around dusk and there was just a sea of cars. I looked at George and said, "See what you've got us into." He looked at me and said, "Look what *you* got us into."

We worked mostly out of United Sound in Detroit and Hollywood Sound in L.A. Once in a while, we used Mathis Sound and Toronto Sound in Toronto. George and I moved up to Toronto to live for about four or five years. Things are being mended between us now. An old-home week is back in the works.

I'm always learning. When I do different projects and meet different people, I get excited. I don't like doing the same old thing. That's why I joined Talking Heads. I didn't even know who they were when they asked me to join them. But I could see what there were trying to do and that they recorded similarly to P-Funk, in jams, or they had snippets of things and used the overdubbing process to add in different elements. And they knew where to go and who to get to get the rhythm they wanted. I mean everybody has their own rhythm. But they wanted to get that thing. Even before they were musicians, when they were just students in Providence, Rhode Island, David Byrne and the others wanted to sneak into Funkadelic shows.

Boyd Tinsley

Lead Violin

Violin Player, Dave Matthews Band

I never intended to play the violin. I always intended to play guitar. But I played mostly classical music from the time I was in fifth or sixth grade all through high school and I fell in love with the instrument. I progressed fairly quickly, took private lessons, and got some scholarships from the local music societies. At the same time, in the back of my mind, I was aware of people like Stéphane Grappelli, Jean-Luc Ponty, Papa John Creach, and that sort of jazz-rock thing. I was definitely aware that there was another route that you could take for the violin, but it took a while before I actually delved into that.

When I started college I put the violin away for a while. I was interested in drama, history, going to law school. So I put it on the back burner. But the fraternity I wound up joining was Sigma Nu, and in Charlottesville in the early to mid eighties, it was a big music fraternity. I think every other person there played something. In Charlottesville, they also had this coffeehouse where they would have acoustic music going and you would sign up to play, and local musicians would come by to play until about midnight. And then from about twelve until the sun came out there would be electric bands playing. A lot of cats would show up and play there. You paid a dollar and depending on how early you got there you got to see up to twelve hours of really good music. Leroi [Moore] would come down there and he would bring his sax and play. Tim Reynolds would come down and play. People like Bob Margolin from the old Muddy Waters band would come down. One night Jorma Kaukonen played an acoustic set at a local club and afterward he came down and I got to be onstage with him and jam. It was a pretty amazing time that since has died out. But back in the eighties it was probably the most happening scene in Charlottesville. I'm lucky to have been around at that time and to have been exposed to all those musicians and all that music. That's where I started to dream about what I could do as a musician. Seeing all of these musicians jamming, playing all night long, was where I fell in love with the idea of being a performer and being onstage. Then I'd get together with some of the guys in the house and we'd play some Grateful Dead tunes, some Neil Young tunes, some Dylan, and sometimes we'd have some original tunes. And I'd improvise on the violin while these guys played acoustic guitar. That was my first exposure to playing in front of a crowd.

I had the Boyd Tinsley Band just before I joined up with the Dave Matthews Band. It was a rock band but the only difference was instead of having lead guitar it had lead violin. We did some really cool things. That was probably the biggest training ground for the Dave Matthews Band. So Dave knew me from there, and also this acoustic duo I had called Down Boy Down, guitar and violin. He knew where I was coming from musically, that I wasn't necessarily a background musician. So he asked me fill a role in the band as somebody who steps up to play.

In this band it's always been about playing like it's your last gig, from the very beginning. At first we didn't have enough songs, so we had to play the hell out of the six songs that we did have. And then it was like people would keep coming and coming and coming and we knew that our job was just to play our hearts out. If I'm really feeling what I'm playing, the audience is going to feel it too. They're not just hearing, they're feeling what's going on. It's pretty amazing, because they sort of push you on, beyond what your limits are. In those magic moments it's like there's this huge musical connection between me and the audience and I'm pushing and they're pushing and I'm pushing more and they're pushing more.

The cool thing about the band is that we're very critical of our music—even though our worst show might one of the best the audience has ever seen. The audience might not know, but we know that it could have been a lot better. I think our last three tours have been really good. But some nights start off bad and they stay that way. It's usually that individually and collectively we're just not performing correctly. People's heads aren't in the right places. We're not thinking about the music. We're not locked in together. When things aren't working, everybody knows. Sometimes people will say something, because we all have in-ear monitors now. Dave wears one. We all have microphones nearby so we can actually talk to each other during the show, so if something is happening we can talk. If a show starts off kind of rocky, we'll talk through it. Carter [Beauford]'s usually the musical leader of the band. He'll just say, everybody, we all just need to relax, put your ears on, listen, and just play this tune. And then everybody will sort of come back into focus and the rest of the gig will be great. It's very rarely that we'll start off a gig on a bad note and end it up that way. Usually after one song everybody readjusts, and we're in there.

Last year at this time we went into the studio for about six months, then we went right onto the road, then back to the studio to record a whole bunch of new songs, and then on the road for a little while, and then back. It was like back and forth, and every time you did it, you had to be a completely different person. You had to go through completely different mental processes, emotions, physical preparation. I find it really tough to go back and forth like that. I like recording and I like playing live. But personally, in this particular band, playing live is more fulfilling to me than being in the studio. At the same time, coming from the studio and going back on the road, the positive thing is that it teaches you a little bit about musical discipline, where you're really thinking about the music in a critical way. You're really listening to everybody carefully, more so than if you'd just stayed out on the road. After you've been on the road for a while it does become sort of an unruly kind of thing. You're not really listening as much as you're just playing. There's no dynamics, it's like bam, go up there and play as loud and as hard as you can for a couple of hours. When you come back from the studio you carry a little bit of that discipline and being aware of dynamics, you're aware of each other and how everything fits together.

But our life is being on the road. In the last five years we've always been one of the top five grossing acts in the country because that's where our life is. People like to hear this band play and we like to play. The thing about what I do, it's still so new to have a violin in a rock-and-roll context, the book is so wide open, that there's so many places to go and so many things to explore that haven't been explored. I'd just like to sort of go where it takes me.

Lisa Kaplan
More Like a Rock Band

Classical Keyboard Player, eighth blackbird

We probably spend about three hours a day rehearsing. I usually spend about two to three hours practicing individually, which may or may not include music for our rehearsals. I'll practice Brahms or Schoenberg as well as things I know I need for our rehearsals. Sometimes the day before a concert we'll have a rehearsal that's really terrible. And then we go out onstage the next day and it's a totally different experience. Everyone turns it up a notch. The reason we put up with all the rehearsing is because we love the performing. And we've gotten a lot better at liking rehearsal. But some people will never like it. Just like people will not like practicing. But we obviously deal with it because we love the performances.

The way we're trying to do it now is to do no more than four concerts a week. We've done it where we've gotten up in the morning, driven somewhere for four hours, gotten there, set up the percussion, had a short rehearsal, taken a little break, played the concert, struck the stuff, and started all over again the next day. That just ends up compromising the quality of the show. Next year, we're just going to have one show that we tour with, so we'll see how that works. And we're going to hire a roadie to drive our percussion so that we can start flying more

places. When we were in Korea for two weeks, we did about ten
concerts and it was the same concert at every place. The first
week we played every other day and then almost every day after
that. We'd never really done that, just traveled with one show,
and that was a lot more feasible. Last season we had three different shows with some overlap. That was difficult because you
would get to thinking, what program are we doing tonight?

Lately we've been commissioning a lot of work. People send
us material all the time—cassettes, CDs, scores. A fair amount
of the pieces just sound generic, in a new-music sense. They can
be really academic, these processes of math, some sort of construction that doesn't sound like music to me. It is music, but I
don't love it. The group tends to be drawn more toward things
that have tonality as opposed to atonality. We've played atonal
music too, but more often we play pieces that are more
tonality-oriented, often with a driving, rhythmic energy. To
play this contemporary music you definitely draw on everything that you've learned before, but you can't approach it too
traditionally. You have to be very open to new sounds and new
approaches. You have to look at what all the other parts are
doing. You have to look away from the score and look at the
other people and play with them. You have to be so aware of
everything that's going on. I remember when our group first
formed. Learning how to cue was a huge part of the rehearsal
process. We were making these huge motions in order to play
together, and it worked, but that was the only way it worked.
Now we've got it down to where we can raise our eyebrows and
each play exactly together. It's awesome.

A piece we're going to start playing on tour in January is
called *Divinum Mysterium,* by Daniel Kellogg. We met Dan in
1997, really liked his music, and finally commissioned him. The
piece is based on a medieval chant that Dan used to sing at

church when he was growing up. It is about the creation of the world, but instead of seven movements, it's just five. It's about a half hour long. The first movement is called "Beginnings" and it's marked, "fast, soft, ready to explode." Everybody's playing these soft, unison chords in an irregular meter and all of a sudden, out of nowhere, we play a forte chord. Every time we've done this, audiences have just gasped. They're so surprised. The first movement is so amazing. We love rehearsing it. We could rehearse it forever and not get bored. Whether that's evidenced when we play it or it's just through the music, I don't know, but some combination of that just makes people react.

I'm not going to say we don't care about what the audience thinks; you have to care a little bit. But mostly, we care about what we think and we try to pick music that we think other people will also like. Sometimes it doesn't work. Last year we played a piece called *Notturno*. The composer was awarded the Pulitzer Prize for it. I really love it. It's a piece that we worked on at Oberlin in 1995, when we were a conducted group, and it was the hardest piece of chamber music that any of us had ever worked on. It is academic. That's what people would say. It's about all the thoughts that go through your head just before you fall asleep. They could be very schizophrenic or whatever. That's how the piece sounded to the composer and I think it does sound like that. When I listened to it I said, "This is fantastic." It doesn't sound like a strict twelve-tone, hexachordal, combinatorial composition, even though it is. At some point in the past two years we thought it would be great to bring back that piece without a conductor. At first we said, that's just not possible. We'd have to work on it so many hours. But then we decided to do it because we thought it would make us much better players. So we did it and it was such an accomplishment for us that we decided we just had to tour it because of all the hours we'd worked on it. Sometimes we'd spend a three-hour rehearsal working on twelve bars! So last summer we started to play this piece and basically most audiences just didn't like it. They enjoyed watching us play it, because there's so much interaction onstage because of the constant cueing. But it definitely was not a crowd pleaser. Honestly, we didn't even care that much because it was such a huge accomplishment for us to have performed it unconducted.

Before a real high-profile event we do a lot of planning. We think, okay, we're going to be premiering a piece at the Metropolitan Museum—how are we going to make it sound really good, and make it memorable? So recently we've been memorizing some of the pieces in our repertoire. But, premiere a piece from memory? People would be amazed! The reason we decided to do this isn't just because we want to knock people's socks off. When you memorize something, you really internalize it, so you know the piece better and you play it better. That's not to say you can't play it well with the music; even if you are using the music a lot of times you're not even looking at it, it's just there.

A lot of it is thinking about how you're going to feel when you're on the road doing this, what kind of expectations people are going to have after you do something like that. I remember us saying, after we had memorized this piece, "Well, now what are we going to do?" Well, I don't know, but we'll definitely think of something. We just keep developing and keep on pushing. The show we're going to do the season after next, we want it to be fully produced, with lighting, maybe costuming, maybe even some multimedia stuff going on, so that it will be more like a rock band going on tour. It's a constant development. And the cool thing is that there's not a lot of groups like ours, so it's always new territory. That's why nobody gets bored.

Lou Reed

Self-Taught

Lead Singer, the Velvet Underground

Most musicians out there are attempting to be virtuosos, which I'm not. I'm self-taught and deal in just three or four chords and have no technical virtuosity. On the other hand, when I listen to most guitar players it seems to me that they're playing in public stuff that should just be practice. And I think it affects their playing because it's all clichés; the guitarists don't have an original thought. It's just very dull. They're technicians. If you give them a piece, they'll play it for you, but it's feelingless and meaningless. I found a lot of times self-taught people who don't know there are any rules to it or anything can come up with a part that just might have a little more to it. The object is not who plays the fastest. Feeling and taste should be the main things, and you can't teach that. That's when you're talking about someone who's talented. It's an ability they have. They do it naturally. It's hard to teach someone taste.

I have these different musicians I work with and a lot of times I say, "For every ten notes you play, you could play nine or one or none. Just because there's a space there, you don't have to fill it." Getting people to play simply is really difficult. Theoretically, how hard could it be to play one chord? What could be such a big deal? Of course, you've got to find musicians who don't mind playing these simple lines, who don't feel they're being wasted by playing simple stuff. It's incredibly difficult to grasp the whole of something, to see and hear what the part means and know how important it is that you do your part to make it work, 'cause if you don't do your part then the thing collapses. I get a guitar player and I say, "All you've got to do is hit these chords, that's all." And immediately they do notes going in and coming out. I say, "No, no notes going in, no notes coming out. Just play the chord and stop." They can't do it. The chord is almost secondary. It's like "Sweet Jane"—straight hits, no frills. Everything is chopped off. It's just a straight hit—that's it.

It's been excruciating trying to find other musicians. What I'm talking about is not what they're interested in. I tell them if they get bored, they should not be in this band. I understand you're playing the same thing over and over and maybe that's boring, but the strength is in staying solid. It's not moving. It's a part, doing this thing where it grows stronger each time around. What they don't understand is this thing that's happening in the listener's head and when you break it, it's got to be for this really great move you're going to make. If you break it because you feel like it, then you're just an undisciplined musician. It's taken me a long time to really intellectualize this. Almost without exception these guys could take out 99 percent of what they play and they'd be a lot better off. And then when they do play the note, it should be a killer.

I used to love the guy who played rhythm guitar for James Brown. What he's doing is the pure rhythmic chords without all that garbage. These guys will do everything else but. They seem to think if they don't do that, they don't play well, or that I can't possibly mean what I say. But even though you show them, they seem to be missing the point. So you tell them. You just say, "Don't play anything other than that." After that, you just get rid of them.

Robbie Robertson
Playing with Van

Guitarist, the Band

Van Morrison played in L.A. a while back and I got up and played with him, and it was one of the worst experiences of my life. Now, Van is an old, dear friend of mine, one of my best buddies in all of music. I visited with him in the afternoon and we had a wonderful time talking and catching up and everything, and he says, "Are you coming to hear me play tonight?" And I said, "Yeah, I'm gonna come to the show." Then Van says, "I'd like you to come up and play a song with me tonight," and I said, "I've come to hear my old friend Van play. If I have to play, all I'm gonna be thinking about is getting up and playing with you. Will you leave me alone and let me enjoy the show?"

And he said, "I'm asking you, as a friend, to come up and play with me." And I said, "You son of a bitch! You're putting me on the spot." He said, "I'll tell you what. When I do the encore, you come up and we'll play 'Caravan' together, okay?" So I said, "Okay. What am I gonna do? We'll do it." So I watch the show. Then I go backstage, and they have the guitar, they have the amp; he comes over and he says, "I'm gonna start doing 'Caravan.' I'm gonna do some of the song, and then I'm gonna break it down, and introduce you. I want you to come out, plug in, and start playing. We'll kick into this thing that we do on the end." So he goes out and starts doing "Caravan," but he's doing it really fast. And then he ends the song! And I think, "I'm off the hook!" And just then, he turns around and they kick into this jazz song, and he's saying, "Ladies and gentlemen, I want to introduce . . ." And I'm saying, "What are you doing! Don't introduce me on a jazz song! This isn't my calling! This isn't what to use me for!"

I go out there, I plug in, and I say, "What the hell are you doing?" And he kind of twirls around me and says, "I don't know!" And as I'm standing there looking like an idiot, he whips around, grabs the microphone, comes right over and sings in my face, "What a wonderful night for a moon dance." And I'm saying, "This is a lovely song, Van, but this isn't what you called me for!"

So he's singing "Moondance," and in the middle of it, he introduces me again, and points, and like, I don't even know what key they're in. I don't know the chord changes. So I start making these god-awful noises on the guitar. Then, all of a sudden, these noises start to turn into something, and it becomes kind of interesting. It's like Pharoah Sanders kind of stuff, and I keep doing it. I'm playing weird harmonics and all kinds of ridiculous things, and the next thing you know, the guys in his band are screaming, "Yeah! Yeah!" And I'm thinking, "What's wrong with these people? I'm out of control, and they're cheering me on!"

And then I look, and the audience is standing up! They're standing and clapping along, and I'm like, "What's the matter with these people? Don't they understand that I'm in hell, and I don't know what I'm playing?" But pretty soon it starts to turn into something, and then the guys in his band are wanting to trade eights on it, and it builds, and it builds, and finally everybody's applauding in the place, and it turns a nightmare into something kind of interesting.

The song ends, and as I leave, I say to Van, "Well, I'll never forgive you for what you've done to me, but it was quite a wonderful experience."

INSTRUMENTS / SOUNDS VIII

Rick Nielsen

The Collector

Guitarist, Cheap Trick

Cheap Trick is one of the few bands where I walk out onstage and the guitar gets more applause than the band. People know I'm going to have some vintage junk, some new stuff. I used to see these guys onstage and they'd be doing the mouth movements and be in ecstasy using their tuners. I said, "Holy cow, these guys are carrying it a bit too far. They've watched too many movies or seen too many pictures in *Circus* magazine." So I decided to have fun with it.

My staples are some of the goofball stuff. With my personality it's okay. If the guys in Ratt come out with a five-neck guitar, it's going to look even more ridiculous than I do, 'cause I look like I should have a weird guitar anyhow. If anyone else did it, they'd say, "Oh man, what are they trying to prove? Are they trying to outdo Nielsen?"

I liked the idea of a double-neck and I've got loads of double-necks. Then I saw Greg Lake or Steve Howe, who had a three-neck thing. I thought, well, this is getting out of hand, so I figured, let's get it over with. The five-neck does give me a backache, because it weighs a ton. I use it for one song a night. Actually, I wanted it to be like in ZZ Top, where they have Billy Gibbons's guitar on some sort of belt buckle, so it can go around in a circle. I wanted it to be like the Wheel of Fortune. But it didn't work out. It would be ridiculous to spin a thing that weighs one hundred pounds.

I think I was one of the first guys who really started dragging a lot on the road with me. Instead of, I got my ax, let's play; I said, "I need more." Now I revolve my stuff; I've got about thirty on the road all the time. Uncle Dick is the only one I've got a name for. That's the one that looks like me; otherwise they don't have names.

When I was growing up my father owned a music store, but he never really had any of the good new stuff. He always ordered the wrong things, I thought. He'd order the Jaguar when I wanted the Telecaster, or he'd order a Jazzmaster when I wanted a Stratocaster. People would say, "Oh yeah, your dad has the music store; hence you have free goodies forever." Not true. I guess I did get good deals, but my dad never gave me any guitars. He gave me encouragement. He gave me a discount. But I had to buy everything I had.

I have about 125 guitars now. I got it up to about 175, but then I was just hoarding and not collecting. If you walk into my house you wouldn't know what I do for a living. I've got insurance on all of my guitars, so if something happened I wouldn't cry. It'd be rough to lose one, and that's why my stuff is in a fireproof vault, but if the fire is hot enough it could melt the things. You should take care of your guitars, but there's no flesh and blood in them. They're not people.

James Durst

Searching for #77

Singer-Songwriter

In those days, Monday night was Hoot Night at the Troubadour, L.A.'s preeminent folk stage. When I had some new songs I wanted to try out, I would hitchhike from my two rooms in Silverlake to Santa Monica Boulevard at Doheny, arriving early enough in the afternoon to park myself and my guitar on the sidewalk out front, so that when the box office opened, I could be first on the sign-up sheet for the evening's roster. Although February 1, 1971, was such a Monday, it loomed larger for me because at the end of the month I was to embark on my first official European tour, with concert and coffeehouse stops spanning the U.S., then numerous appearances scheduled throughout Iceland, Sweden, and Germany, after which I planned to stay on in Holland or Denmark for a time.

Gracing this same Hoot Night stage had been such aspiring folk luminaries as Jackson Browne, his brother Severin, Karla Bonoff and her sister Lisa, Steve Martin, and Ed Begley Jr., although I can't recall ever seeing any of them in line outside the box office. That night, following my four-song set, I loaned one of the other performers my guitar strap, then left my guitar among friends in the upstairs dressing room, returning downstairs to hear the evening's other players. As the final notes of the last singer faded, I went to retrieve my guitar.

She wasn't there.

No matter how many times I scoured every corner of the dreary room, my beloved guitar was nowhere to be found. I say beloved in part because this was no ordinary guitar. She was a twelve-string built to my specs by Cuban émigré Miguel Company in Miami some four years earlier. Descended from a long line of string and instrument makers, Miguel, together with his son and son-in-law, had been turning out singular twelve-strings for only a couple of years when I acquired my first one, #11, in 1964. Sharing a bill at West Covina's Knight's Rest Coffeehouse with Florida folksinger Mike Piel, I was entranced by his Miguel and ordered my own with Mike's help. When it was destroyed by Railway Express en route home to me from minor repairs by Miguel in '67, I used the insurance settlement to order another, #77. Her rich though delicate, full and balanced sound was due no doubt to Miguel's having employed classical-guitar-style fan bracing. I've quite honestly never heard before or since a twelve-string like it; quite different from Bob Gibson's Bozo, any of those made for Pete Seeger by Bruce Taylor, or anything built especially for Leo Kottke.

And now she was gone.

Troubadour owner Doug Weston phoned the police and I dutifully filed a police report. However, I was convinced even then that, despite the odds against it, I would somehow see her again. My friends, though sympathetic, were not especially encouraging.

The next day I began distributing homemade flyers to as many pawnshops and guitar stores as I could find, as well as the various area clubs. I had recently played the open stage up the street at Paul Colby's Bitter End West, so I dropped in there with flyers to post. One of the waitresses, who I had been friendly with in the past, suggested that her roommate, Susan, was good friends with a well-known psychic, and perhaps she would take me to see her. We made arrangements for me to come by the apartment to meet Susan, a single mother of a one-year-old daughter named Sundi, who made an appointment with the psychic, Edna, for the following day. As it was within walking distance, we strolled to Edna's house above Sunset Boulevard for a session. Edna's gift was remarkable, as she described with no prompting or information from me the physical setting of the Troub's dingy dressing room at the top of the stairs. She then implicated three people, two guys and a girl, as having been responsible for walking out with my guitar.

According to the details revealed to her, the first guy had a ruddy complexion and scratched his face habitually—a possible sign of drug addiction—and the second was younger and fair, while the girl seemed to act as a lookout. They made their way unchallenged out of the chaos of the club, as folks had been coming and going with instruments all evening. Edna's first impression was that my guitar was gone for good; but from somewhere deep inside myself I challenged her assertion and insisted that I knew I would get it back. She returned to a deeper place within and then said, "Yes, you're right. And you'll get it 'in a four.' " We interpreted that to mean I might retrieve it within four hours, four days, four weeks, who knows—four years! And that was the end of our session.

Concurrent with concerns about my elusive guitar, a romantic subtext was unfolding. Susan was a strikingly beautiful and streetwise woman, with whom I was instantaneously smitten. Within what seems an unbelievably short period of a week or so, I had given up my little place in Silverlake and moved into Hollywood with her. It was an earthquake of a relationship, both figuratively and literally, for it was here we were awakened one morning soon after that by the *Exorcist*-like dancing around the room of our bed; those then living in Los Angeles will vividly recall the '71 quake.

Of practical consideration was the fact that I was now no longer living where I could be contacted at the phone number on my stolen-guitar flyer. And Susan—true bohemian child of the sixties—had no phone. I soon persuaded her of the importance of getting a phone installed in the event anyone might be trying to contact me. Early in the fourth week of February we went to the telephone business office to place our order. We were told to expect installation the following week. But only a few days later, the phone installation guy unexpectedly showed up at the door—ahead of schedule! By noon, we had service.

Literally within hours we received a call from our friends at the Bitter End: "There's a young woman here who says she knows the whereabouts of your guitar. She came up from San Diego, and she's been trying to find you, and she's just about to give up and leave. You'd better get down here right away!"

Instead of having to waste valuable time trying to hitch to the club, I was able to leap into my sister's precious '68 burgundy Mustang, which she had generously offered to loan me the previous weekend—something she had never done before. When I got there an exhausted-looking young woman proceeded to tell me the following story: She had accompanied her boyfriend and his cousin to the Troubadour several weeks before, where her partner had spotted an easy way to score some drug money. He simply grabbed one of the guitars from among the many stashed in the dressing room, and they slipped unnoticed out the door and into the night. He was an abusive mate, a druggie, prone to physical violence. And he had sold my guitar to a musician out in Malibu for one hundred dollars. They had then moved from L.A. to San Diego. Somehow the boyfriend had come across one of my flyers and, finding it amusing, kept it in his wallet. That's how she—supposedly un-aware of the theft—knew how to find me. When she at last grew tired of his abuse and threw him out, she felt obliged by conscience to try to set things right. So she had driven the two-plus hours from San Diego with only the phone number from my flyer to go on. After searching all day, unable to reach me at my disconnected phone number, just about to give up and head south, she decided to stop in at the Bitter End, where the wait-ress, Susan's former roommate, knowing where I was, was now able to call us on our freshly connected phone.

Armed with her assurance that she could remember how to find the Malibu musician's residence, we picked up Susan and the baby and drove into the encroaching night. Finding the ground-level apartment, but no one at home—it was Saturday night after all, and the guy was no doubt gigging somewhere—I left a note in his mailbox asking him to call. We returned home disap-pointed, but hopeful. In the morning, the phone rang. The gen-tle male voice in my ear was resigned. "I knew it was too good to be true," he sighed, as he acknowledged that he'd paid only one hundred dollars for this exceptional instrument. He agreed that I could come right over and be reunited with my old companion.

And so, on Sunday, February 28—four weeks to the day after it was stolen—I recovered my prized guitar. Thank you, Edna.

I subsequently informed the police that I had retrieved my guitar and, as I was reading *The Prophet* at the time, referred to Gibran's chapter on crime and punishment to help me resist their insistence that I press charges, accepting and embracing instead the law of karmic inevitability.

I departed the following week on schedule; toured through-out the spring and then settled in Copenhagen, where I would base myself on and off for the next several years, often playing as many as five coffeehouses on a weekend, in the meantime building the foundation of a song repertoire that still includes a handful of those first composed on Miguel #77. In three decades, I've told this story a few times, but never until now paused long enough to write it down. Even from this distance, impressions of the events of that single month are etched deeply across my inner landscape.

POSTSCRIPT: I sent tickets for Susan and Sundi to join me in Copenhagen, but unfortunately, our time apart had since exceeded our extremely intensive and fortuitous time together and, perhaps not surprisingly, we discovered we had grown in disparate directions. But I enjoyed the sublime company of my Miguel #77 handcrafted twelve-string for another thirteen years—until the spring of 1984, when she was kidnapped by person or persons unknown from my van parked in front of my flat on Howard Street in Chicago.

I remain hopeful that one day, across a crowded performance room, I'll recognize her distinguished form poised elegantly across the lap of a stranger. I can't wait to hear her story

Wallace De Pue

Selling the Family Violins

Founder, the De Pue Family Musicians

My four sons, Wallace Jr., Alexander, Jason, and Zachary, are musically gifted. When each son became five years of age, he began studying the violin. For twenty-two years, from 1976 to 1989, the four of them and I were known as the De Pue Family Musicians. We played and sang together and gave numerous concerts all across the United States. We performed in restaurants, serenading customers; we performed on national television; we performed on the Bowery in New York City and in many other places. In 1989, we were named "Amateur American Family of the Year" by the American Education Foundation of Chicago. President George Bush wrote us a letter of congratulations for representing over fifty-four million amateur musicians in the nation. The Bowling Green State University TV station did a documentary on the family entitled "String Music for Every Occasion." Producer Shawn Brady won an Emmy award with this documentary.

All of my sons have since performed in Carnegie Hall and are now well on their way to fulfilling lives as professional musicians. Wallace Jr., has finished his course work for a doctorate in violin performance at the University of Texas, in Austin. Alex is making and selling his own CD recordings for a living. Jason is a member of the Philadelphia Orchestra and Zach is a student at the Curtis Institute of Music in Philadelphia and concertmaster of the Curtis Symphony.

When Zach, my youngest son, graduated from high school in 1996, the De Pue Family Musicians and Friends stopped performing. Not long thereafter, nearly all of the violins—quarter-size, three-quarter-size, seven-eighth-size, and full-size—were sold. The half-size violin will never be for sale. It had been my intention to give these progressive instruments to the first son who would organize the De Pue Family Musicians, number two. However, none of the boys expressed much interest in raising a musical family. Maybe they had observed how hard raising such a family was for me to do. Maybe none of them wanted to learn violin-repair work, or how to be an advertising and booking agent, a talent manager, and a pre-concert fight referee. Probably they had seen how much I had to learn and how much time it took just to keep them playing in front of people. After some thought, it seemed advisable to sell most of these instruments, so that they could wind up in the hands of potential violinists.

When the family had to stop playing together, the violins were put to rest upstairs in our storage area. The five of them were lined up in progressive order, like performers waiting to be called; each had its own concert memories. At one time or another, all four of the boys had played each of the violins; however, as I looked at each instrument, special flashbacks came to mind. The quarter-size violin, first in line, had come to me through a close friend whose daughter had outgrown it. Unlike many small instruments, this violin had an exceptional tone quality. This was the violin that Wallace Jr. was playing when he asked me not to practice with him anymore because I couldn't play in tune. Jason's half-size violin was made by hand and given to him by a fine luthier named Fred Warren. Fred was retired and in his eighties when he made that wonderful instrument. Many times, we went to see Fred in Findlay, Ohio, and to visit his remarkable shop. His intuition told him that Jason would someday be a world-class violinist. Alexander's three-quarter violin was next. It was so dark in color that performers on the fiddle-contest circuit called the instrument "Black Magic" because of the way that it sounded when Alex played. Even the most advanced fiddlers feared him. In the year 2000 Alex became an international champion. The seven-eighth-size violin was the instrument Wallace Jr. used to win a huge amateur contest. When the family left the fairgrounds, Wallace left the violin behind! I can still remember the relief I felt when I got the phone call from a groundskeeper who found the instrument under the spectator bleachers. He wouldn't accept any reward, he said, because hearing Wallace play had been reward enough.

Zachary was using the full-size violin when he won the Toledo Symphony Orchestra's annual competition for young people. He was the lad who gave his father gray hair because of his indifference to practicing. How he won that competition was nothing short of a miracle. He knew that he gave a terrible performance and started making apologies as soon as he saw me. That experience was the turning point in Zach's life. After that day, he was always fully prepared for concerts.

Nearly all of the family violins were sold, one by one, to parents who wanted their children to play like my sons. I do not recall who those buyers were. All I can say is, there were no string ensembles in town when we started playing; now all the Bowling Green city schools have orchestras. Maybe our many performances in Bowling Green had something to do with building the town's string program.

I acquired my own instrument, a quasi-Martin guitar, by trading a quarter-size violin, a mountain dulcimer, and a mandolin. It is still in the family. Although I never really learned how to play well, I performed with the boys in a host of concerts and even on TV. The biggest laugh that the family ever had was when my guitar strap slipped off during a concert. As I tried to grab the instrument, it went straight up into the air and then landed on the hardwood stage some fifteen feet behind me. Everything happened so fast that I lost track of where the guitar was! My frantic search for it made the boys cry with laughter and made the audience howl. As things quieted down, Alex, struggling to keep his voice clear, told the audience that they had just witnessed the best performance their father had ever given with that guitar. The main reason I keep the guitar is because it was not damaged in its fall to the hardwood stage. In terms of sheer fairness, any instrument that could survive treatment like that should be given a home for life.

The other instrument that will never leave the family is Jason's half-size violin. It was a gift from a man who literally kept us playing by rehairing our bows and fixing our instruments. For years, we purchased and played his excellent violins. They were used when we performed at his funeral. The varnish Fred Warren used on his violins proved to be impervious to the moisture of tears.

Mike Mills

Covering the Basses

Bass Player, R.E.M.

The first bass I ever had was an old Gibson double f-hole. It belonged to a friend of my mother's. Then I had a Guild Thunderbird and an old Fender Precision. After I got rid of those I just used the school's Jazz bass. I took it home and used it in my band. I don't know if they knew it or not, but I don't think they really cared.

Then I got a black Fender Musicmaster, which everybody thought was a Mustang, 'cause it looks just like it. Then I got one of those Dan Armstrong clear-acrylic-body basses. That was a lot of fun. The Dan Armstrong had one high-intensity pickup. You couldn't turn it all the way up, 'cause then it sounded like a fuzz bass, totally distorted. After that, I was shopping and I said, "I'm either going to get a black Rickenbacker or a black Jazz, whatever I see first." I walked into this music store and this early-seventies black Rickenbacker with a checkerboard binding was on consignment and I got that for like $350. That was my front-line bass until the pickups finally went out. Right now I've got a couple of Rickenbackers and two of those new Guilds. The Guild is really easy to play. The neck is just a little bit smaller and very smooth. It's not a very pretty guitar; I really don't care for the shape at all, but it's so easy to play and it really sounds good. I'm trying to get some EMG pickups into my old Rickenbacker. Then I'll have two front-line guitars.

When you see a band you're hearing everything out of the PA and who knows where they're getting their sound from. The sound man's got his harmonizer and all kinds of equalizers. You can get any sound you want with any number of equipment pieces. So is it the sound man, the bass, or the bass amp? I've always preferred two amps, because a solid-state is so sterile and clinical and clean. I like a little bit of dirt. I have a midrangy bass sound and I like to have a little bit of buzz in there. As long as the amp faithfully reproduces what I can get out of the guitar, I'm doing all right.

Technology scares me, because I don't understand it. For example, wireless guitars. I once saw Sammy Hagar get out fifty yards into the crowd and his wires quit working. I felt so bad for him. I know they don't quit like that now, because the technology has gotten better, but I still don't want to use one just because that shocked me so badly. I feel more secure with the cord coming out of the back of the guitar. There are some friends of mine in England in a band where it's bass, guitar, and drums and the singer wears one of those headset mikes. I prefer a microphone and a stand. I feel that the more gadgets you use the less human the music is. People go ape over toys and gadgets and you end up being Thomas Dolby instead of a rock-and-roll guitarist. You can get a great sound, but then you start thinking, "It's not me; it's the Peavey Corporation making a great sound." I want it to be me making that great sound.

Sean Hopper

Invasion of the Giant Sounds

Keyboard Player, Huey Lewis and the News

The thing about music these days is the level of gear from one end of the chain to the other, from the instruments to the recording, is so high-level compared to what it used to be. You hardly ever hear a bad snare drum on the radio, one that's got a lousy tone. They're all huge. I think it's just a natural evolution. The first good snare drum I remember hearing was Earth, Wind and Fire. They always had a good snare when a lot of people didn't. As people started to get hip on how to do it, how to get those tones, everyone's tones got better. All the tones now are pretty big and impressive so it's almost like an arms race of the giant sounds, so that everything has to crush you. Sometimes I just want to hear a record that's got small production in it and a great tune. Otherwise it's just one crusher after another.

Your sound hinges a lot on the gear you can get, and the gear has gotten a lot better. It's a good time to be a keyboard player; that's obvious. On stage, the Kurzweil replaced the piano. I've used a Korg organ for years with a Leslie Tone Cabinet and I've used a Jupiter 8 for quite a while. I have a T-8, which is tied to a Prophet, which is tied to a Roland Juno 106, which is tied to a Super Jupiter. The Super is used on "The Power of Love." That's a factory setting, but that's what's on the record. I've tied it to a 106 and the 106 kind of rings over the note a little bit, just to spread it out.

In the last year or two, because the explosion of gear has gotten so intense, I've spent most of my time just studying the gear itself and not working with any one instrument much. Right now my rig is working real well. I've straightened it out and done everything I wanted to do. Actually, we're a very old-fashioned band. We don't play to a sequencer. The drummer always sets the rhythm and I play to him. So we don't have any automatic parts. The only thing I would MIDI for is just to change tones. So I'm lucky, I can just sort of disregard all this junk that's going by. If I had the thing running like a science lab, I would need to be even further into it.

My playing is probably stronger than it used to be, but in a way it's also weaker, because I do more background playing. I've had more actual facility at other times, when it was demanded of me. It's hard to keep up a lot of facility if you don't use it day to day. I used to take a brief solo, a piano piece in the middle of the set, but that was last year and we kind of knocked that on the head, so I'm not doing anything independently now. On the road there's really no chance to play. I can get there a little early and play for twenty minutes at sound check, but it's not easy. The only other playing I do is at home. I've scored one documentary and I want to do more of that. Now that I have a Kurzweil it would make film scoring very easy to do, just because of the number of sounds it has on it.

I don't need solo chops so much as a good ear as to where to fit in. And that's fine; that's appropriate to what we're doing, so it doesn't bother me. My ears are definitely sharper in terms of what's working and what's not as it's coming together. If you have five synthesizers and they can make a lot of different sounds, you can pick. There's probably fifty sounds you can put in any one place that would all work, and the questions is, which one works the best. That's a subjective question, but you hone your discernment as time goes on. You get better at picking the right one. Of course, by the time you've finished your album you've heard it so much you may never have another clue as to what you think of it. It's ground into your bones.

Roland Orzabel
A Complex Arrangement

Synthesist, Tears for Fears

A lot of people know how to program synthesizers, but there aren't many who use synths organically and interestingly. *Tin Drum* [by Japan] has got to be one of the best electronic records ever made. "Ghosts" on that album is a masterpiece. They're the people who really got me hooked on synthesis and made me work at playing synthesizer. After I spent a few hours with a synth I was very enthusiastic about using it. A lot of it is very straightforward.

If you're a piano player, you're used to pressing softly on the keys and getting a soft sound, pressing hard on the keys and getting a hard sound. For instance, we had this sound, which was a very hard Wurlitzer DX7 sound, sampled onto the Emulator, and even if you just tapped the Emulator keyboard you'd get really an attacking sound. And Nicky Holland, our keyboard player, just couldn't play it in time to save her life, whereas, when she played the part on the piano it was really straightforward. Piano players generally respond to the instrument like a piano, but if you've got a trumpet preset, you've got to play it like a trumpet player would. Having never really played the piano much, I didn't find it hard at all.

We never decided to make electronic music. The first single

we did was a thing called "Suffer the Children," and it just lent itself to synthesizers. On the next tune, "Pale Shelter," I thought it would be nice if I added a sequencer-type background like Moroder, strings with acoustic guitar over the top, and use it as quite an attractive juxtaposition. The only synth we had was a Roland JP4.

Our arrangements are not the simplest in the world; they're quite complex. Therefore, playing live is not the best medium for them. We do it as best as we can. There are seven of us live, and that's how many people we need. We rehearse forever before going on the road. It takes a week or two to program all the things onto the keyboard. In the studio you use any keyboard, but live you have to squash it all onto certain keyboards. You're aware that one person's got a Prophet, so he's got to play X, and you've got to translate some sounds onto the Prophet. Nicky Holland was starting from scratch. She was not used to synthesizers at all. She had a copy of both albums and she scored out for herself the parts she was going to play. We then took about a week with myself, a Linn 9000, Nicky Holland, and Ian Stanley getting all the keyboard parts together. Meanwhile I was auditioning a couple of guys on guitar. After keyboard rehearsals were over I had to sit down with the new guitarist and teach him everything. It was simple stuff, but I have my own style that's sometimes difficult for somebody else to pick up.

These days I'm less interested in synthesizers than I've been for a long time. I'm more interested in players. The thing that gets on my nerves about some of the things we do is that they're so painstakingly crafted that they're not in the end free. I'm responsible for that. I want to get into more spontaneity, get people to do things, instead of me trying to come up with everything or put things in their place, get people to be inspired, in a band sense. I've been mucking about with trying to come up with original stuff for ages now and I'm trying to get back to a more orthodox setup. I want originality to come from the musicians within that structure. I'd like bass, drums, piano, guitar, and saxophones, and for the musicians themselves to come up with the original things.

Darren Lighty
Redemption Time

Keyboard Player, Producer, Songwriter

I had a job as a security guard and I worked at Macy's putting together stereos and wall units. It took me thirty or forty applications until I got a job at the Sam Ash store in Paramus, New Jersey. If you want to be a banker, you have to be around the stock market or people who are investors. So I wanted to get a job in a music store, because I knew that a music store is a melting pot of struggling musicians. If I could get into a music store, it would put me in a better spot to get my songs placed and my ideas heard.

I was always very technically inclined. A lot of people had a hard time understanding MIDI technology, but, for some reason or another, it was easy to me. I didn't have a problem with it. I knew a lot about keyboards, so when anything new came into the store I learned it in depth and I would do consulting and little seminars teaching people how to use the equipment. Most of the keyboards these days are computers; they're just computers downgraded to do one specific thing. A lot of the newer computers coming out have capabilities to do anything you want them to do. It just may be adding or writing the software and providing the hardware box. In the past if you wanted to do certain things, you'd have to go out and look for it; you'd find out nobody wrote the software, or they didn't have the box that goes along with it that makes the computer see what you needed to see. Now the computer is pretty much doing it all.

But the piano is still by far the best way to learn music. You can't beat the feel of a regular piano in terms of creating. As a matter of fact, when I used to sell keyboards, I always told people, if you could afford it—new or used—a piano is always the best thing to start off with because of its weighted action. When you learn how to play, like anything else, you've got to build up the muscles in the fingers. A piano brings about a level of expression where if you play soft it sounds soft and the tone is different. If you play hard the tone is more aggressive. On most of the bargain-basement keyboards you have these days you can't do that. While they might be touch sensitive the louder they play, they're not weighted, so you're not getting the same level of dynamics as when you learn how to play. So I always suggest a weighted-action touch-sensitive keyboard if you can afford one.

One time I had a session with Marley Marl. He had bought a keyboard called an M1 and I went to his house to show him how to use it. Well, he was a couple of hours late, so while I was there I came up with a sequence to illustrate how he could use the keyboard. When he came in and he heard it, he said, "What's that?" I told him it was just an idea I had to show him how to use the keyboard. He said, "I have a deal right now with the Force MDs, and you're smart and you're together. How about if I produce it and you write it?" I only came there expecting to set up his instrument and it just so happened that I was in the right place at the right time.

Marley introduced me to LL Cool J. He had commissioned Marley to do a whole bunch of production for him and since I was already working with Marley, it just fell in line. I helped create "Around the Way Girl," but I only got credit for playing the keyboard and doing the backgrounds. After that I helped create two other songs with Marley on TLC's first album. On some records it may say written and produced by one person, but if you're part of the creative process the people who know who does what tend to pay attention to you and you can build a name for yourself indirectly.

I'm producing music now for whoever likes what I'm doing. My partner is Eddie F from Heavy D and the Boys. Recently, me and Eddie have produced some hot records, so a lot of times people will come to us and ask us for that style of record. And if they ask us for that style of record then they just have to sit back and wait for what we come up with. We play on everything that we produce. Normally we'll have a bunch of tracks that we did together that we'll give out to a bunch of different writers who work with us and we'll let them come up with ideas. If they don't come up with anything we want then we have other writers, or sometimes the artists themselves like to create, and we're open to it. But if they don't come up with anything we like then we like to stick with what's been proven, the core writers we mainly work with, because that's what you're coming to us for.

A lot of times what we have to do to get things started is to have the group come in and we'll say, "We'll do four or five songs and if you like them, take them, and we'll work out the budget. If you don't like anything, then it was just an opportunity and we took a chance on trying to establish something." There are a lot of people who I think are really talented and I'd like to do whole albums with them, but ultimately this is the best way for me to approach things. Otherwise, you may come in with a finished product in your thinking but the A&R guy at the label will come behind you and say, "I think we should get one track from this person or that person." They have their own camp that they work with and I don't ever want to get in the situation where I'm fighting for control, because that's what happens in so many projects.

I'd say the biggest success I've had is with the Donell Jones track "U Know What's Up," because it happened at a time when I was starting my own venture with Eddie after having been in Kay Gee's (Keir Gist) situation. I had the record I had produced with Kay Gee, "Too Close," that was four weeks at number one on the pop charts, and then I went in the next year and produced the Donell Jones record and that was nine weeks at number one on the R&B charts. So that kind of felt good. It made me feel as though my concept of producing and collaborating with people is the right one, because much of what I've always done or any success I've ever taken part in has never been just me. It's been me and other people who create as well.

Being nine weeks at number one was like a redemption for me. At this point in my career it seems like it's the younger cats and the flashier cats who are in the videos and having all the PR that the record companies are pinning their hearts to. So having that record come out of the blue was great in many ways. First of all, this was Donell Jones's second album, so he was contending with the sophomore jinx. Also, he put out a first single that the record company couldn't break.

But as far as the aftereffects of success, it's almost like when you're hot and you do a record that's dope, you got people calling you and they're thinking they can work with you, but then they want to say, "What can you do next?" Or, "That's a fluke, they lucked out on that one." They commend you and they like it, but it's not like they just open the floodgates and everybody starts calling and wanting us to produce. We were still auditioning acts, still doing stuff for free, doing remixes and handing them in, and if people like them then we say, "Let's work out something."

It wasn't until the Ruff Endz record "No More" hit and

that was like, "Okay, they did another record that went to number one, and it crossed over well, so it's like, okay, maybe they're not just a fluke. Maybe they might have something." As much as you're successful in this business, there are a lot of people who don't want you to succeed for whatever reason. Eddie and myself have been in this business for over ten years and that's a hard thing to do. So much so that we're honest with ourselves in thinking that okay, it's redemption time for us every time we get in the studio. Every group we work with, we tell the people when we're producing them, "This song and this project is just as important if not more so to us as it is to you." We're not just in there to cash a check and hand out garbage. That could be like the knife in the back and we'll be dead. I think there'll be more people who will talk about us once we put out that one wack record than if we keep putting out good records.

I love music, but music does not consume me. Success to me is being able to enjoy life and spend time with my family. So far as people acknowledging me, getting write-ups and PR, I don't crave the spotlight. I like being a behind-the-scenes guy. People don't know me and have no idea what I look like. That's great. A lot of people probably don't even know what I've contributed to unless they pick up the album and read the credits, and that's fine. With the spotlight and the notoriety, people view you a certain way. You're under a certain amount of pressure. I think one of the hardest things for people in this business is trying to live up to people's expectations. At the end of the day, those things come and go; if you really have someone you love, if you have a family and a life, those things don't matter. If something just happens to come along and I get this rush of notoriety and fame, I'm not gonna deny it. And if it happens that I turn into the guy that conducts the first hip-hop orchestra at fifty, I'd love that.

John Flansburgh
A Statement of Defiance

Guitarist, They Might Be Giants

I originally got into music through recording. I think my first interest in sound was working with a tape recorder my father brought home when I was ten years old. Success has its advantages. One thing I've done is I've actually bought the tape recorder that we recorded our last record on, and brought it back to my house.

Working with your own semi-pro unit is much more flexible. Like, if you go into the Power Station and you tell the guy operating the twenty-four-track thing, "Flip those two-inch reels over, because I want to do something backward—maybe it won't work, but that's what I want to do," he won't do it, because he's got to align the whole damn thing, and it'll take forever. The striking thing about studios is that they're totally focused on making passive, commercial music that has no edge to it at all; they just want to make it sound like everything else on the radio. It's mostly fear that somehow transforms you into sounding like that.

Most of our aesthetic judgments are pretty random to a lot of other people, but they make absolute sense to us. When we do a piano sound, for instance, there's almost an aesthetic of making sure that it's so loud it makes your head kick back a bit. If it doesn't have that kind of quality, then it's really not important putting it there. I think that the big problem we have with people who make commercial music is that they don't understand why you want to have stuff like that. That's the whole thing with the sound of the guitar in the Beatles—it was an incredible guitar sound that you wouldn't have known was possible to get through a modern studio. They wouldn't let you mess up the equipment at that level.

If I hadn't been seventeen in 1977, I don't think that I'd be the kind of musician that I am. I'd have probably worked harder, trying to know what people who went to Berklee know. But when I learned, the entire notion of learning how to play the guitar and being a guitar player was an antisocial act. It was more like a statement of defiance.

Not having a great technical facility right off the bat probably helped me more than I realized, because I had no crutches to rely on. You get into "If I do this kind of trick, it'll have this-and-this kind of impact." When you really can't play, you have to have ideas. That's the only thing that you can present. A lot of the best musical ideas are really simple ideas.

For instance, we realized that the best way to get a convincing kick-drum sound was just by tapping your thumb on the top of the microphone. I recorded the vocals to "You'll Miss Me" through a Chandler Tube Driver distortion unit, which is, by the way, one of the finest things available for the guitar. It's half of my live sound. The Chandler Company makes really inventive and interesting stuff.

The great thing about being in a band that nobody cares about is that you can really hone your fine points. I think we were graciously granted total obscurity when we started, which allowed us to be brave and to develop. That's a nice place to be, as long as you can pay the rent.

Ted Myers
Lost and Sound

Guitarist, the Lost

I think it was the Sonny and Cher gig that put us over the top. For a long time there, back in 1965, we were highly dissatisfied with the PA systems we encountered at almost every gig. By "we" I mean the Lost, my first rock-and-roll band, a raggletaggle bunch of white punks on dope, stumbling toward ecstasy at the dawn of the psychedelic era.

So here we were, opening in Troy, New York, for Sonny and Cher. They were *huge,* man! Second on the bill was Len "1-2-3" Barry. "1-2-3" was a number-two *pop smash* in 1965. So why, then, *why,* I ask you, was it that when we took the stage (the very first act of the night) and started to sing, *absolutely nothing came out of the stinkin' PA system!!!?* It took a few moments to sink in that the words to the song we were singing were going completely unheard—then, thinking fast, I remember calling out to my lead guitarist: "Instrumental!" At first he looked at me, uncomprehending. *"Instrumental!"* I yelled again, and we shifted gears—quite seamlessly, if I may say so—to the Stones' "2120 South Michigan Avenue," one of our staples. We vamped on this a good long time. I knew the guys in the sound booth were doing their damnedest to fix the problem, so I wanted to buy time for them as well. I was actually thinking of *their* well-being! We went on for what must have been ten minutes, then ended the song. Scattered applause. I approached the mic, said, "Hello, can you hear me?"

Nothing.

I guess it was this experience that got us to thinking we should bring in our own sound system. In 1965 there was no such thing as onstage monitors. There were no high-tech multitrack mixing boards. There were no sound roadies accompanying every act, busting the balls of the promoter if the sound wasn't just right during the sound check. There weren't even sound checks! You just walked onstage and played. The people doing the sound at these places didn't know or care about your music. They didn't know you from P. J. Proby and could care less!

I don't remember who suggested the Hanley brothers. They were developing a rep around Boston for being the cutting edge of live sound. Four years later they would do the sound at Woodstock, which would put them on the map. The Lost would be long gone by then. But in 1965, we were, briefly, the flavor of the year. We were the new wunderkinds on Capitol Records, the "hairs apparent" to the Beach Boys and the Beatles. So when we were booked to open for the Supremes at Brandeis University, we called the Hanley brothers. We would not be *unheard* again!

The venue at Brandeis turned out to be this huge indoor gymnasium. The Hanleys brought in a pair of speaker stacks that looked like Godzilla's Porta Pottis. They miked every amp, every *drum*. There were monitor speakers at our feet, a luxury, as I said, virtually unheard of in 1965. Even the Supremes and their backup band, the King Curtis Orchestra, would be relegated to the house sound system. We were *so ready*. We took the stage at eight o'clock sharp, ready to rock the socks off those collegiate snots. There had been some talk backstage, and we didn't like it one bit. It seems the Student Activities Committee had settled for us as second best. They had really wanted the Blues Project (some of whom apparently were Brandeis alumni), not us. So we had a sort of chip on our shoulder from the start. The moment we walked onstage, we could sense a certain air of hostility.

Our first number was an original that started off with a big, ringing guitar chord—sort of a *"brang!"* I remember hitting that chord and seeing the first five rows go down. The sound was so big, so loud, so unexpected, that I guess they just dove under their seats. When we started to sing, another few rows went under. By halfway through the song they were standing up and booing with their fingers in their ears. It began to dawn on us that we were killing our audience with volume—the sissies.

As the first song ended there was a cacophony of boos and cries of "Get off!" We were insulted, but doggedly pressed on. We tried to turn our amps down, but with the close mics that did little good. I searched the horizon frantically, looking for one of the Hanleys, but, alas, they were nowhere to be seen. After the second song the boos were even louder—the deafening din of rejection. We couldn't face it. At last we walked off the stage, flipping them off as we fled. If these fools weren't ready for state-of-the-art technology, someone else would be, sooner or later.

Unfortunately, later turned out to be sooner for the Lost. We lasted only about a year on Capitol, which never picked up any of the six options we had left on our contract. We did, however, make one or two sound breakthroughs during that lone quarter hour of my rock-and-roll fame. We were the first (that I know of) to use psychedelic lighting as part of our show. We were among the very early users of feedback and other sound effects generated from a weird array of honkers, tooters, sirens, and other gizmos. And, as stated above, we were among the first to pioneer the live-sound technology routinely used today.

I like to think of it this way: a few eardrums were sacrificed so that many could rock.

IN THE STUDIO IX

Earl Palmer

Playing It All

Session Drummer, New Orleans, Los Angeles

I always say what made me get so much work was that I never thought I was the best at any kind of music I played, but you couldn't find anybody who could play it all and that's the reason I worked. The concept is the main thing. A lot of people can read the notes but they can't savor the concept.

In the studios you might do something in the morning with a symphony and then go out and do something with Big Maybelle at night or play with Lightnin' Hopkins in the afternoon and Frank Sinatra at night. And back and forth like that. Let's say you have to play some rock and roll and then you go from there right to working on the score for *Judgment at Nuremburg*. Now that's switching gears. Then you go from *Judgment at Nuremburg* to a record date that's jazz and you got a five-minute solo. So it was all day from one kind of music to another.

When I began doing movie scores, that's when I really began to feel comfortable with myself as a musician. That's when you start realizing you're sitting next to people that you've heard about, read about, and you're right there next to them. In the beginning you can feel a little bit shaky in a situation like that. Then you realize, well, I'm right here with them, I must be all right, and you walk away knowing you've done a good job, regardless of who pats you on the back. Anybody can walk up and pat you on the back. But when you know you've done a good job, honest within yourself, that's when you feel, I guess I am pretty good. I'm gonna make a living at this and I never thought I would. A lot of people forget about what year I was starting out and that everybody in the studios was white. I resent the fact that people don't realize what a person like me had to go through and how good you feel when you made it through that with it staring you in the face.

As you get older you learn how to temper what you want to do to fit in with what you have to do. I'm basically a jazz player. But that wasn't where you made the money. I knew that. When I first started getting better work I had four kids to take care of and it didn't really matter to me what I had to play, what mattered was feeding those four kids. Once you understand that, you don't say, "My kids are going to starve cause I want to play jazz."

In New Orleans in the mid-fifties, when we did the rock-and-roll records, that's the only rock and roll we did. We were playing jazz on our gigs. I wasn't in a rock-and-roll band. There was no such thing then. There were no bands playing rock-and-roll day and night. Until those records came out, there was no rock and roll. Rock and roll didn't come till later, when the white parents didn't want the white children listening to that black music. So the kids said, "That ain't black music, that's rock and roll now," and the parents said, "Okay," because they didn't know what it was. Our folks didn't want us to play bebop, but they didn't know what bebop was, so you changed it a little bit. "Okay, that's better."

I didn't recognize rock and roll as anything special. It's like asking Rembrandt if he thought what he was doing was classic.

I was doing a gig, just do the job, hurry up, go play my jazz. Have some fun playing bebop. I didn't really think that much of the music. After having studied, it wasn't that musical. I always wanted to play jazz and I never considered myself as good as the guys I used to try to emulate jazzwise. It's the only thing people know me by, I'm sure, but honestly, it wasn't very musical. It didn't get real musical until more studied musicians began playing it and making some songs that were more than rhythm and basic blues lyrics.

I was glad to finally get some credit for what I did, through the Rock and Roll Hall of Fame. I also got the award from the Rhythm and Blues Foundation. In the beginning, frankly, nobody ever heard a thing about the musicians who were on those records. The music itself was fairly new, so the only person who got any credit was the artist. They weren't concerned about the background musicians. But Fats [Domino] and [Little] Richard knew. That's the reason they came down to New Orleans. I don't mean only for me, but from a drummer's standpoint, there was no other drummer playing like that at that time. There were other guys who came along, of course, great drummers. But Richard always gave me credit. And Fats and I were friends long before he became a big star.

Out here in L.A., one of the best dates I ever did was an album with Sarah Vaughan. Benny Carter was the arranger, so you can't get much better than that. Of course, you were surrounded with all good musicians. To be there among them, with Sarah singing, was really special. I think she's the greatest female singer I've ever heard, cause she could have done anything as well as she did what she did. If she chose to be classical, she could do that. That was a very special thing to me, playing jazz by one of the top arrangers, with the top singer, and wonderful music. That session lasted a couple of days. Later on I went to the Middle East with Benny Carter on a State Department tour.

Once my kids were educated I went back to playing jazz. I recently got back together with George Gaffney and Ernie Mc-Daniel, who I worked with for eleven years. George was Sarah Vaughan's conductor and musical director. We play jazz along the lines of Miles Davis and John Coltrane. I'll take a solo, but not long. We split eight bars or something. I might play a chorus, but not too much. I like playing fours or eights and switching back and forth like that between George and Ernie. It's nice to work with experienced musicians because they know how to set things up for each other. We never had a rehearsal in eleven years. We play every Thursday. Frankly, it's kind of a therapy for me to be able to play that one night. It keeps me healthy.

Carol Kaye
Getting to First Bass

Session Bass Player, Los Angeles

Someone didn't show up for a record date one time at Capitol in late 1963 and I was elected to play a Fender bass. It could get any kind of sound you wanted, was dependable, had a great overall response and sound, and the neck was great—not too small or too large. The recording I accidentally had to play Fender bass on was a hit, and I quickly became the number-one call studio bassist in L.A. I saw the future for that instrument and knew I was lucky to be in on the ground floor of creating styles for it while playing on so many styles of recordings back then.

It was not only fun to create and play improvised lines on electric bass, but I liked the feel of the instrument and its role. Being originally a known jazz guitarist, I was getting kind of tired of playing rock sounds, so the switch to bass, which was more creative, worked out. I got tons of calls to play electric bass, starting with that first date at Capitol. The hard pick I used, plus my string-muting system, got a great recorded sound. They loved that pick sound and asked all the rest of the bass players to get the "Carol Kaye" bass sound.

I never set out to do studio work, but it paid well, it was a nice environment, there were no drugs or booze on the dates, and good people to work for. I worked on records for Sam

Cooke and Ritchie Valens at first, many pop stars, then the Beach Boys, Phil Spector, and on and on. We weren't called the Wrecking Crew back then. We were all freelance studio musicians, all independent of each other. But we did so much to make the music happen, not only in performance, but also creatively—a fact that is just now emerging. We all were an experienced bunch, mostly fine jazz musicians in the rhythm sections and fine big-band horn men, with a few rock or country musicians mixed in, like Al Casey, Glen Campbell, Leon Russell, and James Burton. We never believed that the music would last more than ten years, but we must have done something right.

It was strictly a business and professional—sometimes you tried to pull all kinds of rabbits out of the hat to make a hit out of some very mediocre music. I got interested in the process of helping to create a hit record. It's intense work when you're creating lines to make a recording happen, helping to boost a singer into stardom. Soon the arrangers started learning their arranging crafts from the jazzers who were on the dates. Improvising jazz, you continually "arrange" the music, and I believe this was the biggest creative influence on the earlier hits—until music became highly arranged in the middle and late sixties.

In the early sixties, there were as many as three basses on dates, then it narrowed down to two, string bass and electric bass—especially on the Nancy Sinatra dates. (Chuck Berghofer played the string bass; you hear Chuck on many cuts in the movie *Bird*.) Lyle Ritz was on string bass on practically all the Brian Wilson Beach Boys dates, mostly with me, although on some you can really hear him ("God Only Knows"). While Lyle used to kid that he was just "ghosting" on the Beach Boy dates, his string bass is blended into my electric bass parts very well. Brian always asked me to put on more highs (treble) than I normally would use on dates (like Simon and Garfunkel's "Homeward Bound," "Feelin' Alright," or Andy Williams's "Love Story," or some films where I played deep bass parts that sound like fingers). People would swear I played with fingers when it was always the pick. Where there was only one bass, the electric bass was always miked off the amp, with no EQ or compression either. This was to get what Brian wanted from the string bass too, so he could get a good blend. The pick sound worked great, especially when it came to the sixteenths—and the down-up 8/8 picking technique came in handy for that, down-up-up for the fast triplets. It was even and dynamic and recorded very well, plus the feeling came off well.

Brian always wrote his parts out and this endeared him to us. He was also fun to work for. He was totally demanding, which we loved. He wanted the best from us and we gave it to him. Only the finest musicians can do studio work and it helps to have good music to play too.

Forest Rodgers
Playing with My Heroes

Session Guitarist, Nashville

Nashville is a great place to network. One person you meet connects you to ten more. Jim Rushing was a writer I met at Ovation Records. I did some demo recording for him at Dane Bryant's studio, Wild Tracs. Of course Dane Bryant's mom and dad, Felice and Boudleaux Bryant, wrote so many great songs for the Everly Brothers. One day Jim called me to do a session and said Randy Scruggs, Earl's son, was going to come down and help. I met Randy and the three of us put down three tunes of Jim's. Randy was so quiet and humble. It was surreal to finally meet and actually play with the son of one of my early heroes.

I joined the local union and auditioned for a few folks, but most gigs came by word of mouth. I met Howdy Forrester (Roy Acuff's fiddle player) at Acuff-Rose one time. He was involved in putting a band together for the legendary artist Roy Orbison in 1980. One thing about Nashville is that you can't wait for opportunity; sometimes you have to go where the work is. I met Don Helms and the Driftin' Cowboys (Hank [Williams] Sr.'s band) through another contact at about the same time. Don (steel guitar) and Jerry Rivers (fiddle) worked day gigs at Buddy Lee Booking Agency. So I went out as an add-on to their rhythm section to back other artists on package shows.

The University of Texas in Austin was our first show. Me, a steel player, bass, and drums backed Ferlin Husky, the Wilburn Bros., Slim Whitman, and Kenny Price. But I'll never know if I would have gotten the gig with Roy.

Bruce Bouton and I played another package show in North Carolina and backed O. B. McClinton at a twenty-thousand-seater concert, my biggest gig at the time. Bruce went on to play with Ricky Scaggs and become an A-team session player. He and I still work on some projects.

I called Gordon Payne (ex-Waylor with Waylon Jennings) after I saw him at the Exit Inn one night. He didn't know me but I liked what I heard and asked if he needed a guitar player. He did and we met soon after and worked together. Through Gordon I met Dave Osborn, who was playing drums with Gordon and lived in Dickson, Tennessee, where I lived. I went to his father Joe's house out in the country and met Dave and Gordon for practice and Joe's fine chicken-fried steaks. Joe Osborn, the legendary session bass player, was another one of my heroes.

I got invited out there for the Fourth of July fireworks and was knocked out by guests like Sonny Curtis, Jerry Allison and Bob Montgomery (The Crickets), Larrie London and Reggie Young (A-team session players). A few demo sessions followed for me with Joe, Dave, Gordon, and Reggie Young. One was at Sun Nashville for Fabor Robison and another was in Franklin at the Castle with Neil Wilburn. Gordon and the band evolved a bit as we played Buddy Killen's Stock Yard and the Bullpen Lounge. Kurt Howell, who would become part of Southern Pacific in later years, was on keyboard and vocals. Buddy Killen did a regular set at the Monday night performance. Many greats sat in, like Vern Gosdin, the Burrito Brothers, and Dan Fogelberg. Russ Kunkel was with Dan, and I got to jam with those guys, as well as with James Brown. It was unbelievable when

James turned to me on "I Feel Good" and gave me an extra solo. To have him look at you and say "Hit me again!" Wow!

Soon a player named Gene Dunlap (Loretta Lynn's original piano player) called to see if I would be interested in playing with the Vassar Clements band, the legend who had been a part of the Earl Scruggs Review that I had wanted to play with back when I was fifteen. Yes, I said, and I left Gordon to join him. I auditioned at his home in Mount Juliet. He liked my tone, a great compliment to me. I was using a strobe tuner to tune up and he told me, "If you ain't good enough to tune it, you ain't good enough to play it!" We toured the East Coast for about three months in the spring of '82. That tour ended suddenly. After one of our best shows, at Jonathan Swift's in Cambridge, Massachusetts, Millie (Vassar's wife and manager) informed the band that "the group just wasn't working out." We were scheduled to play the Lone Star Café in New York City the next night. It was a long, quiet bus ride back to Nashville.

Then I heard of a group called Calamity Jane on Columbia Records that had a single on the country charts. I called to try out for their band and we hit it off immediately. They were one of the first all-girl groups, consisting of Pam Rose and Mary Ann Kennedy, who later formed Kennedy/Rose on Pangea Records. I was told to wait a few weeks until they would have their tour together and then they'd let me know. But just as the Vassar gig was coming to an end, I got a call from Florida about another gig. It was five nights a week with good money. After two years of Nashville and the uncertainty of it all, I just couldn't pass up this offer. The day after arriving in Orlando, I got a call to go out with Calamity Jane. What might have been.

Joe Osborn once said something on a ride to a Nashville demo session that stuck with me. I asked, in my young, naive way at the time, "What's it like being a top session player?" He looked straight ahead as he drove and said in his quiet manner, "It's the ultimate in prostitution!"

For a young guy starting out in the music business, I sure didn't see that one coming.

Mario Winans

The Vibe Is Definitely Here

Session Drummer, Producer, New York City

I work on lyrics, music; I love it all. When it's time for the artist to do the vocals, I even love to sit in there and sing with them. From the beginning to the end, I love the whole thing. Even when I'm not in the studio I could be on a plane and I'm creating in my mind. So pretty much I work every day, all day. I have a six-month-old daughter now, so sometimes I won't get here until about two or three in the afternoon and I'll work till two in the morning. I'm usually working on a hundred different things, but all of them one at a time. We complete everything in its time.

Every day we have great moments. I'm blessed to be able to come into the studio every day to create. I try not to get too attached into a set studio, but I know where home is. It's Daddy's House, Sean "Puffy" Combs's studio. That's Bad Boy Entertainment, with over five hundred million records sold. The vibe is definitely here. I wouldn't call it a sacred place. Sacredness is for the individual to determine. I've had good vibes at a lot of different studios, but there's a comfort level here, just knowing it's home; it's like the difference between sleeping at your house and sleeping at a hotel. Musicians walking in here definitely get a sense of the vibe. It doesn't mean it's going to come out in the things that they do, but it often does. That's why we always pray before we start.

I started out with drums. When I was a kid I was playing everything. I played pots and pans. I was always getting into trouble pulling out the pots and pans and breaking off hangers.

I grew up in the church, so there really were no DJs around. But once I started producing R&B, I heard people sampling. There's definitely different levels of sampling and a lot of ways to be clever with it. I've heard from the worst-case scenarios to the best. There's some rules involved. I mean, you should never put a song out without clearing it. But as far as in your creation I think you should do what you feel.

The first person I ever heard sampling was definitely Teddy Riley. I'm not saying that's the first person who ever did it, but that's the first person who caught my attention and made me say, I gotta find something that can sample. The way he started using all the James Brown stuff made me say, I gotta get a drum machine that samples. No more factory sounds for me. I used to sample from CDs or off of drum machines or even cassettes when I first started. Then you'd see people finding stuff from old records. That was something I really picked up on when I moved to Atlanta. I was living with a couple of really talented producers, Tim and Bob, and I saw them doing it. They weren't doing it for the loops; mostly Tim was doing it at first for the hi-hat, kicks, and snares, to give records a different fill. Or sometimes he'd sample a different guitar loop. I'd see that and I'd go crazy with guitar loops, because it opened up a whole new avenue. A creative person is going to take that to the next level.

I love being behind the scenes; that's my favorite thing. But I also understand responsibility. I have things to say in songs that I want to get out and that need to be out. As far as my solo career, I'm never really satisfied; I always want to do more and do it better. But I'm happy with the way things are going.

I learned a whole lot from being in a musical family, the Winans. I know God directed my life. As far as music was concerned, gospel was the dimension I learned. That's where all the depth and the feeling is. They're singing about the truth. That's my basis. That's the best basis you can have. You learn what it takes to survive as a musician. You learn how to have a relationship with God, so if you pray that the check is in the mail . . . it will be there.

Paul Evans

(paul@paulevans.com; www.paulevans.com)

One Block from the
Brill Building

Former Session Singer, Teen Idol, New York City

My introduction to recording was making demos of my songs at Audiosonic Recording Studios, which was located in the Brill Building in New York City. It wasn't long before Audiosonic closed its doors and I was forced to look elsewhere for my demos. That's how I discovered Associated Recording Studios, one block from the Brill Building at 723 Seventh Avenue. Associated was destined to become one of my homes away from home.

First, I recorded my own song demos there, but soon I was earning a small living singing demos of songs for other writers who had to hire a singer because they couldn't carry a tune. Sometimes I'd work on two or three sessions there in a day. I think I got paid twelve dollars for a session. It was a great place, very funky, very friendly; it didn't have any panache at all. But who needed panache? All anybody wanted was a great sound, and Associated delivered the goods.

It was a demo studio. I don't know anybody who went into the studio intending to cut a master, but many demos came out sounding so good that labels purchased them and released them on vinyl. That was the story of "Seven Little Girls (Sittin' in the Back Seat)." I had recorded the demo for the writers, Lee Pockriss and Bob Hilliard. I think they originally pitched the demo to Carlton Records for Merv Griffin. However, Joe Carlton, the owner of the label, wound up releasing my demo "as is" on his subsidiary label, Guaranteed Records. "Seven Little Girls" became my first Billboard Top 10 recording.

I hung around Associated whenever I had free time because I knew all the talented musicians and engineers who worked there. The same crew worked at the studio from the late fifties through the mid-sixties. There were two drummers, Buddy Saltzman and Gary Chester. Dick Romoff and Russ Sanders played the bass and Leroy Glover and Frank Owens were the first-call pianists. Charlie Macey was the busiest of the Associated guitarists. Al Gorgoni and Bucky Pizzarelli were also first-call guitarists.

If a session was called for 10 A.M., we'd all come in at ten, say hello, and get down to work. First the songwriter would sit at a piano and play the song for us. Generally, he'd give us lead sheets—just the notes of the melody with chords above it. I'd sing the song with him a few times until I learned it and then it would be up to the rhythm section to start running the song down and come up with a groove. The good writers knew what they wanted to walk out of the studio with. They relied on the singer and the musicians to make it even better than they envisioned. With some writers you had to sing it exactly as they said. But the writers that we loved to work with would allow us the freedom to do our thing.

It would take about twenty minutes till we'd get it grooving, and then we'd get in front of the mikes to get sounds. Drum sounds were always the hardest to get. However, the process was made faster because the drum set was always ready for us in a corner of the studio, so all the engineers had to do was adjust the sound for each drummer's style of playing. I remember that there was a little round electric heater sitting next to the drum setup and Buddy Saltzman used to play on it with his brushes. The sound of that heater is on many records—and many of those records were mine.

Everybody made demos there. That's where I'd run into super talents like Paul Simon, Ellie Greenwich, Burt Bacharach, Tony Orlando, and Jerry Keller. Phil Spector also worked up at Associated. He was known for flinging garbage cans around to get his sound.

I actually wrote the big Bobby Vinton hit, "Roses Are Red (My Love)" at Associated. Al Byron came in with the lyrics while I was doing demos of some other songs. I thought I would pull a joke on him, so I said to the band, "Take five minutes guys, I'm gonna write a hit song." I took Al's lyrics over to the piano, looked at them for a few seconds, and wrote the melody. Al said, "Hey! That's real good." I laughed and replied, "Come on, Al, I'm just kidding around. I'll take it home and work on it." But, fortunately, I could never top that original melody.

I wound up producing and singing on the demo for "Roses" at Associated. Then my co-publisher took it to Bob Morgan at Epic Records, who first played it for Guy Mitchell. Guy's manager wanted the publishing on the song. But Bob said, "There's no way the guys will give you the publishing." So the manager said, "Well, then I'm not cutting that song with Guy." That's how Bobby Vinton wound up with it. A little while later we heard from Bob Morgan, who said, "Hey, wanna hear this record I just cut with your song?" But at that time I had so many songs floating around that when I first heard Vinton's recording I thought, "Oh, that's nice." I don't remember falling off my seat.

"Roses Are Red" was practically sabotaged by the record

company. The powers that be didn't like the record and didn't want to put it out, but Bob Morgan convinced them to give it a shot. They said okay, but they went to work on the other side of the record. Vinton gets the credit for making it a hit because he believed in it and he put his money where his mouth was. He's a Pittsburgh guy and he broke the record by himself in Pittsburgh. He hired a girl, legend goes, who brought one red rose up to every radio station in Pittsburgh along with the record. The record wound up being number one for four solid weeks on the *Billboard* charts.

Everyone in Tin Pan Alley knew when you had a hit. I remember sitting up at Associated with Jack Keller, who co-wrote the Connie Francis hits "My Heart Has a Mind of Its Own" and "Everybody's Somebody's Fool." Jack was explaining his formula for writing songs to me. He obviously believed that the form of a song had a lot to do with its success. He told me that he would take the lyrics from a hit song and write a new melody to them. Then he'd write new lyrics to go with his new melody. I said to him, "Jack, don't you dare do that with 'Roses Are Red.'" "It's too late, Paul," he said. "I've already done it."

Lou Barlow

Great Expectations

Bass Player, Sebadoh

The first time I recorded at Fort Apache studios was with Dinosaur, for the *Bug* album. That was with [Fort Apache engineers] Sean [Slade] and Paul [Kolderie]. On that I was the bass player of the band, so I showed up and did my tracks and high-tailed it out of there. I wouldn't say there was a scene. It wasn't like, Juliana Hatfield's recording, so I'll just pop in. It was just a very friendly place for me. It was a place where I knew that I could set up time and walk in there cold. At the same time, the whole thing was sort of being run by Juliana's manager, who owned Fort Apache. He did well with Belly's "Feed the Tree," so there was money floating around at that point and they really started spending on the studio.

I lived in the area. That's another reason it was so perfect. When Dinosaur started there was a place called Chet's Last Call, which was near Boston Garden and we played there with bands like Salem 66 and the Moving Targets. We definitely had an affinity with those bands 'cause we were all on labels like Homestead at the time. So there was definitely something going on there; I don't know exactly what. I was so young at the time. And we were a very aggressive, extremely loud band. So there wasn't exactly a lot of good time feelings going on, although I did like the bands we played with.

When Sebadoh did our third album we literally had a recording budget of $1,750, which is nothing. But we walked into Fort Apache and Paul and Sean—who I think even at that particular time period had already done Radiohead—spent two days with us recording on the eight-track machine, so it was cheap enough for us to use. We did a whole record in three days. A lot of the record was four-track stuff that I brought in, but we're talking about really low-fi four-track stuff that they took the time to mix and master really well and the album ended up sounding really good.

When I did the Folk Implosion record we were working for the film company of *Kids* and just giving them four-track demos. They said, "We really want you to go into a studio." I said, "Well then, why don't you get us some time at Fort Apache?" So, two weeks later, John Davis and I just walked right into Fort Apache and this guy Wally Gagel, who had recently been hired by the studio as a house engineer, happened to be there. And within a couple of weeks we did a ton of work, out of which came our little hit song, "Natural One."

I just knew it would be okay because it was Fort Apache. I knew, even if I wasn't necessarily working with Paul and Sean, that I could walk in there cold and it would just work out. Nevertheless, to end up with a hit single was completely unprecedented for any band of our type. It was totally weird. How the hell did that happen? But it was just a feeling that it didn't matter. Not that it didn't matter—I just knew that ultimately we were doing it for ourselves. There was no pressure.

We recorded the song in six hours. How beautiful is that? For me it was the creative thrill of it and also flying in the face of any kind of doing what you're told. Well, you really need to get a producer. And you've got to do this and that or it's not going to work. Maybe even at that time at Fort Apache there was a certain feeling that there was a right way to do things. The right mike to put on this. A right guitar to play this part. But I always really disliked those notions. I think anything can happen as long as you have the spirit behind it and the timing is right.

Also, I think because I was coming from an indie rock sort of low-fi thing, people thought I had an incredible sense of purity about the music I listened to and played. A lot of people still approach me as if I would be really offended if they mentioned a heavy metal band. They imagine that I have this real specific idea of the way music should be played and performed and I have all these ideas of integrity. And that song, in particular, flew in the face of that too. For one thing, we sampled—we used a lot of hip-hop influences. Even though it doesn't sound particularly hip-hop, that was the prevailing influence of the song. Also, I wrote the lyrics about the movie instead of writing them about myself. Everything I had written up to that point were these very sort of uncomfortable descriptions of my personal situation. So I stepped outside of myself, which for me was kind of a cool challenge. It was really unexpected and that's beautiful when that happens.

Once we had that success we obviously completely complicated the situation. That's almost because for myself I find it's not so much the money, but it's more like the feeling of expectation. I like surprising people. I hate the feeling that when I walk into a situation someone's expecting me to do something brilliant. I would much rather be in a place where people have no real idea what my background is or what I'm actually capable of. I find that to be more conducive to having a good, confident, really fun experience recording. But when it comes to expectations—here we are following up our major-label hit song—that sucks.

Byron Nemeth

(www.byronnemeth.com)

Switching Gears

Guitarist, Studio Owner, Cleveland

I work in my recording studio about forty to fifty hours a week. I have twenty half-hour guitar lessons after sessions and on weekend mornings. I rehearse with my band four to five hours, one night a week and two nights a week before a show. On the nights that I get done with sessions and there is no rehearsal or students, I'm usually doing Internet publicity with my agent, going to clubs to cool off a little and do some promotion of my CD and the studio, or scheduling complete time off to relax, play a little guitar, or just do nothing. It's hard to switch gears from being a businessman to being a teacher to being a rock star, but if you really love music as a spiritual part of your life you take the pain and look toward the brass ring.

Music picked me.

The main reason I went into the studio business was to have free rein of the gear so that I could record the album of my dreams with unlimited time. To pay for the gear meant that I had to go into business. To this day, on the rare occasion that I miss a client's call because of a session, I always return the call within an hour. I have been relentless in this habit and it has paid off. It has allowed me to produce a stunning instrumental guitar CD that was totally financed by my intense work ethic for the studio.

In my experience I've found that most bands have a very limited knowledge of how studio procedure works. It's an involved process and it takes a while to accomplish a professional production. Bands want a Ferrari-level production and they have a Volkswagen-level budget. They want to do ten to twelve songs for a couple of thousand dollars and then complain when it doesn't sound as tight as the latest Creed or Madonna or Jay-Z or Metallica album. They think that in the studio everything just happens instantly with magic instead of focused time on a specific song done right the first time. They spread themselves way too thin and in the process drive me and themselves crazy.

I go to unbelievable lengths to explain the procedure to all bands. Bands with "studio-type" people in them, even though they may not have necessarily worked in a studio, always have the best sounding results. They have a specific budget and the guy in the band who understands the studio has educated the band so that everything runs with correct expectations.

An ever-increasing trend that I see with other musicians is whining and complaining about how they don't have enough time for their music. It never dawns on them that the key to success is focus, the ability to follow your dreams and execute a plan of attack. A lot of them do not supremely sacrifice their own personal time to have more time to bring control to their career. I love a good party, but the night life does not rule my life. Personal issues are absolutely secondary. What makes me feel this way is that music is a spiritual gift that must be pursued and cannot be ignored.

Strict professionalism is an important habit of mine. Nothing is worse than a band or musicians who are late to a gig, disrespectful to an established national promoter, or who ignore talking to fans after a concert. People in the business remember a bad situation faster than a good one. The reason I have opened so many shows at the Odean Concert Club in Cleveland is that the promoter always says he likes to call me first because of my reputation as a serious guitar player. Also, when he calls (usually at the last minute) he knows I'll answer the phone and be able to give him a decision on performing the opening slot right away or not.

When I was on the bill with Zack Wylde at the Cleveland Agora, you should have seen the look on his face when he heard that an instrumental band would be opening up for him. But after the show he came up to me and said how much he enjoyed the show and how he wished more bands were like this. He mentioned how he was tired of "Zack" clone and "Ozzy" clone bands opening for him, because they all sounded the same and had no originality. Comments like this make me feel I'm right on target with what I'm doing.

Onno Lakeman

(redtoviolet.com)

A Different Recording Process

Guitarist, Red to Violet

After our previous band broke up and the contract with the record company expired, we had the chance to make a fresh start. We started to write songs again and visualized a different recording process. Instead of limited time in an expensive studio, for which we would need another record company for financial support, we thought of a way to record independently. We knew that sound engineer Kees van Gool, with whom we did the last series of gigs, was also very much into recording. He had gathered some great recording equipment and a large microphone collection over the years and had previously done recordings with the Dutch group Golden Earring. As we got along fine, both musically and personally, we played Kees some demos of our new songs and discussed the idea of recording an album on location. It clicked! We decided to set up a production company in which all three of us agreed to have maximum input and in which we would all benefit equally.

Wishing for an inspiring environment, we booked a remote vacation house on a green Belgian hillside, rented a van, brought in the studio equipment, and had the studio working in less than a day. Beds and mattresses were used as sound-blocking devices against walls and there were cables running through almost all the rooms and stairways. We were extremely happy to be able to use the Otari MTR 90-II twenty-four-track analog recording machine of Golden Earring's guitarist. We invited Holland's most groovy session bass player and drummer to this remote location to lay down the basic tracks. The atmosphere was very good. Recording and sleeping in the house and chatting away in between sessions created a relaxed atmosphere. A mouth-harp player we knew, who had later joined the Hare Krishnas, invited us to come over to a Hare Krishna castle nearby to eat there every day with the devotees. This not only added to the positive vibes, it also meant there was less time and energy needed for the daily catering. We only had to fill the fridge twice a week and that about did the job as far as eating and drinking in the studio house.

During recordings of the basic tracks the bass guitar went into a DI box and to a Drawmer 1960 preamp compressor and then straight to tape. The drums were miked in the large attic of the house. Because of all the wood on the ceiling and on the walls, the sound was great for live drums. As the recording console and desk were placed two floors below and the doors were taped with foam for acoustic isolation, it was possible to record and to be able to tell the difference between live sound and recorded sound.

Having the luxury to record until we were satisfied with the sound and the part, we moved forward a bit slower than planned, successfully finishing five songs in three weeks. For the recording of El's deep-sounding voice we would often use a classic Neumann U-47 mike, which complemented the warmth of her vocals. We also tried the weirdest sounds and sometimes let the smallest amps make the biggest sounds. One night after we came back from a dinner party at the castle we used the combination of a cranked-up small Birdie amp and the dirty sound of the Epiphone Casino to produce a great Elvis Presley kind of solo guitar sound, for the song "It Comes Again." We used a drumstick to produce an off-the-wall percussion sound on the Fender Strat guitar in the bridge of "Let There Be Light." The five-dollar red-painted first guitar I got from my parents turned out to be perfect for a moody mandolin kind of sound on the ballad "Mr. J."

Recording acoustic guitars, we would not only mike the guitar near the sound hole but also near the neck, near the bridge (for the percussive strumming sound), as well as 1.5 feet away from the guitar and even all the way back in the room, to use the room sound as well. On his sound board Kees would mix several microphone channels into one sound for the acoustic guitar, depending on the need of the song. For some electric-guitar parts, like the continuous solo on "Inner Peace," we would go straight from the black Gibson Les Paul Custom into a classic fifty-watt Marshall head and two Celestion speakers, but again using mikes for the room sound too.

Although we were happy with the first five songs, we still needed another ten to be finished. So we came up with a new plan. Instead of again moving equipment and installing a studio on location, we dreamed of a steady recording place in the same kind of environment. Kees knew people who were setting up a new studio and needed some extra recording equipment to make it work. He offered to help out with his equipment so they could record their first project and after that was finished, we could move in and finish our recordings. This studio was located on a small estate in the south of Holland—with some free peacocks flying around. According to people from India these are holy birds.

Working in this new remote studio, we got in for mostly

three days a week to fill in all the vocal and guitar parts of the song we chose to work on. We felt very inspired as well as free and explored the soundscapes even further. On "Here I Am," which turned out to be the opening track of the album and debut single, we sent the EBow part through a Hammond cabinet, which resulted in a heavenly rotary sound for intro and choruses. The combination of the blond Epiphone Sheraton with the crunchy 1970s London City tube amp gave exactly the right drive for the dramatic feel of "Mercy." For this song we also recorded some Hare Krishnas singing their morning mantra "Govinda" in their temple. The recording was done on eight-track and added later.

Once we had recorded all of the vocals and the guitar parts, we invited some more session players on percussion and an occasional Hammond organ. After we rearranged the studio and brought in some extra sound equipment, like the Yamaha NS-10 speakers for sound reference, we also did the mix here. Every mix we did was an experience in itself. Feeding Kees with our ideas, we would leave and he would set up a mix. After a few hours or sometimes a whole day, we'd come back in, analyze the rough mix, after which the three of us would bring it to the next stage. Producing the album while being the band and songwriters was something that went naturally. Somehow we knew exactly in which direction the songs needed to go—including to the smallest room in the house, the bathroom, where El sang a percussion part for the song "Mercy." We used the weirdest effects or used the most normal effects in an extreme manner—like a flanger on the drums of the up-tempo track "It Comes Again." Or the bass guitar in heavy "Mother Earth," that automatically followed the regular kick-drum sound by keying it through the noise gate—an idea Kees got while lying in his bed in between sessions. Using a vocoder on the backing vocals and on the bass guitar in the broody number "The Way You Are" did wonders for the song.

The electric tabla in the bluesy "Don't Wanna Lose You" was sent through a simple Boss Metal Distortion and resulted in the weirdest percussion sound.

Once we finished the final mix, we knew, having recorded on location, that it needed an expert in mastering to get the overall sound spectrum right in place. We all had a special affection for Abbey Road Studios in London, so that's where we went. The three of us came in one morning with the collection of analog masters on quarter-inch tape. We agreed it would be an attended session, as we wanted to add our ideas to the mastering process too. Inside the legendary studio, we were welcomed by Lucy, who informed us that the mastering engineer we had booked, and who had earlier worked with the Beatles, was ill. But she had an alternative for us: a young and upcoming mastering engineer with good credentials named Sean Magee. We decided to try out a few songs with him and if the result would make us happy, we would continue the mastering session with him. Sean turned out to be a miracle in disguise. His way of approaching our music and adding his sound colors was ideal. The team effort resulted in a high-vibe session with lots of capuccino coffees, and lots of in-spiration. And of course we felt privileged to be able to work in a place with such history. The quarter-inch master tapes were played on the very same reels that once played Pink Floyd's *Dark Side of the Moon*. In Abbey Road Studios the music went through an old EMI console, a Prism EQ and compressor for analog pro-cessing, and was converted to digital thereafter. At the end of that day, we enjoyed the late night vibes of Abbey Road Studios, as we knew the Beatles used to record lots of times in the evening and night hours. In the cab that brought us back to the hotel the three of us were silent. Without speaking a single word we knew we all felt what an uplifting experience this magical ride had been.

John Hiatt

Getting in the Spaceship

Singer-Songwriter

I've always been into sound, but it generally never went past, "Leo Fender had it down, and it hasn't gotten much better since." But since I've had the good fortune to be able to set up my own little home recording studio, it's had a very positive effect on me as far as kind of demystifying the whole studio process. The studio experience in the past was always sort of like a photo session to me. You go in, smile, say cheese, take a quick picture, and then get the hell out of there. This time, I wanted to not do that. I wanted to get a little more friendly with the studio and the process of record making, for maybe the first time.

I mean, you're talking to somebody who, beyond volume, bass, and treble, is lost. Now I've got a terrific Peavey board. It's a wonderful little tool, to learn how to twiddle those knobs, and I've got a sixteen-track Fostex and some outboard gear, and I'm learning how to punch stuff up and get some echoes going. When I make demos I go in and usually play all the instruments. I'll either punch up a single drum track on a drum machine or sometimes I'll play the drums or I'll get a friend in to play the music that I can't do. The high point of a song for me is when it's finished and I feel like it's a good song. But I so enjoy the process that that's also the low point, because it's over. Getting the idea is a high point too; feeling those endorphins shake loose gets you kind of pleasantly high. It's kind of a compromise after that point, good or bad. But it's fun to hear what happens, how it sounds when you put a band to it, how other people perceive it, what they might add to it.

We spent two and a half months making my last record, which for me is like an eternity. It was an incredible learning experience. The only snag I had was in the mixing process, which I have managed to avoid, lo these many years of making albums. I have always ducked out during the mixes because it was too excruciating for me. It's just a sinking feeling, being the artist and the singer, and you realize that there's such finality to these damned mixes. It was just too terrifying for me in the past. But I was bolstered by Glyn Johns, the producer, who in fact loves the mixing process. I'd watch him mixing and go, "How come he loves mixing so much, and I hate it so much?" I realized that he was able to just sort of be there in the moment, with the excitement and the fun of having it take aural shape in the final mix, whereas I was already down the road and had it coming out and in people's living rooms, sounding funny.

Once I got in the studio, I was merciless as far as what I wanted to have happen. I didn't want to hear anything where I could say, "Been there, done that." Which was what Glyn and I kept saying to each other. We said we could go in and make a record played by a mean little four- or five-piece band, with live performances, nice and tough and all that, but we've already done that. Let's try something else. I'd never done much in the way of overdubbing stuff. So on these tunes, we'd get a good live performance, but then we'd go back in and put some other pieces on, and this was a new experience for me. I mean, I'm no stranger to the overdub, and I have no qualms about it not being music if it's got an overdub. That's part of the art of the craft. But I never relied on it that extensively, and I found it to be intriguing.

I was really going for what Ry Cooder calls "getting in the little spaceship and going on a trip," and having enough trust in the process that you're going to come out the other side into some sort of interesting world.

Karl Wallinger

Studio Rat

Guitarist, the Waterboys, World Party

I'm hardly ever not in the studio. I just go there and lie in wait like some sort of biblical thief behind a rock. It's like fishing; you go to the river every day, and if you have a bite and it takes you all night and all the next day to haul it in, you just stay there. I've gotten jet lag in the studio without going anywhere. You end up going to bed at two o'clock in the afternoon and you get up at ten o'clock that evening, and you're totally backward as far as what the world is doing. I definitely like working at night; I find it's very peaceful. There's no phones ringing, there's nobody out there—you're not missing anything.

The reason I got my own studio is that I just hate the feeling that you have to do it in a day. This way it's open-ended. There's no booking. I don't have to panic because it isn't finished in a month. You can be working on something, and it's quite good to just take it off the machine and say, "Well, I'll come back to that . . . whenever." Not tomorrow—or it might be tomorrow, if you fancy that, or it might be in two months' time.

"I Fell Back Alone" happened one evening and I mixed it, and that was it, and I never got the tape out of the box again. And then there's something like "Rainbow," which has been recorded with different bunches of people. There are two hundred mixes of each version. "Thank You World" was an eight-minute groove and it had a different melody. It was slower and hardly had any vocals on it at all, and I knew there was something in there. I edited it down to 3:39, just crashed into it every sixteen bars, and built up sections, and that's how it ended up. It was very enjoyable doing that; it was really great, making something out of something else.

At one point in "Message" I actually made each two-bar phrase into a one-bar phrase by editing. That's a lot of edits, making every two-bar B-major chord one bar, but it works. I love tape editing. You get a razor blade and you have the tape, and as long as you can remember what piece of tape you've got round your neck, you're all right. It's when you get a bit mixed up that you think, "Oh, where's the chorus?" You have to go and look around the studio; you might have thrown it away. You've got pieces of two-inch tape everywhere, and that's brilliant. I love that.

For me the best part comes somewhere midway in the process of everything, when you're not mixing, you're playing, and you're really into it and you don't exist for however long the song exists. You're just part of this music, and that's really great, that feeling. That's why I do it, for that feeling. I'm a junkie for that feeling. It's just so incredibly good for you. I think if it could be bottled, it'd probably be a cure for cancer.

SONGWRITERS X

Paul Simon

He Wrote Aretha's Song

"Bridge over Troubled Water"

There's this guy in the garage where I park my car, a black guy in his fifties. Somebody there must have tipped him off about me. So one day he comes up to me and says, "Who are you, are you famous?" So I said, "Well, yeah, you know, to a degree I'm famous." He asked, "What do you do?" So I'm trying to grope for the broadest common denominator that anyone would know. I said, "Did you ever hear of Simon and Garfunkel?" No. Then I said, "Did you ever see *The Graduate*?" No. Finally I said, "Do you know that song that Aretha Franklin sang, 'Bridge over Troubled Water'?" Yeah! I said, "I wrote that." So he called his buddies over. "Hey, he wrote Aretha's song!"

When you do a piece of work that's good and it becomes a hit, it gets into the mainstream of the culture and has a great impact. "Sounds of Silence" has had a greater impact than "Hearts and Bones." I wrote "Sounds of Silence" when I was twenty-one and "Hearts and Bones" is, I think, a better song. But "Sounds of Silence" was a big hit and it's in the culture.

When you talk about a popular art, as the writing gets more complex and more layered, it's harder to have a lot of people who really like it. It is easier to have a smaller group of people who are more intensely devoted to you. It's natural that this should happen in my development. I wouldn't have it any other way. I was a rock star at one point. I had many years of being a rock star. I don't want to be a rock star anymore. So that's not the criterion I apply to my work. I'm interested in the work. I hope that the work is popular. I try and make it popular, but I try and make it popular with my own ears and I know that my own ears are far away from the marketplace at this moment in time, and have been for several years now. Nevertheless, it's still possible that people will find that my work is interesting. If so, I'll be even more gratified because I will have shifted thinking/listening habits, sort of, just a little bit, in another direction.

When I wrote the *Graceland* album I had a cassette player that had an automatic memory and I'd just keep playing it over and over, thousands and thousands of plays. I didn't have a guitar. All I needed was the tracks. A lot of writers write backward from the tracks, particularly writers who are writing groove records and dance records. They find the groove, then they write the song. I've done it before, but never for an entire album. All the elements that became mainstays of this album, juxtaposing music from one culture against music of another, recording with musicians from another musical culture, writing backward from track to song, I had done in little bits and pieces in the past. So it wasn't a new move for me. The only thing that was new about it was the proportions. The other thing that was new is that I found it didn't really inhibit what I was writing lyrically. In fact, I think it helped.

A high percentage of my lyrics are products of my subconscious thinking. Part of the impulse to write is to have a catharsis. As the writing continues you can get into a little pocket where things are coming easily. You find yourself with this inexplicable flow of images, ideas, thoughts that are interesting. You also have to have a very low level of critical faculty operating.

The opposite is when you experience periods where nothing comes because the critical faculties get heightened and you won't allow a line to come out without criticizing it. You have to loosen up on yourself to allow things to come. I found that reading different books from people who were writing in the mood that I was writing was helpful. When I was writing "Crazy Love" I was reading Chris Durang. When I was writing "Under African Skies" I was reading Yeats. With "Graceland" I was probably reading Raymond Carver. Actually, I did read a book called *Elvis & Gladys,* but I don't think it affected me.

Most of the time, though, what I'm writing is about music, not about lyrics, and critics pay scant attention to the music. I mean, if you're saying something with music *and* words—if you're saying one thing with words and the opposite with music and you're creating a sense of irony—that's lost. Or if the idea of a song is a musical idea, how to write a song in 7/4 time and make it feel natural, let's say, it's beyond them. I never heard anybody say, "Now that was a clever way of doing 7/4 time." Instead, most critics are basically analyzing words. It's English lit all over again.

I was always free to do exactly what I liked during my career, but what I liked was also very much in sync with what the vast public liked. There's something in me that's singles oriented. You start to make a track and all of a sudden it's got a great feel to it. A kind of magic happens that you couldn't have predicted. "Let's pull out all the stops and make a single." That sentence comes up a lot in the studio. I've been making records for years. That's my profession. I first started trying to peddle songs with a friend of mine, Carol Klein (who would later become known as Carole King), back in the 1950s. Carol would play piano and drums and sing. I would sing and play guitar and bass. The game was to make a demo at demo prices and then try to sell it to a record company. Maybe you'd wind up investing three hundred dollars for musicians and studio time, but if you did something really good you could get as much as a thousand for it. I never wanted to be in groups. I was only after that seven-hundred-dollar profit.

But I know that what I like is not at all what's happening now on hit radio. So I'm not thinking, will this be a hit, because the stuff that is a hit is not of interest to me. I'm not writing it, so I don't think about it. I just try to make what I'm doing as interesting to me as I can.

Desmond Child
The Cool Hits

"Livin' on a Prayer"

I was poor and Hispanic and Catholic, going to a school of upper-middle-class Jewish kids who had everything in the world. It was very difficult being there, so I was drawn to the artistic types at school, the musicians. I joined the choir and it became my special world. Eventually I began to feel more and more confident in the things I was thinking about and talking about, 'cause these kids were reading special books and knew about special things. It was a magic time, really, when I became Desmond Child.

I was always going to these three-day pop festivals and sleeping on blankets. I hitchhiked to Canada when I was fifteen. The next year I quit high school and my writing partner named me Desmond Child and I named her Virgil Night. We took my Buick Skylark convertible and drove to Montreal and then, heading back, we ended up in Woodstock, New York, and lived there in a hippie house for nine months. We packed apples in Poughkeepsie for money and hung out at the Joyous Lake with Taj Mahal and Van Morrison and Dylan. Todd Rundgren was making an album up there called *Something/Anything?* that really influenced me because he was moving into rock, which was more aggressive than the folk-based things I had been interested in previously.

My mother is a singer and a songwriter and also a heck of a stage mother. So writing songs and trying to get covers was something that was going on ever since I was a baby. She put a lot of value on being an artist, expressing yourself, but also to get a lot of applause for it. That desire to be known, to have the world approve, was something that was programmed in me from infancy. It's really thrilling when I go to see my friends performing and I see an arena full of people singing the lyrics that came out of my brain.

But it's deeper than that. We are reflecting the aesthetic of our time in the music, the consciousness of our times, and as times change then we should change as artists. For instance, I wrote "If You Were a Woman and I Was a Man" with Jim Steinman in 1985. Bonnie Tyler put it out and it was a bomb. In writing it, Jim had said, "I want the bridge to be like Hall and Oates and I want the chorus to be like Bruce Springsteen." So it was very funky, and then had an anthemic chorus, with "Because the Night" kind of chord changes, and the bass line was kind of R&B-ish, but it was played with a heavy guitar. When the song stiffed I was heartbroken, because I thought I'd stumbled upon a really important new style, so I brought that groove and the chorus to my first writing session with Jon Bon Jovi and Richie Sambora. I also had the title, "You Give Love a Bad Name," and they had written a song on their previous album called "Shot Through the Heart" and so we started the song off with that line. If you listen to the music it's exactly like "If You Were a Woman and I Was a Man." All those elements came together and created something new. And from that point in 1987 on, rock bands that had never been played on the radio before were able to be played on Top 40.

With "Living on a Prayer" I knew immediately that it was

one of the best songs I'd ever written. I felt it the minute me and John and Richie hit that chorus. "Oooh, we're halfway there/Wo-oh, living on a prayer." Forget it! This is big. And it almost didn't make the record 'cause it scared the record company. They thought, "Oh, it's too pop; we're gonna lose our rock credibility." Yeah, well, fifteen million albums later, I think they have some kind of credibility. It ended up being number one for four weeks.

I think there's a window where a song can make an impact—like "Luka." I love that song and it meant something. Or "Janie's Got a Gun." Or "Fast Car." I don't think those songs have lost their impact. I don't think they're a cliché. It's all in how well something's done. There's an aesthetic involved even in writing a hit song and there's certain kinds of hits, and I hope that when, in the sum total, you look at my work, you'll see that they were the cool hits. They were songs that meant something. Songs that, even if they were just fun, had an attitude that reflected a poignancy, the poignancy of our time.

Donald Fagen
(Steely Dan)
The Bill Murray Effect

"Hey Nineteen"

I don't think Walter [Becker] and I are songwriters in the traditional sense, neither the Tin Pan Alley/Broadway variety nor the "staffer" type of the fifties and sixties. An attentive listening to our early attempts at normal genre writing will certainly bear me out. It soon became more interesting to exploit and subvert traditional elements of popular songwriting and to combine this material with the jazz-based music we had grown up with. In college we were both intrigued by certain humorists of the late fifties and early sixties, such as John Barth, Joseph Heller, Kurt Vonnegut, Thomas Berger, Terry Southern, and Bruce Jay Friedman. I've since cooled on a lot of these writers. Walter read a couple of novels by Thomas Pynchon. We both thought the predicament in which popular music found itself in the middle sixties rather amusing, too, and we tried to wring some humor out of the whole mess. We mixed TV-style commercial arranging clichés with Mersey beats, assigned nasty-sounding, heavily amplified guitars to play Ravel-like chords, etc. The fairly standardized rock instrumentation of the original group added to the schizy effect. We never tried to compete with the fine songwriters of the era (Goffin and King, Lennon and McCartney). We were after a theatrical effect, the friction produced by the mix of music and lyrics—the irony.

At this point I can't remember who wrote this verse or that chorus, but the way it often worked out was like this: I would come up with a basic musical structure, perhaps a hook line and occasionally a story idea. Walter would listen to what I had and come up with some kind of narrative structure. We'd work on music and lyrics together, inventing characters, adding musical and verbal jokes, polishing the arrangements and smoking Turkish cigarettes. Of course, the musicians would kick in with arranging ideas, bass lines, etcetera when we got into the studio.

Because most of our tunes were written to be performed only by Steely Dan, they don't lend themselves very well to cover renditions. The lyrics are not the sort that would inspire singers to cover them. And most of the melodies are instrumental-type lines, and not songs in the usual sense of the term. By that I mean that a real song, it seems to me, has a kind of melody which is, first of all, very easy to sing. It has a natural flow, usually in a stepwise motion, with consecutive notes, simple arpeggios, and so on. That's a quality a lot of the great songwriters had. You can sing the melody without a chordal background and it'll still sound good. The melody is not dependent on the harmony; it's just a really good melody. I think our songs were derived more instrumentally, more in the way—not to make a comparison in quality—Duke Ellington would write. I think his songs in fact don't work that well as songs. He wrote for the people in his band, the specific players. He wrote lines he thought that they could play well. And although we weren't writing for instrumental performers—we were writing for my voice—I think our background, because it mostly comes out of arranging and jazz, made us lean toward melodies that had that kind of structure—they're more chordally situated.

When I hear the occasional cover I almost always experience what I've come to think of as the Bill Murray Effect—i.e., Buddy Grecco doing "Born to Be Wild."

Michael Bolton

Getting Covers

"Love Is a Wonderful Thing"

First you hear they're going to cut your song. Then you find out they never did cut it. The next level is that they cut it, but never put a vocal on it. Then they cut it, put a vocal on it, but it didn't make the record. Usually when I'm told the song is on hold, it winds up on the record. But I don't believe it until I hear it. Then they tell you it might be a single. When they tell you it's going to be a single, that's the only time I feel really confident that the song is going to make the record. I don't believe it's going to really be a single until I hear the version of it. Once I hear the version of it, I can start making noise myself and have whatever friends I have at that label go to see them every other day and say, "Did you hear that track yet?" I don't hype my work actively, but if I think there's a single there, I don't want to lose it. If it's not good enough to be a single, then I hope it's bad enough to be the B-side of a single. If it looks like it may be a single, they'll never put it on the B-side. Then, if it does get released as a single and it makes the charts, that's like going to the races. And they're off . . .

Anybody who says they're not trying to write hits is either in the wrong business or lying, because once you realize what you're up against, the odds of even getting a song on a record, then you'd better write a hit, or it's not gonna be on the record. Hit songs are the lifeblood of the industry. Every company is screaming for songs. The hit song is what keeps the industry alive, because that's all that radio wants to play. I didn't realize that until all of a sudden I started writing for other people. I've got a list right here of about seventy artists and producers who are looking for songs. Right now I've got songs on about twelve or thirteen albums. I have no idea whether they'll be produced well, whether any of them will even be singles, but I'm hoping for hits.

One song I wrote, "Still Thinking of You," has been recorded seven times. Larry Graham did it, France Joli, Rachel Sweet. Through Larry Graham, George Duke became a big fan of the song, and that's when I realized how it's great to have a producer really hot on a song. They're just gonna keep cutting it until they have a hit.

Once you've had a hit record, people start calling you up. There are a lot of writers who can sit down and write a song that sounds just like their last hit, only sideways. Those are not true songs to me. The writers I enjoy working with want to write songs that will be around ten years from now.

Travon Potts

It's About Time

"Angel of Mine"

I studied classical music since the age of three. By age twelve I started playing for my church's youth choir. In high school I was introduced to one of the creative directors at a publishing company. She took an interest in me from hearing me play and I recorded some demos. I wound up getting my first publishing deal right after graduating from high school, for a whopping seventeen thousand dollars a year. I knew at this point I was on my way to becoming like my music idols.

In about two years I was dropped from my publishing deal and picked up by Motown music publishing. I had not written any hit songs at that point but I felt that being with Motown meant that every song I wrote would be viewed as a hit and Whitney Houston would be knocking on my door. I also felt that if I wrote about five or six songs a year that would be five or six hits. My publishing representative urged me to be a tad more prolific but I felt that was unnecessary.

In a year I was on probation with Motown because of my low song output and lack of song placements on commercially released CDs. I was able to get a few remix gigs here and there to pay off some of the debt I was mounting. At this point Polygram bought Motown. My publishing rep survived the merger and somehow had enough belief in my raw talent not to drop me. To motivate me she figured out a way to advance me money to purchase some studio equipment to add to the equipment I already owned.

One day I got a call from an old friend, who told me that the popular producer Rhett Lawrence had an opening for a staff writer/producer. I had a meeting with Rhett and in a week I moved my small studio into one of his studio rooms and his engineers integrated my small setup into a computer program called Pro Tools. In his studio I cranked out about two to three tracks a day and with each one he became more and more impressed.

One particular track I liked I took to Rhett. He listened to it in passing and didn't say much more about it. But I didn't give up on the track. I played it for him again in a different setting and ironically he loved it this time. He went into my studio room and asked me to set the track up to be played over and over as he wrote lyrical ideas. He was stumped on lyrics for the second verse and bridge so I wrote those parts. When we finished "Angel of Mine" we sent it to Tamia. I don't think it even got to Tamia. Whoever intercepted it didn't like it and thought it wasn't a hit. So we sent it to Clive Davis as a long shot for Monica and the next day he called us and put the song on hold. Six months after Clive's hold a popular act from England named Eternal came to town with their manager. They heard the song and loved it. Two days later we recorded and produced it and the following week it entered the European charts at number five.

Clive still wanted the song but he wanted Rodney Jerkins to produce it here in the States. Knowing Rodney is not cheap told us just how interested Clive was in the song being a single. We made calls and found out it was going to be the second single on the album, but I was not sure until I saw ads for it in the trades.

I don't remember how long it took to go to number one, but I remember it entered at number eighty-five. I thought that was too low for it to go to number one. It's a ballad, so I thought it would move slowly, but it seemed like it took forever. But more and more the video kept being shown and more and more my family would call and tell me they saw it. And pretty soon I started hearing it over and over on the radio, which was cool, 'cause when I would look over at other people in their cars, they were bopping to it. It wound up being number one for four weeks on the *Billboard* charts! But it only started to sink in that it was a hit when I met Jam and Lewis and L.A. and Babyface for the first time.

Before this, my only other big hit was a song called "It's About Time," which was a Top 5 R&B single for a Chicago-based group named Public Announcement. Needless to say "It's About Time" was one of the biggest songs of the year in Chicago. I met the program director at WGCI at the group's record-release party and after having such a big hit he asked me to come speak on a panel at WGCI's conference. I thought the panels would be led by a bunch of midlevel writers like myself. Little did I know that Jam and Lewis and L.A. and Babyface would be there. This program director did not know I wrote "Angel of Mine" until he saw my discography. Then he made it a point to make sure everybody at the conference knew I wrote that song. What was weird was that Jam and Lewis and L.A. and Babyface, the two songwriting teams that are the reason why I even wanted to write and produce, congratulated me on the success of the song. I mean, they even came up and shook my hand. That's when I started thinking to myself, Wow, this must be a hit!

Hank Ballard

I Thought It Was Me

"The Twist"

The members of my group, the Midnighters, were doing the dance. They were twisting, so that's where I got the idea of writing the song. But the company thought it was just another record. Dick Clark did a pretty good job duplicating my record of "The Twist," man—note for note, gimmick for gimmick, phrase for phrase. He auditioned about twenty people before he picked Chubby Checker. And I could have sworn it was me; that's how close he came to my sound. I was wondering why they were playing it on the radio. I didn't find out it wasn't me until a few weeks later.

I can't complain. It's one of the best copyrights I have. Dick Clark did me a favor; otherwise the song would never have been heard. I made a lot of money on that song. Of course it was just a drop in the bucket compared to what Chubby made.

I didn't know there was so much money involved in publishing. The company I was with said there's no such thing; if you asked for publishing rights, they'd give you your contract back. They would tell me, "You've got to write a hundred songs before you can even get a BMI contract." I got it later, but they didn't even tell me I had to apply for it. Man, I hate to even think about the way we were took. But what can you do, man?

We were ignorant, and they were the beneficiaries of that. Very few people were lucky enough to find a manager like Elvis Presley had.

I should have had my own production company and everything. But we didn't know anything and there was nobody that was ever going to tell you about it, because you had some dues to pay. But I don't hold anybody responsible for my being ripped off but myself. I just read in the paper the other day where Bo Diddley said he sold all of his copyrights. Otis Blackwell sold the copyright on "Fever" to Henry Glover for fifty dollars. Glover also bought "Dedicated to the One I Love" from Lowman Pauling of the Five Royales for two or three hundred dollars. I can understand the circumstances. Circumstances can make you do a lot of things.

But a lot of people don't realize that when "The Twist" broke for Chubby Checker, we got hot too. We were working 365 days a year. We had to beg for time off. The Midnighters were into a real sweet Sonny Til and the Orioles style. I had them change to a more driving, up-tempo thing. You know, let's get funky! The South was our territory. We didn't do too much touring in the East. They were afraid of our act. Like the Apollo, they threw us out of the Apollo. We went to Philadelphia, we sold out for the whole ten days. The Apollo wouldn't let us do our act; now you can do anything. As far back as I remember we had a white audience, because they loved those dirty records, like "Annie Had a Baby," man. We sold a lot of damn records. We used to play colleges. They'd yell, "Get dirty!" Most of the stuff that Alice Cooper did, all that stage shit, we were doing that years ago. They weren't as liberal then about a lot of things. They're even cursing on records now.

We always had plenty of work, even when we didn't have a record out. We were red hot for a good ten to twelve years. We were a very glamorous group, but mentally I didn't get into it. I'm very low key. I don't care for all that glamour. It never does anything for me. I call it "commercial admiration." I've never tried to rise above ordinary people. I like ordinary people. I've never been on that star trip, but I've seen a lot of my associates destroy themselves. Take Clyde McPhatter. He was my idol; I was crazy about Clyde McPhatter. But he had an emotional problem that he never did outlive. He drank himself to death; Little Willie John, the same thing. You have to condition yourself for the decline. I've never had a star complex, thinking you're God. How the hell are you going to be a god when you got a Top 100 out there? Everybody with a hit record thinks they're a god overnight—you got a hundred gods!

John Lee Hooker

She Gave Me a Song

"Boom Boom"

I used to play at this place called the Apex bar in Detroit. There was a young lady who was the bartender there named Luilla. I would come in there at night and I'd never be on time. Every night the band would beat me there. Sometimes they'd be on the bandstand playing by the time I got there. I'd always be late and whenever I'd come in she'd point at me and say, "Boom boom, you're late again." And she kept saying that. It dawned on me that that was a good name for a song. Then one night she said, "Boom boom, I'm gonna shoot you down." She gave me a song but she didn't know it.

I took that thing and I hummed it all the way home from the bar. At night I went to bed and I was still thinking of it. I got up the next day and put one and one together, two and two together, trying to piece it out, taking things out, putting things in. I finally got it down right, got it together, got it down in my head. Then I went and sang it and everybody went, "Wow." Then I didn't do it no more, not in the bar. I figured somebody would grab it before I got it copyrighted. So I sent it to Washington, D.C., the Library of Congress, and I got it copyrighted. After I got it copyrighted I could do it in the bar. So then if anybody got the idea to do it, I had them by the neck because I had it copyrighted.

About two months later I recorded it. I was on Vee Jay then. And the record shot straight to the top. Then, after I did it, the

Animals turned around and did it. That barmaid felt pretty good. She went around telling everybody, "I got John Lee to write that song." I gave her some bread for it, too, so she was pretty happy.

A lot of people think blues singers write when they're sad and lonely. They think you gotta be down and out to write the blues—hungry, broke. It's not true. I write when I've got a good feeling, when I'm happy. When things are going well for you, you write. You have to be in the groove to write. You can't be upset and worried and write the blues. You've got to have a clear mind. The songs are sad, but they think you're sad when you're writing them, but you're not. You're just in a good mood for writing blues. When you write like that you're not writing for yourself. There are millions of people out there. Maybe some of them are sad and when they hear the words you said, the song will hit them. "Goddamn, my old lady just left me." Anyone in the world who's been in that position will buy it. I'm not feeling that way, but I'm writing it for people who are. Sometimes you feel something deep down and write it to get it out, get it off your chest. But I cannot write a song when I'm feeling blue. I can't think when my mind is on my troubles.

When the blues first came out it was only among black people. We used to sing them in the cotton fields, on the farms. They didn't care about lyrics, they whistled the blues, moaned the blues. They didn't have set words; the words didn't rhyme. But you have to roll with the times. I'm doing the same things as I used to, but it's more modern. I'm playing the same basic beat, but I build different instruments around it. My fans know me from playing the blues and the boogie. When I sit at home I can play beautiful ballads. I can do Brook Benton's style real good. I love Tony Bennett's voice. I can do country and western, too. But I don't do it. If I started to do that, I would lose my blues audience. I would lose my fans.

Karl Williams

Thinking Globally

"To the New Century"

In 1998 I came into a modest inheritance. With the end of the century and the millennium just a year or so away I decided to invest my windfall in a song I'd written in 1982 called "To the New Century." I hired Robert C. Welsh, with whom I'd been writing country songs, to produce the album, to be called *From One Millennium to Another.* It would be a musical snapshot of the end of the era. "To the New Century" would be the song I'd promote.

Bob's a bass player as well as a songwriter, but he also owns the Green Room here in Harrisburg, the studio that launched the career of the Badlees. Bob took an interesting approach, choosing from a wide array of instruments—drum kit or djembe or chime ladder, oboe or clarinet or Gypsy violin—to set each of my songs. When we got to mixing "Century," the drums and piano and electric guitar worked well with my vocal and acoustic guitar, and the layered background vocals on the choruses, which we'd also used a cappella to kick things off, were great. But the song still seemed to need something, and neither Bob nor I could figure out what that was.

I played what we had for my wife, Nancy, one Friday night in the spring of '99. The next morning she said, "What if you had

toasts in different languages, as you're singing those last choruses?"
So, with a used Marantz tape recorder and two wineglasses, I proceeded. I had some help from the folks at the International Center
in Harrisburg, who obliged me with toasts in Vietnamese, Chinese, Korean, Russian, and French. A phone call to Bob's
girlfriend's sister-in-law in Japan and another to Israel to the as-
sembled family of my wife's best friend produced two more toasts.
Various other contacts and calls and meetings in or around Harrisburg resulted in toasts in German, Hindi, Lebanese, Polish, Span-
ish, Italian, and Yiddish, as well as in a Nigerian dialect, an Irish
brogue, and an Australian accent. Finally, we had what we needed,
I hoped, to pique the interest of a worldwide audience.

Bob introduced me to a graphic artist who did the artwork
for the CD and designed a Web site for me. From a Nashville co-
writer I got a lead on a radio-promotion company. And my first
few searches on the Web yielded such gold mines as the MIT
database of radio stations, the International Association of Student Radio in Europe, and the World Association of Community
Radio. As we sent the CD off to the manufacturer, I was hiring
the radio-promo guy who would work the U.S. stations, putting
the song up on my Web site and at mp3.com, and beginning a
campaign on the Internet aimed at the rest of the globe.

I wrote an e-mail query in the third person from my record
company, hoping to make the best first impression possible,
since I knew that what I was attempting was a bit outlandish, to
say the least. I began by apologizing for being unable to write in
the addressee's native tongue. The gist of the message was
"We've got an upbeat song with a hard-edged message called
'To the New Century,' with toasts in seventeen languages. We'd
very much appreciate your taking a moment to listen at
mp3.com or at our Web site and, if you'll get back to us, we'll
be happy to send the CD out to you." If the e-mail was going

to a station in a country in whose language we'd recorded one of the toasts, I noted that.

The fall of '99 was the most exciting I've ever lived through. Days were jam-packed with e-mailing queries, searching on-line for more stations, answering the stations that had responded, charting the progress I was making on a map of the world I'd found in the attic, and packing up the CD to send out (along with a one-sheet and a little green Customs form which the U.S. Postal Service requires on every package going outside the U.S.). Then I would follow up to see if the package had been delivered, if the program director had had a chance to listen, if he or she had given it to a DJ, if the song had been aired, and, finally, if there had been any reaction.

By the week before the big event, "To the New Century" was being played on AAA, Americana, college, community, public, independent, and Internet stations across the U.S. It was also being aired in Canada, England, Ireland, Scotland, Denmark, Sweden, Norway, in the Netherlands, France, Germany, Lithuania and Russia, Albania, Italy, Romania, Moldova, Zambia, Malawi, Nigeria, and South Africa; also in Israel, India, Indonesia, and all the way to Fiji. The most exotic-sounding address I mailed to was Kangaroo Point, Australia. The station in Russia e-mailed to ask me to record, "Hi, this is Karl Williams on Radio Samara!" for use on the program that was playing the song. I had to send the CD to a friend in Canada to mail it to two stations in Belgrade since the U.S. was not delivering mail to Belgrade for political reasons. One of the stations named "Century" Song of the Month in January! *Millennium* was named Album of the Month in February on one DJ's show on Radio Marabu.

"To the New Century" was not a resounding commercial success, but it did find an audience worldwide: it touched a chord in people who persist in believing that, despite all the misery and cruelty in the world, there is something else as well. We are now, for the first time, whether we choose to be or not, One Planet. Music can and will play an integral role in the work of uniting us, across borders and traditions and languages, into what we will certainly one day become: One People.

Jimmy Webb

Lyrics Have to Come First

"By the Time I Get to Phoenix"

I seem to have most of my problems at the beginning, when I'm trying to decide what actual shape the song is going to have. I would think that painters have the same difficulty when they're first laying out a work; the composition of the work is important and the shape of it. The tone of it is very important, and it takes a long time to work that out.

Once you see how it's going to go, then it's a race for the finish line, and that's the way it is with me. If I can get through the first verse, then I know the shape of the second verse. So all I have to do is fill in the second verse, which is harder than it sounds, because—just as a completely unfair rule of thumb—songs in general tend to open stronger than they finish. So you have to discipline yourself to work as hard on the second half of the song as you worked on the first half of the song, and not give in to that impulse to just fill in the blanks. I've probably been guilty of that when I was younger, and when I was in a hurry just trying to get finished. But Joni Mitchell and I were very close friends for a while and I've watched her work and I've seen her notebooks. I've seen how many times she rewrites something, how completely meticulous she is. If there's a possibility she could go back and make just one line better, you'll turn over the page and see where she's recopied the song and changed things. Paul Simon also does a lot of rewriting and does a lot of free association on legal pads, where he opens up the idea that a song could go in any direction, rather than be obsessively controlling about which way it's actually going to go. Stephen Sondheim works that way as well—free associations on a page, where every idea is given entrance and then they're honed away until the very best ones remain.

Lyrics have to come first, and I've never said that to anyone. But I think that lyrics have to come first. Or at least the central idea and intent of the song has to come first. You have to know what you're going to say. That's when it's great to have a good title, because if you have a good title you have a tremendous clue about what you want to say. It's great to go off with some great melody or some great chord change, but talking about pure songwriting, you've got to know what you're writing about.

There are two kinds of discipline involved with writing every day. There's the discipline to get up in the morning and go to work and work on something for five or six hours. And then there's a reverse discipline to leave it. I don't play the piano at home, even though I might be tempted to worry a tune some more. And since composers are obsessive by nature, it's tough. You have to say I'm not going to look at that until tomorrow. I know from playing tennis, sometimes I play my best after I've been away from the game for a couple of weeks. It's about letting yourself breathe a little bit. Plus, I have five kids, so when I get home they have a way of blowing everything else out of my head, whether I like it or not. I used to be quite a lot more obsessive about what I did, but then when I listen to the old stuff, I sometimes see where I could have stood back a little bit and been a little more objective about what I was doing. In retrospect, if I were going to rewrite something, I'd probably rewrite "MacArthur Park," because I feel that maybe it wasn't my best work.

Working on Broadway, I've learned a lot about making things clear. Because on Broadway everything has to be clear and it has to relate to the book. If the person singing the songs wouldn't sing those words, you're in big trouble. You're in trouble if it doesn't resonate with the character. On Broadway the music serves the book, serves the scenario. It can never become more important, for a second. But it's good discipline. It teaches you to work with other people and it teaches you to put across an idea that isn't totally selfish, that isn't totally your own. You have to be of service to the idea.

Neil Peart
(Rush)

W o r d s   a n d   D r u m s

"Vital Signs"

I'm a musician first, not a lyricist. I only spend two months out of every two years writing lyrics and the rest of the time I'm a drummer. Being a drummer helps me because words are a subdivision of time. Being fairly adventurous rhythmically as a drummer, I'm driven that way lyrically. I like to stretch lines and play with phrasing. I have a good sense of the music of words and the poetry of words and what makes a nice-sounding and even a nice-looking word. I find that the more layers a word or a series of words offers to me, the more satisfied I am. So if I can get a series of words that are rhythmically interesting and maybe have some kind of internal rhyming and rhythmic relationship, plus at least two layers of interpretive ideas in there too, the more pleased I am. I love to sneak in little bits of alliteration—even if it would never be recognized. It *is* recognized. I do like to get away with unusual words, but there are limits. There are some words that can sound good and look good and feel right in the context of a piece of verse, but when I go over them with Geddy [Lee], he'll complain to me that I've gone overboard. There are certain vowel-consonant combinations that are very difficult to deliver because you have to think so much about the elocution of those syllables that you can't possibly deliver them with the necessary emotions. The first time I hear words sung is really when they come alive for me. When they're written on a piece of paper it can be satisfying technically, but whether they work or not really happens when I hear Geddy sing them for the first time.

Writing lyrics is a tremendously demanding form of discipline; it requires precision. I don't like lyrics that are just thrown together, that were obviously written as you went along, or the song was already written and the guy made up the lyrics in five minutes. I can tell. Craftsmanship speaks. I'm not happy with spontaneity musically either. I think you take such a chance. It's the same with those ideas you wake up with in the middle of the night. Sometimes you write them down and you wake up in the morning and you go, "What?" And you rip it up and throw it away. Other times you save it. We do have improvisational periods during sound checks and we record them and at the end of the tour we sift through them and look for anything that happened that was magic. And there are ideas that we can mine out of that, taking advantage of the spontaneity of one day's mood. But to go onstage and expect people to indulge you—that doesn't work. I prefer organization.

I think the joy of creation is very overrated. The irony of it is that the moment goes by so fast. When I'm working on a piece and I have the theme of it going and I'm working away, there is that moment when I realize, yes, this is going to work. But then I'm gone. I'm gone into making it work. And then the knots in the brain start to become untied. I'm figuring out, "Okay, this line goes to that line, this verse to that verse." You can't just sit back and feel fulfilled by it. To me the most satisfying time of making an album is the writing period. We listen to a demo, and yes, this is exciting, and it's what we wanted it to be and it gets you off. That is the ultimate return that you will get from that song. And then you'll spend another six months recording the basic tracks, doing the overdubs, doing the vocals, doing the mixing. At the end of it all, there's no joy of creation, there's no sitting back going, "This is finished and wow, I'm so happy." Because you're so tired and drained from all of the mental demands you don't have anything left to throw a party.

In the demo period the rewards are instantaneous. But by the end of an album it's impossible to judge which songs will truly be popular and which won't. We're inevitably surprised. And then there are songs like "Vital Signs," from our *Moving Pictures* album. That song has a marriage of vocals and lyrics. I'm very happy with. But it took our audience a long time to get it, because it was rhythmically very different for us and it demanded the audience to respond to it in a different rhythmic way. There was no heavy downbeat. It was all counterpoint between upbeat and downbeat and there was some reflection of reggae influence and a reflection of the more refined areas of new-wave music that we had taken under our umbrella and made happen. That song took about three tours to catch on. It was kind of a baby for us. We kept playing it and wouldn't give up. We put it in our encore one tour—putting it in the most exciting part of the set possible. We just demanded that people accept it because we believed in it. I still think that song represents a culmination—the best combination of music, lyrics, and rhythm. It opens up so many musical approaches, from being very simplistic and minimal to becoming very overplayed. Everything we wanted in the song is there. So that song was very special to us. But we had to wait. We had to be patient and wait for the audience to understand us.

Frank Zappa
(Mothers of Invention)
Building an Airplane

"Joe's Garage"

I think the basic idea of being a composer is if you're going to be true to yourself and write what you like, you write what you like without worrying whether it's going to be academically suitable or whether it's going to make any mark in history or not. My basic drive for writing anything down is I want to hear it. I didn't start writing songs per se until I was about twenty-one years old, because all my compositions prior to that time had been orchestral or chamber music. The very first tunes I wrote were fifties doo-wop. It's always been my contention that the music that was happening in the fifties has been one of the finest things that ever happened to American music and I loved it.

Usually after I finish writing a song that's it. It doesn't belong to me anymore. When I'm working on a song it takes weeks and weeks to finish and the orchestra stuff takes even longer than that. It's like working on the construction of an airplane. One week you're a riveter, or you're putting the wiring in, or something like that. It's just a job you do and then you go onto the next step, which is learning how to perform it or teaching it to somebody else. I feel that all the material I've written goes through a cycle—especially if it's something I'm going to record—where you work on it so much that by the time you finish it you can't stand it anymore. You just get saturated with it. When you get to hear it played right for the first couple of times, that's the get-off. After that I don't like it again until it's a few years old and it's been recorded and I'll pick up the record and I'll say, "That's hip."

Sometimes I'll get my wife to read the lyrics to me so I can see what the sounds are like, because part of the texts are put together phonetically as well as what the information is supposed to be. I change lyrics all the time. A lot of them get changed by accident. Somebody will read them wrong and it'll sound so funny I'll leave it wrong.

I've always hated poetry quite a bit. The whole idea of it makes me gag. I don't like books. I very seldom read. My wife and I have a joke, because she likes to read. I say, "There are two things wrong with the world today, one of them is the writers and the other is the readers." The main thing wrong with writers is that they're dealing with something that is almost obsolete, but they don't know it yet, which is language. The meanings of words have been corrupted to the point where—from a semanticist's point of view—how can you convey an accurate piece of information with language? I feel sorry for writers. They have a problem similar to people who write music. It's just hard to write an accurate musical concept down on a piece of paper because of the new techniques on all instruments. There's just bunches of problems in getting true meaning across. The only guy who's really got it made is a painter. All he's got to worry about is whether his colors are going to fade or whether his canvas is properly stretched. He does it and that's it. He doesn't have to send it through a bunch of other processors, because there's no middleman.

Keith Richards
(the Rolling Stones)
A Band Man

"Satisfaction"

To me songs come out of being a musician, playing. The important thing is to sit down with an instrument. You might spend three, four hours going through the Buddy Holly songbook, and then, out of nowhere, there'll be a little crash, and there it goes. All it takes is a split second. It might be an accident, a mistake that sets you off. All you've got to do is be receptive and recognize it when it happens, because it can come from the weirdest angles. Personally, I cannot write to rhymed couplets and things like that. I can write a song out of a chord sequence, a riff, and eventually come up with lyrics to fit onto it.

I never think I have to put anything down. I never care if I have it on tape or if the tape runs out and the song disappears, because they all come back eventually. I've written songs and lost them and found them ten years later. Once it's there, it's there. It's just a matter of how long it takes before it comes back out again. I find the more I play, the more I'm into it, the more songs pour out. I don't have a problem with being nonprolific. That's all psychosomatic. Music isn't something to think about, at least initially. Eventually it's got to cover the spectrum, but especially with rock and roll, first it has to hit you somewhere else. It could be the groin; it could be the heart; it could be the guts; it could be the toes. It'll get to the brain eventually. The last thing I'm worried about is the brain. You do enough thinking about everything else.

When we're doing an album, I come in with a handful of riffs and some songs. One or two will be fairly well defined. Others I have to wait until I get the Stones all together in the studio to really find out. I can't take it any farther by myself as a song or a structure or an idea until I've got their input on it. If there's no kiss of life, there's nothing you can do. If everybody walks off to the toilet, then you know you've got to drop that one and go on to something else. But when you just sort of pick up your guitar when the studio is virtually empty—people are telling jokes in the back room or playing dominoes—and then within two or three minutes they drift back, pick up their instruments and begin whacking away, you know they're into it.

Rarely do I write a song by myself. Even if I actually do write it by myself, I always like to have someone around just playing along with me, going, "Yeah, yeah." I'm a band man, a group man. I can't sit there alone in a room and say, "It's songwriting time, ding ding ding." When Ron Wood and I sit down together to play, we're two guitarists, whereas with Mick [Jagger] and I there's maybe more of an idea in our heads that what we're after is a song at the end of what we're doing. When Mick comes in with a song, usually he's got it worked out pretty much. He may need a bridge to be written or a different beat, or turn it around a little bit. We write in every conceivable combination of ways. It's really an incredibly elastic arrangement. Some songs hang out for years before we feel happy with them and resurrect them and finish them off. Others, in two takes they've come and gone and you've got to relearn it off your own record in order to play it later. In a way I'm like a guitar maker. Some songs are almost at the end, others are hanging there waiting for that special coat of paint—you can't find the right color for them right now. Lots of times you think you've written four different songs, and you take them to the studio and you realize they're just variations on one song.

I remember after "Satisfaction" got to number one—bang bang at the door. Where's the follow-up? I mean, every twelve weeks you had to have another one ready. The minute you put out a single, you had to start working your butt off on the next one, and the bigger the hit, the more pressure there was on the follow-up. But it was an incredibly good school for songwriting, in that you couldn't piss around for months and months agonizing about the deeper meaning of this or that. No matter what else you were doing you had to make damn sure you didn't let up on the writing. It made you search around and listen for ideas. It made you very aware of what was going on around you, because you were looking for that song. It might come in a coffee shop, or it might come on the street or in a cab. You might hear a phrase at a bus stop. You're listening for it every moment, and anything could be a song, and if you don't have one you're up the creek without a paddle.

You use every available tool in the kit. You play on your image, to a certain extent. You get a general feel for what people want to hear from you and when you're good at providing it and they like it—oh, you want more? Here's more. So I'd just come up with a line or a song and lean on it, push it, go for it. Nobody writes a song or makes a record to put it in a back drawer.

I work best when the sun goes down, I've eaten, had a few drinks, and I've got some good buddies around. I love sitting around with an acoustic guitar and whacking out songs with friends and family. Somehow they never sound as good as they do that first night on the living room couch.

Carole King
A Balancing Act

"Will You Love Me Tomorrow"

Music has always been a balanced part of my life and one of the reasons why I periodically withdraw from the mainstream is because I never want it to become out of balance. It's a lot of fun to perform; sometimes it's not fun. I try to structure my life and schedule tours and shows so that it stays as much fun as possible. There's nothing wrong with music, but I don't want the business to take over my life. That's why I don't go out on tour unless there's a very special show, and I only do as much of that show as I feel will keep me fresh. I could not go on a real lengthy tour and still feel I was giving the audience their full money's worth.

With Don Kirshner and Al Nevins I was always singing on demos and they decided to release "It Might as Well Rain Until September" as a master. But it was always a demo to me, and the fact that it had success did not make me want to do any more recordings as an artist. *The City* was another collection of demos. So was *The Writer,* but it included "Up on the Roof," because I had been working a little bit with James Taylor and I liked the song and wanted to do it in a new way. And then when we got to *Tapestry,* it was still demos in my mind. That way there was no pressure for me.

My performing a song is a completion; another performer singing my song is another completion. Most of the songs I write for another artist I can sing. I could be thinking of another artist completely, but since I'm the one writing it and I'm the one who has to sing it to convey it to the artist, ultimately I wind up singing it in one way or another. By the time I've sung it for demo purposes, it has become mine. If another artist takes it and does it, it's expanded into a broader horizon. If another artist doesn't do it, it's still mine to do anytime. As long as a song gets sung and sung well, I'm not attached to whether it's by me—I feel complete as a songwriter.

I've broadened my scope from writing on the piano. Several years ago I did an album on guitar, mostly because I was living in Idaho, in a remote community, and we had no piano, so I had to learn to play guitar. Synthesizers have also taken me in a new direction. And while no drum machine compares with Russ Kunkel, or some of the other fine drummers I've worked with, it does give me a basic beat around which to play, so I don't have to imply it on the piano. Now that I've got electricity again, I have a music room, with an eight-track studio and a Linn drum machine, synthesizers, and all that stuff.

I don't consciously structure songs that will be great live. I write for the song itself. Sometimes a song that I write does not make as good a record as a live performance, but ultimately, if you just look at the song as a song, it should have a cohesive entity to it; it should have a mood, a consistency. I like to try to establish something in the beginning, be it a musical phrase or a lyrical phrase, then go wander around, and then always try to bring it back home in some way.

I had always avoided writing lyrics because I didn't think I could. Gerry [Goffin] wrote lyrics so well that I felt no necessity to do it. Once we were no longer married I had more time to write so I said, "What the heck, I'll go for it." I didn't think about it. They just evolved naturally. In the early days Gerry would start with a phrase or I might give him the music. I think I gave him the melodic opening for "Up on the Roof" and he put words to it. In recent years he will give me a lyric and sing an idea that he has for the melody. Gerry and I have both changed, of course, but there's a connection between us and that connection remains the same.

CREATIVITY

Melvin Van Peebles
Once Around the Stadium

"Lily Done the Zampougie"

I got into songs sideways, through the music that I needed for my films. When I did my first short film I couldn't afford to pay anyone, so I had a kazoo and I hummed my soundtrack. That was 1957. Then, in 1967 or 1968, when I came back to the States from Europe, I was surprised to find that black music, lyric-wise anyway, didn't really mirror any of the everyday aspirations, problems, or lifestyles that were going on. So that's what I tried to do in my original songs. Each song was meant to encompass a lifestyle, a personality, a character. What I had hoped was that my renditions would be taken up by mainstream artists and performed in a more normal format. But it's never happened. In *Don't Play Us Cheap*, the music was for a specific show and for real singers—in the classical or pop classical sense of the word. So they were arranged differently. Now people will say, "Gee, Mel, why don't you do more tunes like that?" Well, the other tunes were like that, or at least that's how I heard them in my head. If the Temptations asked me to take a tune and arrange it in that format, I'd be more than happy to.

Sometimes I'll be writing something and I'll say, "Gee, this is a film, or a poem, or a song." I'll write a feeling or analyze or conceptualize and then it dictates in itself the form that it's going to take. Right now I'm writing a play, I'm writing a novel, and I'm writing a film script. I find each type of writing and each stage of the writing a different experience. Lyrics usually come as a spin-off. Having the discipline, say, of all the time doing marathons, having to go around the stadium once is easy. And since you only have to go around once, I spend an exorbitant amount of time on the lyrics, even though they may seem as though they just fell out. Songs are a gas to work on because you can hold them in one concept and you can see where you're at, whereas with a novel you may have done fifty pages and you'll do another fifty pages and you're nowhere near knowing.

I've been very illiterate in my taste. When I started in films I didn't know the names of directors. When I heard a single, half the time I didn't know who was doing it, but I danced to everything. Growing up, I was influenced by the singers on the south side of Chicago. Sometimes I'll get on stage and people will still question my voice, but I'm not the least bit intimidated, because the voices I remember hearing in my childhood sounded a great deal like I do. These voices didn't have musicality, but that wasn't where they were coming from. Many of the kids in the audience have never even heard those old voices.

Unfortunately, I do not have the commercial success in music that I have in other areas of my career. The songs are succeeding, but on a very limited basis. This enters into my mind only as a fervent hope that they will someday work. But if I change to make them work and if they become less than they were, then they're not working. I won't do it. I won't change them to make them less and end up being just what it was that I was coming away from.

The revelations I hope my songs bring to people about themselves, about the human condition—that's the joy. I had a very good experience once at a prison. The prisoners really dug my songs. They were not intimidated by them. I started to do "Lily Done the Zampougie" and the prisoners all started clapping. They said, "We got a prisoner here who does that." So we brought him up there onstage and it blew his mind. He had a band and everything. And those are guys that became the family that have now done the play *Short Eyes*. That's what it's all about.

Laura Nyro

Growth and Change

"Wedding Bell Blues"

When I was very young I remember sitting at a piano and hearing the notes and the chords ring out in the air and I knew there was something special in that sound, some kind of freedom. More recently, when I was writing, as I was working through the chords, I remember getting that same feeling.

I was still a teenager when I made my first record, and the world around me started changing at the speed of lightning just because I'd written some provocative songs. The sixties started spinning into a whirlwind, and outside of some recognition for my music, I felt like I was living inside a hurricane. My rhythm in life was more of a free-spirited one and then it changed. I kind of felt like I was losing the rhythm of my youth. So many things were happening at the same time. I started slowly moving out of that scene so I could find some peace and experience other things in life without a bunch of people breathing down my neck.

I don't think you should categorize yourself as an artist. You should allow yourself to grow. Growth is the nature of the creative process. You have to accept it, respect it, and move on. When I turned thirty my love songs changed from romantic notions to a deeper taste of life. My mother died right before I wrote the songs for *Nested;* my child was born right before I wrote *Mother's Spiritual.*

The form and content of what I want to say is very influenced by nature. I think my favorite songs come from a certain place of elemental power. I have a love for simple, basic song structure, although sometimes you'd never know it. Take, for example, "Wedding Bell Blues," a three-minute song, like a painting on a page. It's a musical starting point and you could stay with it or take it to the ends of the earth, because as beautiful as simplicity is, it can become a tradition that stands in the way of exploration. I started off in music with simplicity and then moved into abstraction and some uncharted waters with the exploration of it. Actually, some people would say I was going off the deep end. I wanted to learn more and I took freedoms with the principles of composition. I used these dark chord structures, suspended chords, advanced dissonance—advanced for rock and roll—all within the same song. My jazz background put certain inflections in my writing and singing. Throw in all the poetry I'd read since I was a kid, and just being a woman, and that's what made my songs complex and emotionally rich.

The last few years have been so musically abundant that I felt like the goddess of creativity. But who knows? Songs come in cycles; next year I may write one song. That kind of songwriting is cyclical, seasonal; it's the culmination of a deeper experience. It's like nature; it takes time to seed and then it blooms. Like *Mother's Spiritual* was a wonderful idea that flew through my head in a minute and then took years to manifest, because the relationship and responsibilities that were inspiring the music were also pulling me away from it in terms of time. Since I was recording while I was writing, it actually took me two and a half years to complete those fourteen songs. Most of the songs I wrote at night. I would just wake in the middle of the night. I had a young baby and that's when I found the space to write. Subject-wise, the songs were just moments right out of my life.

Once I'm writing I'm very disciplined. I'm there for the music. When I'm writing music there's a certain magic from the music underlying life. It's like you're living at a deeper current. It's a very complete feeling. You're taking care of everyday things, but you're living at the edge of a song.

Richard Marx

Surprise Changes

"Endless Summer Nights"

Locking myself in a room and making myself write a song has never worked for me. When I first moved to L.A., when I was eighteen, there were some songwriters I knew who would write for eight hours a day, so I thought, Okay, I'd better do that if I'm serious. I did that for about three months and it was the worst stuff I ever wrote in my life, because it didn't come from inspiration. It came from making myself write. Something that I really loved to do became something that was painful to do. So now, I never do that. I only write when I feel like it, and now I feel like it a lot.

I find myself inspired on the road; I have a lot of time on my hands, so I use that time to write songs. I write the best songs when I'm in my car and I just start singing a riff, or I start singing a melody without any thought to the chord changes. Usually there's a few scattered words in there, but I don't write lyrics nearly as easily as I write music. Once I've got in my head the basic outline of what the melody's gonna be, what the structure's gonna be, then I can sit down at a piano and work out segues from the bridge back to the chorus, or the bridge into a solo. Lyrically, I have to sit alone and really hash it out. A lot of times I'm not really sure what the lyrics are gonna be about, and then I have to really suss out, Okay, what do I want to write about? What have I been feeling lately, or what have I been thinking about?

The only time I don't want to write is when I come home from touring. I just want to watch TV or hang out with my wife and go to movies. But when an idea comes I don't ignore it. If I'm lying in bed at three in the morning and I get an idea, I don't just blow it off. I get up and write it down, or I sing it into a cassette machine.

I keep a cassette machine with me at all times. I know there are some theories that if you don't remember it, then it wasn't worth remembering. I don't believe that. I've had plenty of songs that I didn't remember, and then I'd hear them on a work tape and go, "Hey, that's good!" So if I come up with a chorus idea or a verse idea, or just a little instrumental hook that sticks in my head, that's usually a good sign. "Satisfied" was written from the guitar line. It was pretty simple, but I couldn't get it out of my mind, and then the song came from that.

I used to write at the keyboard maybe 80 percent of the time and 20 percent of the time on guitar. And then I figured out from touring that I didn't keep a guitar on the bus, and I could almost never get to a piano, except at sound check, and I didn't write much at sound check, so I just started singing into a hand-held cassette machine. I started singing melodies, and because I know what the changes are in my head, I would say, "After D minor it goes to G minor," and then I would work it out later, after I'd pretty much written the song. By doing that, the melody dominated the songs from then on.

I went through a period, especially during the time I worked with David Foster, where what was important to me as a songwriter was to come up with really hip, surprise changes. To me, "After the Love Is Gone" is one of the greatest songs ever written, musically, because it's got so many really cool changes, surprise changes. But you don't hear anybody walking down the street humming that. But you do hear people humming "Lady" and "Three Times a Lady" and songs that are straight-ahead melodically. So I finally started to figure that out, and I think that my melodies have gotten tremendously stronger because I'm not concerned with putting ninety chord changes in a song anymore. If there's only two or three, if they're good ones and they lead the melody to the right places, who's counting?

I don't demo songs for myself anymore, either, because I've already been through the nightmare of having to "beat the demo."

On "Endless Summer Nights," the record is the demo. I went in and recut the song, but it didn't have the magic that the demo had, and so I resang the vocal and everything that's on the demo, the sax solo, the guitar parts, everything is on the record, because we couldn't beat it. We couldn't match the spontaneity of it. So, at that minute in the studio for my first album, I said, "I'm never demoing a song for myself again." What I do is, I write out lead sheets and I go into the studio. When I write a song, I hear everything. I hear the bass part, the drum pattern, the guitar parts. As the producer of my records, it's my responsibility to know what the hell I want, and I sit down with the rhythm section, depending on who's playing, and we just hash it out that day and cut the track. What's really cool is when you hear the song come to life in the studio as you're making the record.

Randy Newman
I'm Capable of Doing Absolutely Nothing

"Lonely at the Top"

Every time I've had to talk about songwriting I've gone into a grim litany. I know I'm making it worse than it is. It can't be as bad as I think it is. But it depresses me. For long periods of time I've been unwilling to do it, to be there all alone in a room. I don't mind if I'm all alone reading, but when I'm walking into the room with the piano in it my legs begin to get heavy and I feel a pressure. Recently I've overcome my guilt about it, which had always acted as a goad. Now I don't even feel bad about not writing. I've had financial disasters, owed the government money. I had an album deadline looming over me. It loomed and went right by. Maybe in a way what I wanted more than money or sales or fame was praise, and I kind of got it. Now it seems I'm worried I won't get it again. But it probably isn't as important to me as it was.

Performing is so easy, so immediately rewarding. Writing, although I know it's more important, is just rough. It might be that with performing I'm getting the gratification that I used to get through writing, without all the grief. Actually, I could quit both performing and writing, and just do nothing at all. I'm capable of doing absolutely nothing for long periods of time without much remorse. But every once in a while I'll wake up and say, "Jesus

Christ, what a waste. What a big talent I used to be, like a meteor across the sky."

I've always worked the same way. I just sit there. Very rarely, maybe a couple of times, I've jumped out of bed with an inspiration. But usually it comes while I'm sitting at the piano. I hardly ever have the words first. A piece of a melody or a figure of some kind will be enough to get me going, and sometimes the song will be right there, where you can see to the end of if. Usually, I just say what I have to say and that's all I have to say and I'm done. There are songs that could have been longer, I guess. But I'm just happy to be done. I can generally feel when they're finished, but I've been wrong a few times—more than a few. I have urges to change them all the time. I would do it, but I know I could never get them right. There's ruin there if you start to do that. But I can't think of many songs where something musically or lyrically doesn't really bother me. Which is a deterrent from working. You bust your ass with a crazed kind of worrying about every little thing and then you wind up seeing all these bad things about it two weeks later. It's a psychosis. In performing they all seem okay. It's only when I have to think about them.

Writing was easier for me when I was writing for people. I'd have someone in mind and then I'd write the song and file it away and I wouldn't have to think about it anymore. When I have to think about writing for myself, it's another matter. In fact, at one point I said to myself, "I'm going to write a song for Tom Jones." I didn't give him the song, but I did write it, and it made me feel pretty good for a while. I like being able to do things like that. Now all I have to do is be able to make songwriting seem less unpleasant, or I just won't write. It'll be all over and I'll have to go back to North Hollywood and play in a lounge somewhere.

Andy Partridge
(XTC)

Billy Bolt

"Dear God"

I like to play our records when the family goes to bed and I get really drunk and my vanity completely disappears and I get over the guilt of listening to my own stuff. I ram the headphones on and lay there on the floor with the empty cans rolling on the carpet and I go, "Yeah, great, I'd forgotten about that." Like playing something from *Drums and Wires* or *English Settlement* and I'd forgotten the chord changes; I'd forgotten the lyrics, and right in the middle I go, "Of course, yeah."

I always have this terrible dilemma that the last song I wrote is going to be the last song ever and it gets worse every time. It always resolves itself, but I feel like I must worry about it. If I don't worry about it, it's not going to resolve itself. At times I can write a song a day, but sometimes I can go for months without anything, absolutely nothing comes up. I have to just click into a writing mode. Then songs come, but if I don't run home and sing them into my answering machine quick, they go. There are tunes that come just as you're falling asleep. A few times it's happened where I'm dozing off and I get into that incredibly relaxed state and a whole song will just pop out—melody, great lyric, and I think, "Oh, I'll write it down in a little while," but I never do. It's the best thing you've ever heard and then you go to sleep. And you've just dreamt "Hey Jude" or something.

We try not to give ourselves really specific deadlines, but you begin to see one on the horizon, like some big distant city, and that increases the anxiety. A sure sign of desperation is when you just turn on a drum machine and play anything. Sometimes, just by the brute banality of it, you might kick down a door that you thought was never going to open and suddenly you'll see something in there. You'll hit a chord and think, I'm just going to keep squeezing and squeezing this chord and you play it for hours and hours and the drum machine is bashing away. And then suddenly you'll slip with your fingers and make a mistake, and you'll think, this is so banal, it's a battleship. Battleship! It sounds like a battleship! Some stupid thought will blow the thing wide open.

But usually the case is, you get tuned in and this stuff explodes, takes you over. You play too late into the night and your dinner's going cold downstairs. Then it gets like the air changes and you're breathing a sort of different atmosphere somehow. It's like you really have tuned in and the first program's come in and suddenly you feel wonderfully receptive to a load of stuff, things that wouldn't have meant anything a couple of weeks before suddenly all come crowding in real quick. Things suggest other things. A chord can mean a phenomenal amount; just one chord brings you a lot of pictures. You hit a chord and think, that chord is so foggy; if somebody could get fog and turn it into a chord, it's that chord. And it'll be like the tip of the iceberg for a song, and you'll work on this foggy chord and all these lyrics cascade out under fog, like some sort of school essay. You know, give me five hundred words on fog. You try some other chords. No, that's not foggy, that's too rainy, that's too sunny. And then, oh, that's really foggy. How does it sound with the other one?

Maybe I'll use that as the middle. Then you kind of round up all the foggy chords and you build this set for yourself. Sometimes when I come up with something really exciting I'll start tingling, so I run downstairs and force it on my wife. She's very cool and my worst critic, my stabilizer. Her opinion is usually, it's not commercial enough, or I don't like the bit about the porpoises.

In the middle of this kind of creative period you get your brain so wound up you can't turn it off. I go to sleep but my brain is going crazy, inventing or searching, and I wake up screaming. We call it the Billy Bolts or Billy Bolts upright. I just sort of sit up and become this person, Billy Bolt. You just get into the process of thinking and sending your brain out to search, getting those tendrils going everywhere. You find this piece of string and you think, This is a really good piece of string, and you're pulling and pulling. God, there's something on the end of this. And I can't turn my head off from doing this at night. And there I am, I'm awake, and I'm yelling like I'm being murdered and I'm facing the wardrobe and it's 4 A.M. and I don't know what I'm doing.

Phil Ochs

A Layman's Revolution

"Power and the Glory"

Everybody said go to New York and I figured, well, New York is the lion's den. I can't go up against those guys. But I went to New York and right away I met Dylan and I said, "Oh, my God, this is the guy!" As soon as I heard him sing his first song I flipped out. And of course there were also a good ten or fifteen other people around who wrote songs. The breakthrough was at Newport, 1963, with the Freedom Singers, Dylan, Baez, the songwriters' workshop, where it suddenly moved from the background into the foreground in just one weekend.

After that I got an album out and I was completely prolific. I was writing all the time. Quickly followed by another album, followed by a concert. Everything I wrote was on instinct. There was some sort of psychic force at work and I don't know what it was. When the songs came, they came fast. I don't think I ever spent more than two hours on any one song, even "Crucifixion."

That period in the Village was incredibly exciting, super-euphoric. There was total creativity on the part of a number of individuals that laid the bedrock for the next ten years. But everything goes in cycles, everything has a life span, and I guess this life span just ran out. The old-time songwriters were more trained. The sixties were very instinctual and untrained and that's what's showing now, the lack of discipline and training as inspiration runs out. A lot of these people were laymen. It was basically a layman's revolution.

Now the question is will these songs stand the test of time? That was always one of the things from the early days, when Dylan and I were writing political songs. Will the song be meaningless in a couple of years because it's topical? So to sing "Outside of a Small Circle of Friends" seven years later and still get the same response gives the lie to that attack. Whether the audience is hearing it for the first time or the fifteenth time it still holds up. It could be nostalgia for some people, but on the other hand, there's some essential truth locked up in that song and it's locked up to a thirteen-year-old kid who hears it today for the first time. He responds because the truth is there. My favorite recording of one of my songs is Anita Bryant doing "Power and Glory" on her patriotic album, *Mine Eyes Have Seen the Glory*. It's unbelievable, I mean really incredible. I think if a song has enough meaning it can survive anything.

For me songwriting was easy from 1961 to 1966 and then it got more and more difficult. It could be alcohol. It could be the deterioration of the politics I was involved in. It could be a general deterioration of the country. Basically, me and the country were deteriorating simultaneously, and that's probably why it stopped coming. Part of the problem was there was never any pattern to my writing. The point of discipline is to create your own pattern so you can write, and I haven't done that. I always make plans to do that. Ever since the late sixties that's constantly on my mind—discipline, training, get it together, clean up your act. I haven't been able to do it yet, but the impulse is as strong as ever. I'll never make the conscious decision to stop writing. To my dying day, I'll always think about the next possible song.

IS THERE LIFE AFTER XI

Steven Tyler
We Owned the World

Lead Singer, Aerosmith

We were down to whether we thought we could even write again. I mean, that question came up. "Are you going to be able to write without drugs? But don't you realize you gotta get off drugs, or you ain't gonna have a band?" I mean, these questions came up. Everything was a paradox, and we had to settle on one thing, and that was that we were gonna give up the drugs and play like we owned the world and we want it back again, and that's it.

We went into the studio with Rick Rubin, right after the "Walk This Way" video, and Joe [Perry] and I were just up against a wall, a flat black cement wall. We couldn't come up with jack. We listened to the thing that we put down the next day, and it was so bad. But I heard this parable about this guy who lived in a cave, and a big tree grew up in front of it, and he had this small, tiny hatchet, and for years he thought, I'll never get out of here, not with this thing. But someone told him, just tiny swipes, a little bit at a time, and eventually the tree comes down. And in a month's time, that huge tree was chopped down. I looked at that with Joe Perry, and we went into the studio, and we just rehearsed every day for five hours, Joe on guitar and me on drums, with a little tape recorder. We did that for two or three months, and that's how we came up with *Permanent Vacation,* and *Pump* as well. One of the very first things we wrote was "Monkey on My Back." I knew that that was the kind of song I wanted to go on-stage and play to people. That's what I wanted to play in front of ten thousand screaming Aerosmith fans live. That was what I thought Aerosmith was, the definitive Aerosmith.

The journey of a thousand miles starts with the first step, and for me, the joy is taking that very first step, when I look behind me and I see that I've moved. It's a real challenge, and it's the hardest part, but I've just found, in the last four years, that walking that extra mile, doing that one more thing, when I used to say I was too tired, is what's worth all the work. You collect all those things at the end of a month, and you've got a gemstone, man, and it's polished already. And it's a strange thing how it works, but it's one of those little secrets of life.

The definitive way for me to do an album is to get it down with 99 percent of the lyrics, and work it up till the thing shines. So it stinks from the groove. In preproduction, I work it up and then drop it and forget it. Go up into the studio a month later and play it again, and you go, "Whoa!" You play it with such vim and vigor it's unbelievable. That's a major-league get-off, and you know what? You can feel the sparks through the tape from that magic moment. There's another magic moment; that's when you're in a studio, you put it down, then you spend three weeks mixing it, and adding instruments, and you get the finished product, and you listen to it and you go, "This is it, the album's finished!" You put it in your back pocket, get on a plane, fly home, and then a month or two later, the record's been released, but no one knows jack from shinola about the rest of the songs. You play them live, in a huge hall, and you hear that song like a monster, and then you get goose pimples like crazy. I remember when I first did "Angel." We did it a couple of times, but the kids only wanted to hear "Walk This Way" and "Sweet Emotion." And then when "Angel" came out and became a hit, and we played it, the place went "Waaaaaaaw!" I remember going, "I'm alone . . ." and I couldn't sing the next verse, 'cause I got choked up and started to cry, onstage, in front of twenty thousand people. I started to cry because the place went crazy. I'll never forget that night. I'll never forget that. I started to cry. I loved it, and I accepted the feeling. I didn't hide it with coke. I didn't hide it with booze. I loved it. It was the moment for that song.

Neil Sedaka

Vengeance

Pop Singer-Songwriter

I had a lot of good years, but no one knew what I looked like. I wasn't in too many of the teenage magazines. I was just a voice. They didn't want to take a chance on me bombing in the United States, so my first gigs were in the Philippines, Brazil, and Japan. I never did the Dick Clark tour. I was on *The Ed Sullivan Show* once. I played the Copacabana once. I played the Brooklyn Paramount with Alan Freed and Murray the K, had beer bottles and cigarettes thrown at me, four shows a day. I played the Steel Pier in Atlantic City. Then came the bow tie and tuxedo—everybody wanted to be Bobby Darin. So I played the Twin Coaches, the Holiday House.

I stayed the same old Neil. I never changed. After "Next Door to An Angel" was "Alice in Wonderland," which made the Top 20. Then "The Dreamer," which only got into the forties. And my brother-in-law at the time—married to my sister—said, "You know it's going to end." I said, "I know it," but it was not easy to accept. At that time Neil Diamond became popular, and his parents were right across the street. They owned a clothing shop on Brighton Beach Avenue called Diamonds. And everybody said, "Well, whatever happened to you? Neil Diamond is doing so great." But little by little, the records stopped, and I got over it. I got over it. I had made a great deal of money, but a lot of it went astray because of mismanagement, because of bad investments. I had an accountant who made me buy a building in Birmingham, Alabama, for $150,000. That went down the drain. I didn't have charge of my money. I was living in a fantasy.

I wrote with three lyricists, five days a week. I was writing with Carole Sager, Howie Greenfield, and Roger Atkins. I said I could write like Paul McCartney and I did write like Paul McCartney, but it was very hard to get records when I wasn't singing the songs. I made one record for Colgems, which was a part of Screen Gems, called "Rainy Jane," which I produced with Howie Greenfield, and it was terrific. I heard it once, I think, on WNBC. The only time I'd hear myself on the radio was when an oldie would come on. So I felt, Well, this is it, I'd better get resigned to the fact that I had my shot and it'll never happen again.

When I heard Carole King's album *Tapestry*, it blew me away. I said, "Oh my God, that's my style, the piano, the voice, the whole approach to melody"—we grew up together—and I begged Donnie Kirshner to let me do an album for RCA. I wrote probably the best collection of songs I ever wrote in my life, but the album was too classy, and it was against the market; RCA was not about to promote it. So *Emergence* was a flop, and it shattered Howie and me, and we split for two and a half years. It was very sad. Howie moved to California. Just before he left we wrote two songs; one was called "Our Last Song Together," the other was "Love Will Keep Us Together," which I think was kind of like his plea. We both cried.

The original recording of "Oh Carol" had been rereleased by RCA and was a hit in England. So I picked up my wife, my two kids, and Mary the housekeeper, and we moved to London. I got a job at a real toilet in Manchester. I sat down and recorded a whole album with a group called Hot Legs at their studio in

Stockport. I spent six thousand dollars and recorded an album called *Solitaire*. It had "Solitaire" on it, "That's Where the Music Takes Me," "Standing on the Inside." RCA put it out here—on a shoestring. Nothing happened. But I knew when I heard the record that I was on the right track.

The next album was called *The Tra La Days Are Over*, also recorded with Hot Legs, who were by then better known as 10cc. *Laughter in the Rain* followed that, and the title song was a smash in England and then, in 1975, went to number one in America. By that time Elton John and I were pretty close. We'd met many times at Bee Gees concerts; we were both friendly with Maurice Gibb. One night at my apartment in London we had a big party and I took Elton and [his manager] John Reid aside. I said, "I'm frustrated. I have a hit in England; I'm now a concert artist in England. You've got to help me." It just so happened they were in the process of opening Rocket Records. I said, "Don't pay me. I don't want any money. Just put out a compilation album, some of the things I did with 10cc, some of the things I did in L.A. All I want is your endorsement." And that's what he did. The album was *Sedaka's Back* and he wrote on the jacket, "Neil Sedaka's songs are great . . ."

The next time I went to Los Angeles, it was to headline at the Troubadour. I took over the town. Every producer in town was there. I wanted it with a vengeance. Donnie Kirshner said I would never make it again; that drove me. My old manager said I'd never make it again; that drove me. Carole King; that drove me. I knew I was good, and I spent hours at the piano. I wasn't afraid of it. My voice was a great help to me, too, because I knew that nobody could sing those songs like me. The critics in L.A. couldn't believe that anybody could write and sing with such enthusiasm, with such spirit, and with this vengeance.

Jay Leslie

Hidden Opportunities

Horn Player, the Tokens

I knew Phil and Mitch Margo before the Tokens were formed, but since I was so young at the time I wasn't a member of the original group. I went out to L.A. before them and joined Sha Na Na right after their TV show ended, so they could tour again. I actually hooked up with them through my daughter, who was a classmate of Jocko's son. Jocko and I would see each other at school functions; one thing led to another, and soon I was on the road with a bunch of great people!

When the Tokens reformed in the late eighties, due to a demand created by "The Lion Sleeps Tonight" getting into several major motion pictures, I joined the group. I play all of the woodwind instruments and compose and arrange music for other artists as well. When I am not touring I have done gigs ranging from local blues jams to being the music coordinator on a television show called *The Young and the Restless*.

The Tokens perform today at venues such as state fairs, classic-car shows, rock-and-roll-revival shows, radio-sponsored concerts, and, more recently, corporate dates and cruise ships. Let me say a word about playing the cruises. First of all, the demographic of cruisers has drastically changed. Baby boomers, families, and teenagers now make up a ship's manifest. We recently did a few shows at sea, and it amazed us that people of varied nationalities all had one thing in common. They love to see live musical entertainment and love to hear songs from earlier times in their lives performed by the people who created them.

When we're working on cruise ships, we are usually on board from eight to sixteen days, and perform every four nights (two shows a night). This is followed by a "meet and greet" the next night, where we sign pictures, CDs, tapes, T-shirts, et cetera. Actually, we have found that our signing sessions last twice as long as our shows! I once turned to Phil and said, "You know, the shows are like doing a live infomercial!" We're allowed to bring guests and family along, and have done so. This only pertains to a headline act; the other musicians, singers, and dancers on the ship are considered crew.

At the state fairs we'll be on a bill with anywhere from one to nine or ten other acts. The Los Angeles County Fair is really enjoyable to us as we can invite friends, family, business colleagues, et cetera, who usually don't get a chance to see us perform.

I try to play every day, but I will admit that no matter what level of the business you find yourself at, you just cannot avoid dry spells. These are the toughest times to endure, but they also can act as impetus for creativity and reinvention of oneself. The main thing to remember is that every situation may have hidden opportunities that are not recognizable at the moment. This is why it is imperative to always conduct yourself in as professional a manner as you can. Even on a dumb gig, always try to turn your thoughts to a better situation in the future. This attitude has kept me going during periods of less-than-attractive work or no work at all. Always stay ready for the next gig—practice your instrument, maintain your equipment, stay healthy. It's a good idea to hang out with people who are doing the type of gigs you would like to be doing. This is a little tricky because you have to strike a balance between talking up your abilities and listening to the other cats talk about their projects. If you can truly show some interest and try to weave the conversation onto a common ground, perhaps you'll get invited to the next show, recording date, release party, et cetera.

The typical image of a musician is not one that endears us to the straight world, but it is sometimes those very people who can take your career to the next level—whether it's to finance a demo, act as a manager, or introduce you to their brother-in-law, whose dentist has a patient who works in A&R at a record label.

Remember, there are many genres of music to choose from, so choose the genre that you *absolutely, positively, unconditionally love*! That will be your ticket to success. And if that major record deal or cushy television gig doesn't come through, at least you will be musically fulfilled.

Dave Guard
Life Values

Banjo Player, the Kingston Trio

I was the first in the group to get married, so I was married before the group really started getting heavily into things. But there were always a lot of people who wanted to meet you. I saw a lot of one-night-stand-type business, where people would come up to you expecting one thing and not being prepared to deal with your whole personality, only with your media image. So it was like being stampeded for autographs and as soon as they get a foot away, everybody realizes it's a human being standing there, instead of a statue, and they stop screaming and take a look in your eyes, and a lot of their head trips disappear.

I'd say the quality of our work went up as we went along, but the enthusiasm for the songs didn't. On the first three albums in particular, we were very interested in all the tunes. Those were songs we really liked. Later on, we were just looking for tunes that would keep up the quality of the group. That sounded like Kingston Trio songs. Some good tunes would come by, but they didn't grab you like the early tunes. Finally, we had to record on such short notice that the tunes would be very respectable, but they just didn't get your heart like the other tunes did.

I started to get bitter that the other guys weren't studying music or anything. I just felt we should keep on pushing to learn all kinds of instrumental techniques and to keep getting better every week. I told them we had a responsibility to the fans to be good musicians and that we should all take lessons to improve our stuff. The other guys weren't big hot students in school or anything; they didn't see how taking lessons would do any good. They had the idea that people liked us for what we were and that's how it was. But they kept their musical ears intact. They brought in some very good tunes, even in the last stages. And they were true to themselves, in that I don't think they've taken any lessons since.

I left the group because I wanted to get away from a life of being on the road in a string of motel rooms, where the only food you eat you have to unwrap, and the only people you talk to are taxi drivers. No matter how much bread you could make, you weren't getting any life value. I decided my values lay with hanging out with my kids when they were young and raising a family. So we moved to Australia. I wanted to leave it all behind totally. I didn't want to have anything to do with the Trio. I remember my replacement, John Stewart, wanted to be very friendly and he asked me for a lot of advice, but I didn't want to get involved. It was kind of like graduating from school, you know? I wanted to keep it in the past; otherwise I would have been permanently frozen into it.

I don't feel that way anymore. My oldest daughter, Cathy, and I sat in with John on a couple of cuts from his album *Bombs Away Dream Babies.* We played on "Coming out of Nowhere" and "Run." On his next album we're going to do a song called "Sing at the Wheel," which is a variation of a Druid tune from two thousand years ago—the chorus is—and I added some fresh stuff to it. I'm writing my best songs right now. I guess you'd call them advanced Kingston Trio songs.

Folk music is still pretty vigorous. There's as much now as

there ever was. Peter, Paul and Mary just came through town. Arlo Guthrie plays around here quite often. Joan Baez and Mimi Fariña are still active, of course, and I think Odetta has been recently seen on the boards. I just talked to Pete Seeger and he's as healthy as ever. He's a fine cat; he was my idol. I had the pleasure of seeing him about a month ago when he came out to San Francisco to play for an anti-nuclear concert. There were moments during that concert when he looked about twenty-two years old.

Freddy Parris
They Still Love the Doo-Wop Sound

Lead Singer, the Five Satins

There were originally only four Satins, but you couldn't call yourself the Four of anything in those days. It was uncool. You had to be the Five. So we signed up a piano player when we went on the road. One of the guys in my old group, the Scarlettes, became one of the Satins. He must have been home on leave. We picked up two other guys from the neighborhood. There were different guys each week. The songs were easy to sing. I knew the music was kind of sloppy, that it wasn't done well, but there was just something about it that caught my ear, something about those four chords.

It was an entirely different life than what I was used to. It was all sort of off the top of your head. "Hey, I got you guys a gig." "Okay, we'll be there. Maybe we can get an advance on next week's pay. As soon as we get through we can go out, meet some girls, and have some fun." There were always girls who would wait at the stage door for you to come out. They kept up with your career; I think that's all they did. Living conditions left a lot to be desired. You were only making $750 a week for five guys, and that included room and board. So you ended up staying in one room most of the time. Usually you set something up in the neighborhood with a lady in a restaurant, who let you eat on credit until the end of the week. That's all we worried about in those days. We never looked at our overall career and said, "We should do this or that."

For me it was always a struggle. It was never a situation where I was comfortable. We kept on working even when the Beatles came here in 1964, with the whole British invasion. We all learned instruments; I started playing bass. The club owners got a real break when the Beatles came in. They no longer had to hire two groups, a singing group and a band, because everybody began to play their own instruments.

I should have studied, but I never took it seriously. If I'd had the tools they have these days to work with, I'm sure we would have done a much better job. I could have put everything on tape exactly as I wanted it. But as it went down, I'd have to tell everybody what I wanted at rehearsals; the guys were local musicians who couldn't pick up too quick, and I would end up saying, "Ah, okay, what the hell, let it go that way."

I've had a diversified past. But whenever things were right, I'd go out again. When we appeared at a rock-and-roll-revival concert at Madison Square Garden, one story had it that they found us working at a car wash. They tried to make us as low as possible. But I was making a pretty good living and just singing on the side. After that, there was suddenly a demand for us. I was being booked on tours, working almost seven nights a week, going to Philly and Boston and Washington, plus working during the day. I finally had to quit my job. But if you're just going to say, that's it, then you're not going to do it anymore. If you want to be in it, you've got to keep doing it.

Given our track record, we've played many more places than we should have. I've been to Lake Tahoe and Puerto Rico. A lot of the other guys on the circuit were a little bit jealous. In New York they're still in love with the Satins, the doo-wop sound. But we also genuinely put on a class show. When you've got an hour to do in a club, you can't stand there all night and sing "In the Still of the Nite."

Shirley Alston

Nobody Had a Swelled Head

Lead Singer, the Shirelles

It's very difficult for a person who was popular back in the sixties to have a hit record today. If it happens, you better consider yourself very fortunate. I just recorded two sides. I think they're both good and they're not like the old stuff. But they wouldn't accept it. They wouldn't accept new things from the Shirelles either, because they said they loved the old things. "I like your new things, but I'd rather play your old things." And then if you try to record in the oldie vein, you're out of date to them. They say, "Here you come again with those doo-wop tunes; I can't believe it." Right now I'm peddling the single, but I don't want to drop it here or there. I want to put it someplace where they're going to do something with it. I don't want it sitting on the shelf. I have a whole album with the Shirelles in the can at RCA.

When we left Scepter I didn't care if I worked anymore. I was very blue. Everybody was blue. We did continue performing, but recording-wise we weren't anxious to jump into anything. By then we'd kind of cooled off. We hadn't had a recording in a while. We weren't a hot item. So everybody wasn't exactly breaking their necks to grab us.

As far as I'm concerned the business hasn't changed at all.

·   The crowds aren't that much different either. In the early days I toured with the big packages—Lloyd Price, Dick Clark. Today I'm doing the exact same thing with Richard Nader. So it's not very different work-wise. When we'd go out on a bus with Dick Clark, everybody looked out for the other person. We've done tours where if we went into a town and they said to the black acts, "You can't stay at this hotel," the white acts would say, "Then we're not staying either." As tired as we were from working, we'd drive to another place that would accept us. It was just beautiful. The arenas were always packed, everybody was hot on the charts, and usually we stayed at very nice places.

It was easy to meet people then. Getting rid of them was the problem. They'd recognize us in stores, or on the street. When you'd come offstage after a concert, they'd rush you—not to tear your clothes off. It was different for girls than it was for guys. Still, if you went out there and you looked attractive and you were singing something they liked, they didn't care if you were married or single. It was up to you to keep yourself from getting involved with anyone.

The first time we heard one of our songs on the radio, we jumped up and down, but life still went on the same way, believe me. In school we were just regular people. Our friends were excited for us. When they passed us in the hall they'd say, "How're you doing? What's your new record going to be?" But as far as really going ape over us, forget it. At first we couldn't do much, anyway, because we weren't old enough to play the clubs. Because we were still in school we could only play Friday and Saturday nights, usually at private parties. After we did "Dedicated to the One I Love," we started going out on tour. In our junior year we had to drop out of school and get private tutors. But nobody had a swelled head. And no big deal was really made about us. We never got the key to the city. One of the girls used to say that all the time. "They should give us the key to the city." I said, "I'd rather have the keys to a car."

Though I'm not with the Shirelles anymore, they work and I work on the strength of our recordings. Once you've had a smash, standard-type song, you can always work, just doing your hits. Even these days when I'm playing a high school, sometimes I may fumble the lyrics to a song, but the kids know them. They learned them from their brothers and sisters.

Cheryl "Salt" James
It Wasn't a Mutual Decision

Singer, Salt-N-Pepa

Breaking up Salt-N-Pepa wasn't a mutual decision. I was the one who couldn't take it anymore. People were like, "You know how much money you could make?" Salt-N-Pepa's a household name. Even on a failed album we were still in demand. I couldn't believe it. It was really hard for both of us but it was time to be individuals and have separate lives and do different things. It was kind of rough on Pepa, but the wounds have to heal before you can talk about stuff. We haven't been speaking a lot lately. I can't even lie to say she was like, "Hey, congratulations, you're going solo." But coming home and having some time to myself with my family and getting my personal life in order, which is my priority now, brought me back to a place where I wanted to do it again. Not because I had to or everybody thought I should, but because I wanted to.

My husband, Gavin, was always doing a lot of things with producers, selling tracks and working on tracks himself. So we have a studio at home and he continued to work in the studio. For a while we tried to run an independent label. But that proved to be impossible. With Gavin being downstairs in the studio all the time, the music kept calling me. So I got my little pen and paper out and I called a friend of mine, Rufus Black, who wrote on the last Salt-N-Pepa album, and me and him got together. He really gave me a lot of inspiration to start writing again because I lost my confidence. I had just had a baby and was in real mom mode. So I started writing and just fooling around in the studio. I ended up making a few songs that everybody thought were really good, so I called another friend of ours, James Prince, from Rap-A-Lot, and I asked him to come to New York to hear what I got and maybe I could do a solo album. He heard it and thought it was great and took it straight to Virgin. They loved it too. It all happened naturally, without me even thinking about it or trying too hard. Before, I was doing everything. I was in the studio moving choruses with Pro Tools till three or four in the morning. I was going to different places, hearing tracks, sitting in studios. I was chasing down producers. Just doing everything. This time around, Gavin was doing all of that. I was able to stay at home and help my daughter with her homework and send her to school in the morning and spend good time with my son. I don't have to worry about any of the things I had to think about before. It's almost too easy.

I guess you put could my career in three categories. There was the beginning when it was pure adrenaline. I've never worked harder in my career than when Salt-N-Pepa first started. I'd do anything. I would sleep in the studio and wake up in the studio. Nothing mattered. I would spend my last little part-time-job check in the studio and just drive to any function. Nothing was too far for a little club date. It was more fun then, because I was so excited doing it.

Then there was the middle when it was all hype and glamour and glitz and people on their knees tying your shoes and Grammies and stylists and hair and makeup and drama. Which was fun, but then after a while it got to be exhausting. You felt like you were being pulled in ten different directions. Everyone else dictated what I needed to do—every magazine, every interview, every photo shoot, every television show. My turmoil came because I didn't have control of my life, and that's a bad, bad feeling. I think every artist goes through that when they become very famous. They just lose control. People are constantly in your ear with opinions on what you should and shouldn't do. The business gets bigger than the music and when you're an artist you're totally not thinking along the lines of accountants and lawyers and people fighting over money.

This time is totally different. This is a real peaceful, family time. I'm in control of my life really for the first time. And I get to dictate what I think is important in my career and what I feel I need to do. This time out, I want to do a live band with turntables and with some stuff from the studio, like a D-88—but definitely with a live feeling. I don't like to be stuck to a tape. I want to be able to go with the flow of the crowd. If something's not working, or they're not diggin' it, I can just move on. Or if they're really lovin' it, I can keep it goin'. I love that feeling. This time I'm not going for an all-girl band. I'm going for the best new vision.

Still, when I put my daughter on the bus, I get a little teary-eyed because I think in a minute, I'm not going to be able to do this every day. I know I'm going to do what I have to to make this album successful. I'm just going to have to figure out a way to be able to still see my kids. Even if I have to take them with me, which I did a lot with my daughter, but she's in the fourth grade now and school is getting serious. Hopefully, the album will do well, and I'll have those kinds of decisions to make. But guess what, if it doesn't, I won't be very very upset.

Robby Krieger
The Doors' Guitarist

Guitarist, the Doors

The thing that was great about the Doors was that Jim [Morrison] could do whatever he wanted and we could do whatever we wanted within it. It was more like a jazz group in that respect. In the early days, the Doors were like Living Theater. Jim really lived the life that you saw onstage. He was like that all the time. Our trip was to mesmerize people and get them into hypnotic states and Jim could take them wherever he wanted. In those days we used to get all our arrangements down by playing in person and we had time to work up our songs. It was more the sound and the feel and the environment rather than the notes. When we got into the bigger halls it became harder to reach people. There was no room to fool around onstage. We were just doing stuff that people knew. We ended up playing the same thing every night and it became more difficult to be creative. Eventually, we didn't go on the road that much because, frankly, Jim got too wild to stay out too long. The longer he stayed out the crazier he'd get. So we ended up doing mostly four-day weekends. We did a couple of two-week tours, but we never did any ninety-day marathons. Jim definitely lived for performing, but for me it was a necessary evil. I liked playing for people, but I didn't miss those giant crowds and the traveling.

More or less I was just getting by with the Doors. I would never practice or study or I wasn't really interested in music as such. Mainly I would only play what was right for each song. I learned how to be the Doors' guitarist, and if you tried to stick me in some other band at that point I would have been terrible. If you listen to what I played, it's nothing like anyone else played. It was good for the Doors, but when I tried to put that into another situation it was totally wrong. It was kind of weird, because after the Doors broke up, when I'd go to a jam session or something, I'd be out in left field. I wouldn't know what was happening. It's funny, because if you're from a big group, that's all the more reason they like to cut you down. It's like this big competition thing. Other musicians would be real jealous because we had money from the Doors. And they'd think, Well, here I am, this great musician, but I don't have any money. They couldn't understand that talent comes in different ways. I got really embarrassed a couple of times and I said to myself, "Well, I'm going to practice for ten hours straight and I'm going to get that guy." I had to learn to play all over again.

I had a style of my own with the Doors. Everybody used to say, "I can tell it's you on the radio." But when I started really learning how to play, I kind of lost it through too much technique. Once I started learning music, my songs got to be eight million chords. To me playing is more fun than writing and I don't really need the money to write for money. I still write, but a lot of what I have are just riffs. It used to be in the Doors when I would write something they would do it and not that much was wasted. Jim was perfect for my writing style. A lot of times I'd write music to his lyrics. It seemed like whatever I wrote he could make it sound right. I guess people didn't realize until recently that I wrote a lot of those songs, cause it said on the album, "written by the Doors." Most people just figured Jim wrote the songs. But there were never any ego problems between us. If Jim were alive today I'd have twenty hit songs by now.

T-Bone Wolk
It Changed My Life

Bass Player, Hall and Oates, the Saturday Night Live Band

I remember once sitting in Columbus Circle right by the newsstand when this cop car pulls up. It's like twenty feet away and I think I see out of the corner of my eye that the cop is motioning for me to come over to the car. I, of course, ignore him. But when I look over at him again he's still pointing at me to come over to the car. I'm going, Oh my God. This is really weird; what have I done? So I finally go over and he says, "Did you ever play at the Lodge in the Bronx?" And I go yeah and he says, "And now you play on *Saturday Night Live* with G. E. Smith, the guy with the big head and the hair, right?" I say yeah. He says, "I used to see you guys all the time with Big River and Pip Gillette," and he starts into this whole thing about a bar band I had in 1971. Then he got out of the cop car. Maybe it was a slow day for them, but he just wanted to talk.

TV does strange things to people. Whether you've won on *Millionaire* or you just go on *Jerry Springer*, anybody who's on TV, their life changes. *Saturday Night Live* was so unique and such a huge presence that it put my face in front of people and made it into instant recognition. Also, don't forget that G. E. and I had a pretty heavy visibility from 1981 to 1985 with the

Hall and Oates band, because of MTV. Those were really the MTV glory days and we were one of the big, big MTV bands.

When I joined the *Saturday Night Live* band with G. E. in 1985 we were still upstairs, hidden away. The director, Paul Miller, decided that year that he was going to feature band members a lot more. I remember he said, "I'm going to put you guys on camera this year." It was a very big change in the format of the show and it was a very big change for the profile of the band. It really made a huge difference; it was a wonderful thing he did for us. After that you couldn't go anywhere where someone wouldn't say, "Hey, you guys are great. Who's on the show this week?" As a working musician, you couldn't possibly buy that kind of visibility. People would ask me, "Do you have photographs, a press kit?" I'd go, "Yeah, turn the TV on at eleven-thirty on a Saturday night. There's my press kit."

By the time I joined the show, they kind of had it down for financial reasons to one very long day on Saturday. We'd show up at 10:30 A.M. and we'd do any pre-records for a skit or Cheryl Hardwick would show up usually with something for one of the comedy pieces. We'd play those live on the sound-stage and record them right there at NBC. The only time we had to do more work is when we were backing up the musical guests. We did more of that the first couple of years because there was a bigger envelope of creative bookings in the beginning than there was when I left the show. We played with Elvis Costello twice, Anita Baker, Randy Newman. We did something with Linda Ronstadt and Aaron Neville when they had that big hit together. Eddie Van Halen sat in with us. To be able to stand there on our stage and be ten feet away from Prince or Eric Clapton, I mean, that's one of the highlights. Eric came over during a commercial break and played "Born Under a Bad Sign" with us. I'll never forget the look on G. E.'s face. We got

Robbie Robertson to do "King Harvest" with us. But that happened less and less frequently as time went on. Typically, you'd put in an eleven- or twelve-hour day and when they went live at eleven-thirty that was your big run, that hour and a half. So you really had to pace yourself to keep focused.

I lasted six years and at the end I really needed to move on. I needed to go on the road again with Daryl and John. Cheryl Hardwick retired at the end of last season, which was in June, and I played that show. For twenty-five years she single-handedly wrote most of the comedy music you heard. Talk about a working musician. If they were doing a serious skit, if they did something that required classical music or some heavy piece, that was Cheryl on the air watching the TV set and playing along with the skit. If she wasn't on camera, she was back there watching the TV and playing live. I've never worked with a musician like that in my entire life. She was just a brilliant, brilliant person. So this was the show where Cheryl was leaving and it was really great. She's crying, everybody's crying, the stagehands were crying. Lorne came up. The cameras were on her and then you're watching the monitor. You're watching her and watching what's going out on the air and you're saying, "People are not going to understand why they're doing this with her," but it was a very great tribute. She was one of the biggest behind-the-scenes musicians that the show ever had.

Last year they had the twenty-fifth-anniversary show, but I couldn't make it because I had other obligations. It's hard to get people together. It's hard to get people together for dinner, let alone together for a *Saturday Night Live* reunion show.

I just want to go on record as saying that I did not get rich playing *Saturday Night Live*. People think that you're instantly rich because you're on TV, but it wasn't the kind of money people think it was. It was a union-scale thing. We were paid union wages for the time we worked on Saturday. Yes, you'd get some residuals when they ran it in the summertime, but it was pro-rated, so that means they go down each time they run them. It wasn't ever enough money for any of us in the band to survive on. It was just a piece of the puzzle.

HABITS OF TWELVE SUCCESSFUL MUSICIANS XII

Brenda Lee
Respecting the Business

Country/Pop Diva

Back then you worried about your first hit. Then you didn't worry about the second, because the second was going to ride on the first to an extent. It was the third one you really worried about. If you didn't get the third one, you were either out of the business or it was like you were an embryo all over again, because nobody cared what you had out. It was, "Well, what are you doing now?" You had to prove yourself every time you put out a record. This created a feeling of desperation among some of the people, because they didn't know what to do with themselves, how to pace their careers, or strive for longevity. Most of the ones who survived, like myself and Paul Anka, and a few others, knew, or their managers knew, that you had to have a tremendous amount of respect for the business or you couldn't stay in it. You couldn't even make it if you didn't remember who put you there, and that was your audience, the DJs, the writers—people like that.

My manager would never let me listen to other singers. He didn't want me to start trying subconsciously to sound like them, or take little tricks away from them. But once my style had already been formed, he made me sit down and listen to everything that Frank Sinatra ever recorded. Not so much for singing, but for phrasing. The only other thing that was pounded into my head from the time I got my manager was articulation of words. And then choosing good material. I had all the control on that, because I don't think you can sing a song unless you pick it, unless you feel it. I'm basically a lyrics singer, and I tried to pick songs that would not become passé—that I still could do in front of audiences ten, fifteen years later. You have to think in terms of if you don't have another hit record for a while, then you can still do these things and you won't be out of the public's eye.

Music changed in 1964 with the Beatles. Then it did another change in 1967 with the psychedelic acid. There was just no place for me and I wouldn't prostitute myself to what was happening. You can knock the Beatles all you want to. You can knock the way they looked, knock what they said, but you cannot knock their musical genius. They started a whole new wave of comprehensive intelligence in music. I knew them when they were going under the name of the Silver Beatles. I didn't associate with them that closely. I was a teenager and they were older. They didn't talk a whole lot to anybody. They were kind of cocky, but in a nice way. They were fantastic writers, and they had most of their songs even then. They recorded the weirdest way I've ever seen. To go to a session with them, you'd go into the studio and you'd stay for a month. John thinks up a line and then they may go home to bed. And then the next day Paul thinks up something and then they put music to it and then they do it. It could take them up to a week to do one song. I tried to get them a contract with Decca Records at the time, but Decca didn't want to know about them.

I was still working on the road some at this time. I just didn't record. Now that hurts your career a little, because you're more or less out of the ball game if you don't have some product to put out there. Fortunately, it didn't hurt mine all that bad, although it certainly didn't further it any. While I was working out a new deal with MCA I was unable to record, so I missed "Here You Come Again." Barry Mann, the writer, sent that to me and I held it for eight months. Then I finally had to give it back to him. I also had "She Believes in Me" (I was going to do it as "He Believes in Me") and "I'd Really Love to See You Tonight."

I guess there are a lot of girls out there who probably listened to me, maybe cut their teeth on some Brenda Lee records. I was really proud with Stevie Nicks of Fleetwood Mac. I love her, and I finally got to meet her. I said, "I'm really embarrassed, but would you sign my autograph book for me?" And she put down, "To my greatest inspiration." And I thought, she's heard of me—Stevie Nicks of Fleetwood Mac. I couldn't believe it.

Richard Thompson
Keeping the Shop Open

English Folk Performer

The editor Gordon Lisch said that being creative means you have to keep your shop open. When things come along you have to get them; if you miss them they just never come back. I'm pretty open about half the time. If I see something on the street, I'll write it down. If it's a melody, I'll write down the notes, and it's usually close enough for remembering a tune. For some reason I never use a tape machine. I probably should.

Often sounds are what trigger music for me. I hear the sound of the song. I don't really know the title yet, but I can hear the totality of it. You might hear a gong or a steel rail, the sound of the sea. You have the song in your head before you ever have a lyric. I think that sound is something I try to reach for but never quite attain.

The real struggle is trying to find out what the details are. I like to take advantage of a kind of keyhole effect, where you look at a large subject like you're looking through a keyhole. You're describing a small part of it and you're suggesting everything else. In a way, that's the best use of a three-minute song. I like that kind of discipline. I used to listen to a lot of Scottish ballads—I still do. I think they're probably among the finest songs in the English language. The language is tremendously distilled. You may have a simple love song, but the way it's described, the way it's veiled, is what gives it its power. I could put a lot of feeling into a song when I'm performing it, but I couldn't say it's literally my experience. It has to be broader to be of interest to other people. It has to be a more complete picture of life. It's not that I have a fear of revealing myself, it's just more interesting to use symbols, or a third person. Those are the songs that last.

If a song has real value it'll grow with you; it won't drag you back. A song can have enough in it that you can interpret it in different ways or be happy about singing it in completely different sets of circumstances, or under different conditions. But I can't think of any songs that I really get constant satisfaction out of playing for more than a year without giving them a rest. And it's nice to discover things on the back burner that you might have forgotten about for a few years. I'm planning to do "Did She Jump or Was She Pushed," which Linda (Thompson) used to sing. I might do "Walking on a Wire." There are songs that people always ask for like "End of the Rainbow," which Elvis Costello performs sometimes. I think it's too gloomy to play. I don't want to play a really depressing song. People always ask for it and I wonder why, unless there's a kind of cathartic effect.

You need some sort of reaction, some sort of feedback, because a song has to be communicated. It's not something you stick in a museum. You have to have a reaction to know if something was communicated. The reward for me is performing a song, playing a few notes on the guitar, that moves someone. Sometimes just one person comes up after a concert and says, "You know, I really appreciated this particular sentiment." That means a lot to me. That is communication.

John Sebastian

His Father's Son

Singer, Harmonica and Autoharp Player, the Lovin' Spoonful

I felt much better prepared for what happened with the Spoonful as a result of growing up as the son of a man who was committed to music for a lifetime. I knew how very good you could be and still not have popular acceptance. So I think the various waves of public approval and disapproval might have rolled off my back a little bit better than off a lot of my contemporaries whose parents had nine-to-five jobs, who sort of said, "How can this be a lifestyle?"

I'd say my father was never really able to attain anywhere near the recognition that I for one always wished for him, but that was never his goal. He was a classical musician. He wanted to be a soloist and I think he did have it that way. Eventually he was written for by some of the great composers of the time. He transposed a lot of flute and violin sonatas by Bach. He adapted a lot of classical works to the harmonica. He doesn't have much of a reputation as a writer, but I found his occasional original pieces to be completely magical.

If you think rock and roll was funky in the forties and fifties, believe me, classical music was funkier—because you had to get to more places for less money. Generally, he traveled with a pianist in a station wagon. He toured places that nobody had been at that time. He was in the Orient before that was anything like fashionable for Americans. This was not somebody who was afraid to get his tux muddy. He was usually on tour three to four months a year and then there was the occasional plush gig with an orchestra at the Whatchamacallit Room of the Waldorf-Astoria.

Having a famous father in a given area, you do feel competition. I decided at the age of five that I never wanted to play the harmonica again. But I found at about thirteen or fourteen that I could play it in a very different way and not be anywhere in the same ballpark. In fact, my father got me my first Sonny Terry record. It wasn't even a record; it was a silver acetate of Sonny Terry musically recreating a fox chase that got me pursuing this other way of playing.

My father also introduced me to Lightnin' Hopkins. He had done a Sunday morning television show called *Robert Herridge Presents*, which, in addition to Hopkins, also included a Welsh poet, and an at-that-time-unknown folk singer by the name of Joan Baez. I was snowed by Lightnin' and started following him around. My roommate from Blair Academy had an apartment where I lived part time and Lightnin' ended up there because it was a place he could stay for free. I never played onstage with him. I carried his guitar and bought him gin and that was about it. As time went by I could accompany him in living rooms now and then. He'd sort of nod and smile when I'd play a lick back at him, but ours was not a really tight relationship.

One day after just arriving back in the Village, I got a call from Stephan Grossman, who I knew from the neighborhood. He said, "Hi, you're in our group and rehearsals start today." I said, "How convenient." The group was called the Even Dozen Jug Band. Our only album was produced by Paul Rothschild. Meeting Paul resulted in an enormous amount of work for me as a harmonica player, because Paul was producing all these folk acts for Elektra and needed accompanists to flesh out albums by people who were used to working just with one guitar and vocal. So Felix Pappalardi and I became the Village rhythm section for a long time—Felix on guitarrone (he rarely played electric bass) and me on harmonica and second guitar. Soon I was making fifty-three dollars for a three-hour session. I remember writing to my father about it. Gee, this is great; this is what I want to do. I'm a studio musician. And he wrote me back a great letter that I remember to this day. He said, "You be careful. You'll be selling it note by note and you'll lose your soul."

Bruce Hornsby
I Just Made It for Me

Keyboard Player, Songwriter

When I was growing up, there were two camps at school, the preps and the freaks, and I was popular in both camps but I wasn't totally in with either of them. It was the real hippie era, and the musos were always the longhairs, the guys hanging out in the smoking lounge. As far as social standing, in my southern high school at least, the jocks were certainly more well thought of. The musicians were more of the subversives, not really that subversive, probably, but kind of a little outside of the social circle, and I think that's right where they wanted to be. But I was really kind of in the middle of the two worlds. I was a jock who played music, so that in itself put me in sort of a gray area. I was a little too out there for the preps and a little too straight for the freaks.

I've always likened making it in the music business to making it to the pro sports leagues. There are only so many slots open and so many people trying to do it, so when you attain that status it's like attaining the status of being a pro basketball player. When I got my record deal I thought, now I've made the team, I'm like the twelfth man. When you have a hit and get a little success, maybe you're the eighth man. You improve yourself a little more, and then maybe you're in the starting lineup. A lot of people referred to me, when I won the Grammy as Best New Artist, as Rookie of the Year.

But I have definitely run the gamut of different types of gigs. I played in disco bands with the matching disco zoot suits and frat-party rock bands playing Allman Brothers songs to three layers of dancers. There were lots and lots of weddings. We were real slackers. We never cared a bit about the wedding. We were the guys over in the corner trying to get away with as much as we could. We would just play some standards and then blow, slipping in as much bebop and jazz as we could into it. It was just a gig to us and we hated the gigs. My attitude on club dates was just, let's get out and get wild and screw around and get through it.

Then I spent seven tough, frustrating years trying to get a record deal, but not really featuring the piano at all because I was buying into the notion that you couldn't. You really didn't hear it on Top 40 radio; it wasn't done. It was all synthesizers and guitars. So I would write these songs on piano and translate them to guitars or synths and it was never quite true. I always came away from these tapes disappointed in the way the songs came out. Finally, I just made this tape with no regard to what I thought was commercial. I just made it for me. It was a one-man-band sort of deal, with a drum machine, a synth bass, piano, and a little organ. I sent it to Windham Hill and they offered me a deal. I was elated. I thought, well, okay, maybe I wasn't cut out for the majors. Had I signed with Windham Hill I feel like only one side of my personality would have come out. It would have been the real kind of nice pleasant stuff and none of the harder stuff.

Ironically, my lawyer leaked the tape out to a couple of major labels and they offered deals too. Since then it's just been a question of hard work and persistence and intensity—a gradual growing process. I'd say we're definitely playoff caliber now.

George Thorogood
Going at It

Blues Rock Performer

There was this one review I got that angered me at the time, but the more I thought about it the more it made sense. This was in 1981, and the writer said that my band reminded him of the Oakland A's. It was the time the A's were playing that Billyball stuff. They had an ex-third-string infielder catching. They had no bullpen. And yet here was a team that was in the playoffs and had an outside chance of going to the World Series. So this guy said, "Your band reminds me of the Oakland A's, a band with limited talent stretching it as far as it will go." I realized that he had a point.

Bob Uecker had the best statement. He said making the big leagues is one thing, but for six years making people believe you are still a big-leaguer is a bigger trick.

Critics have always said I could be a superstar if I really went at it. If I really went at it? I really have gone at it; that's what people don't understand. People are always telling me to push myself a little. They don't understand how far I've pushed myself already.

Like when I write original songs, the record company says, "Those are lousy songs. Don't do any more songs." But when we put those songs on the record they're always the ones that get played on the radio. Six months later the record company says, "Boy, that 'I Drink Alone' was great. The band writes great original songs." And the critics go, "Why doesn't Thorogood write more songs? With "Gear Jammer" and "Bad to the Bone" it seems like if he pushed himself he could write more songs." I say, "That's what I've been doing!"

Performing was never tough for me. I went out onstage to perform before I knew how to do anything. I had to make my musical ability catch up with my performing desires. I'd jump up on stage and go, "Da da . . ." And they'd say, "You've got everybody's attention, come back when you know how to play."

I was playing a solo blues gig in Boston and I went back to Delaware because my sister was getting married. When I was there they had this party where a bunch of people were playing and I joined them and we had a pretty good time. Whenever we couldn't get enough guys to play baseball, which was almost every day, the three of us would get together and play. We didn't have any microphones; we had amplifiers, but I didn't even have an electric guitar. I had to borrow my friend's electric guitar. We were just playing old Chuck Berry songs. We didn't really sing or anything, but the funny thing about it was that it worked. It sounded pretty good; it kind of clicked. So then, when I came back home, we got some jobs. Two nights before our first job I bought an electric guitar, and I've been playing ever since.

Basically, everything I learned I put together in the first two years that I studied the guitar. Now improvement is very gradual; like a weight lifter presses two hundred pounds the first time out, but it takes him six months to a year to be able to press 220 pounds.

I guess I was like eighty million other pimply teenagers in America. I wanted to play guitar to be cool. I never really dreamed it would end up that I actually did become cool. The day I realized that I was never going to be cool and should stop trying to be cool was the day I became cool. I just said, "Look, I'm just going to try to play this music for fun, and if I can pay my rent and never have to go to work in a store selling shoes then I'll be happy."

James Hetfield

Lead Singer, Metallica

I tried the jobs at the factory and all that. I was really into wanting to make this a career. I'd jam with my buddies and I'd go, "Nah, you're not good enough." And they'd go, "Oh man, you've got some kind of an attitude." I just wanted to get together with people who really had the drive.

The main idea of going out and getting some aggression was there from day one. The energy and aggression in the music has always got to be there. It's just evolved into growing musically, but still keeping the hard edge. There's power in slow stuff and in fast stuff, and there's power in using mellow stuff to make the heavier stuff heavier, and experimenting with all of it. Lyrically, too, I'm into rapping about some stuff that's heavier than your basic "Let's get down to the gig." So I mean it's aggression, open-mindedness in songwriting, and throwing some intelligence in there—thought-provoking stuff—not preaching, but making people think, or use it in their life somehow.

As far as surviving, there are definitely some tests we've gone through. We've played the interesting clubs and had our equipment ripped off. Test-wise, maybe the second album is make-or-break and the third one you've set a standard for yourself. When we toured with Ozzy we got to do a lot of sound checks. We'd be up there goofing around on Sabbath songs and he'd come out and watch. During the tour he was always saying, "Man, you guys remind me of the early seventies." That was a huge thing. Those few words really hit me, coming from the master.

But we never really thought about any of it as it was coming up. We lived pretty much day to day and had a fairly good grasp of reality, so every time something happened, we could deal with it.

When Cliff Burton was killed it was real shaky. There was definitely no talk of us busting up, but the thought was that we had to just get right back into it instead of taking a hiatus to grieve over it. The best way to get rid of some of that grief or aggression was to get out and slam back into it. After the accident, when we were still in the hospital, getting ready to go back to the hotel, I remember Bobby, our tour manager, saying to someone else, "You take the crew with you and I'll take the band with me," and it was like, "Wow, the band." It was like we weren't the band anymore; we were just three guys now. We weren't the unit that we were and that was a shock.

There's more responsibility now, not in that we have to defend ourselves or what we're doing, but now when we perform we're up there for two hours and we've got to be into it all the time. It doesn't get any easier. It isn't that much harder, either, only in that because of the length of our show, you have to get a good amount of sleep. We used to drink a lot. I love beer. I drink beer all the time. But I've cut down. As far as going on-stage, I want to be 100 percent aware and healthy. That I think is a responsibility I want to live up to. It's not that I have to, I want to. The band has to be tight. You have to go out and play a good show. Everyone has an obligation to the people who come to see us.

Lenny White
A Part of Jazz Lore

Jazz Drummer, Return to Forever

When I was seventeen I played with Jackie McLean here in New York. Jackie was famous for having young drummers play with him, like Tony Williams and Jack DeJohnette, so people said, "You played with Jackie, you're gonna play with Miles." I played a gig out in Queens and a mutual friend of ours heard me playing and said, "Has Miles ever heard you play?" I said no. He said, "I'm gonna tell him about you." I said, "Yeah, right." But sure enough I got a phone call to come to Miles's house on Seventy-seventh Street.

I played on *Bitches Brew*; that was the very first recording session I ever did. The recording was at ten o'clock. I was at the studio at nine. The cleaning lady let me in. I was setting up my stuff and kind of practicing and Miles comes in and he says to Jack DeJohnette, "Hey, Jack, tell that young drummer to shut up." So I was intimidated right off the bat. I had been playing funky-type music, James Brown stuff, for a long time. Of all the guys that were on the session I was the one guy who knew how to play all that stuff. So there was this tune that Miles wanted a funky beat on and he runs through it. I'm playing with Miles Davis now, so I'm trying to play all this slick stuff. He comes over to me and he says, "You ain't getting the chicken." I wound up playing percussion on the tune. Don Alias came up with a real hip beat, so he played the beat and I just played percussion. I was bummed out. When the day was over I said to myself, "Well, I had my opportunity to play with Miles Davis but that's going to be it." And then he came over to me and said, "Be here ten o'clock tomorrow morning." So I was vindicated.

One time Miles was playing at the Village Gate and he asked me to come backstage. The first thing he said was, "Can you play fast?" I said yeah. He said, "When?" I said, "Whenever anybody asks me." So he said, "Okay, be here every night this week. I want you to listen to the whole set." Between sets he would take me upstairs. We'd sit and listen to Les McCann and he'd kind of give me pointers. "What they're doing there is kind of slick, but what they did there is corny." He wanted me to come play with them on the road, in Boston. Jack DeJohnette's wife was having their first child, so that's why Jack wasn't going to do this; that's why I had the chance.

We were going to leave on a Monday or a Tuesday. On Friday or Saturday I went to Miles's house to listen to tapes. When I was leaving he said, "Where you going?" I said, "I'm going to Brooklyn to see my girlfriend." So he said, "Okay, I'm going to Brooklyn too." So he drove me into Brooklyn in his red Ferrari, doing eighty miles an hour on the West Side Highway, with one hand on the wheel and talking to me at the same time. I can't describe the fear that was in my body. But we made it and he dropped me off and I went to see my girlfriend. And that was the night Miles got shot. So I didn't get a chance to go out on the road because he didn't do the gig.

Everybody wanted to be in Miles Davis's band or John Coltrane's band. We wanted to strive to be good enough to play with Art Blakey and the Jazz Messengers, or Horace Silver. Because these were the highest musical institutions that were prevalent at the time. We were young kids, wanting to be part of jazz lore. Being a part of jazz lore meant you had to make records and have an apprenticeship with a master, then people could refer back to it. That was the whole thing. That's what everybody wanted to do, because we had listened to all of these records of our heroes and all these guys did exactly that. Miles played with Bird, Trane played with Monk. It's hard for a young musician to apprentice playing with the likes of a Miles Davis, the likes of a Thelonious Monk. There are no longer musical institutions like those. So they were cherished. I remember Max Roach came to hear me play one time and he introduced me to the person he was with, "This is Lenny White. He's a great drummer, and he's made a lot of important records." And I thought that was a great compliment. When you think about it, it's an accomplishment to have a body of work. There's a lot of guys that are winning polls and doing this and doing that, but how many important records have they been on?

When Return to Forever first started to play and I saw the reaction that we had from the audience I knew it was something special. Right away we were getting complaints about loudness, but the musicianship was stellar. The music was really aggressive. It was like rock and roll with brains. I mean, Elton John, Gamble and Huff, the people from Yes, and all these established rock-and-roll bands came to see us. Kenny Gamble said to us one day at a CBS convention, he said, "Man, if you could get a singer that was on the same level of musicianship, you guys would own the world."

In the latest *Downbeat* they had Weather Report on the cover, and they called them the greatest jazz band of the past thirty years. But I'm telling you, there wasn't one time when we played opposite Weather Report that we didn't smoke them. So, they were the greatest band, but we smoked them, okay? This is when RTF, Weather Report, the Mahavishnu Orchestra, and Herbie Hancock were all vying for the same piece of the pie. Every night it was like the wild wild West. Everybody's out gunning for everybody else. I remember one time we did a tour of the States, started up in Maine, went across country to California, from California we went to Japan, from Japan we went to Europe, and from Europe we came back and did another tour of the United States. Fifty concerts in seventy days. When you're twenty-two or twenty-three years old, you don't get exhausted. You're seeing the world. Every night you're playing, and at that point your testosterone level is like through the roof. You use a lot of energy, but the thing is it's such a great conditioning situation because you're doing all this exercise every night, especially when you're playing this high-powered fusion music. At that time we were into health food, diet, trying to eat right, chewing raw ginseng, taking herbs. I never did drugs. I thought that the music put me in such a euphoric state that I didn't really need to induce it any other way than by playing.

I have a very talented student now, a young kid about nineteen years old, who has all the tools. If he sat down and devoted five hours a day to it, he'd be a master drummer in a while. But the point is, with those five hours, he might take one hour and devote it to practicing his instrument and the other three hours or four hours he's making beats. It's the twenty-first century and that's what guys are doing now. So it becomes a problem. What happened is, since the eighties, you no longer have to be a musician to make music. And that's a real profound thing. Kids that were studying to be musicians now say, "Wait a minute, I'm studying, knocking myself out here, sacrificing, trying to learn my instrument, and I could just get a program and put it together and make five times more money than if I was going

to school studying to become a musician." That's what it's become. It's a whole other working situation. A whole other dynamic. A different chase. Because when you're learning your
craft and the bar is so high and you're trying to get to that level
of becoming a master musician it's a different kind of a chase
than to go write a few songs and take them to an A&R guy at a
major record company. It's a whole other thing.

Nowadays I've taken on a real ambitious project; it's like
putting on a parachute and jumping off a mountain. My intention, with a friend of mine who's a playwright, is to write a contemporary opera. So I told my cousin about it and she goes to
work and tells her co-workers I'm writing an opera. I said,
"What are you doing that for? I don't know how it's gonna be.
It might be junk." She said, "Yeah, it might be junk now, but in
two hundred years from now it might be great." So you never
know.

Leonard Cohen
A Count of Monte Cristo Feeling

Poet, Novelist, Singer-Songwriter

A man visits a master who's living in a very pitiful terrain and the man says, "How can you survive here?" The master says, "If you think it's bad now, you should see what it's like in summer." "What happens in the summer?" asks the man. The master says, "In the summer I throw myself into a vat of boiling oil." "Isn't it worse then?" says the man. "No," says the master, "pain cannot reach you there."

That's really the way things are. If you throw yourself into a kind of effort, it's not better or worse. Like a chameleon, you take the color of the experience if it's intense enough, and the pain cannot reach you there. Performing is definitely the boiling oil. You can't really develop an intellectual perspective on it. I mean, you're in it. You realize the next moment could bring total humiliation, or you could actually be lifted up into the emotion that began the song. But you're already in the boiling oil by the time you've gotten that far.

In Montreal in the fifties when I began to write, people didn't have the notion of superstars. The same prizes weren't in the air as there are today, so one had a kind of modest view of what a writing career was. My training as a writer was not calculated to inflame the appetites. But I put my work out the very best I can. It comes out of my life. It's a very large chunk of my life. I can understand if it becomes important in another life. Whether you involve yourself personally in these other lives is another matter. You can involve yourself totally in the lives of your listeners, and it has got to be disaster. I'm not talking about somebody who has a fantasy of a singer. These are people who really relate to your own experience and vice versa. Now maybe they're living in some kind of milieu where they don't have people to relate to. You set yourself up as a kind of kin of these people and they see it and it's true. That's the fantastic thing about it. You meet them and immediately you see they are people who have your own experience. Over the years I have somehow fallen into some lives that my songs have led me into, and some of these lives have ended—rather violently, rather sadly.

I think everybody is involved in a kind of Count of Monte Cristo feeling. You want to evoke figures of the past. You somehow want the past to be vindicated. My own experience has been that almost everything you want happens. I meet people out of the past all the time. Not only that, I meet people that I wanted to create. It's like Nancy [in "Seems So Long Ago, Nancy"]. The line is "Now you look around, you see her everywhere . . ." This is just my own creation, but obviously there's a collective appetite for a certain kind of individual; that individual's created and you feel you had a certain tiny part in that creation.

A friend of mine said about poetry that the two things necessary for a young poet are arrogance and inexperience. The late teens and twenties are generally the lyric phase of a writer's career. If you achieve enough fame and women and money during that period, you quit, because that's generally the motivation. I didn't get enough money or women or fame for me to quit. I don't have enough yet, so I've got to keep on playing. I know it's rather unbecoming at my age to keep it all going, but I have to do it.

Roger McGuinn

Meeting the Beatles

Singer, Guitarist, the Byrds

It was right after I saw the Beatles that I knew I wanted to get a band together. It looked like a very attractive proposition. In fact, I remember walking down the street in 1964, just before I left New York, and there were these club owners who said, "What we need are four of him." That's when I knew I had something that would work.

I think what initially attracted me to the Beatles was the fact that they inadvertently or subconsciously were using folk changes. I'd been listening to Bob Gibson, who used some pretty slick chord progressions for a folk singer. He used a lot of passing chords like the Beatles ended up doing. Like he'd go G, Bb, Eb, C, Ab, Db back to G, and stuff like that. So when I heard the Beatles, I went, "Oh, I love those changes." I loved their harmonies of the fourths and fifths, which were also folk-music kind of harmonies, like sea-shanty harmonies. I think because they had been a skiffle band and because they came from where they did, that music was just in air there. They were doing their version of the fifties rock and roll/rockabilly sound and the folk thing combined. I guess that was what it really was.

When I got to meet them, I found out they didn't know they were doing that. They didn't know how to fingerpick and they didn't play banjos or mandolins or anything, and they weren't coming from where I was coming from at all, which I'd given them credit for. I thought they knew all that stuff and were just being real slick about it. But it was just kind of an accident. It was a great accident.

When George Harrison and I compared notes, it turned out that he and I had learned exactly the same guitar line at the same time. It was the first thing we both learned. I think it was the break from "Be-Bop-A-Lula." I told George about Ravi Shankar and all that Indian stuff, and he got into it after that. This was 1965 or '66. We'd seal ourselves up in a bathroom or something, get the security guys out of there, and all take acid and sit on the floor and play guitars.

George didn't believe in anything when I first met him. I remember his response because I thought it was really odd. He said, "We don't believe in God," like he didn't have a personal mind or ego of his own. It was a group consciousness. "We don't know what to think about that." They were kind of neat the way they worked, the Beatles. They all used to protect each other. It was like a little gang. If you do something to one of them they'll get you.

Anthony Gourdine
Real Show Biz Takes Years

Lead Singer, Little Anthony and the Imperials

The unique thing about Little Anthony and the Imperials was that we became a great performing act. We spent eight years in Las Vegas and Lake Tahoe. We were one of the highest-paid working groups. And we were the only ones in the whole world who came out of that era and went in that direction. We set the stage for everybody else. Gladys Knight and the Pips saw us; the Temptations came in and watched us very carefully.

After we first broke up, the Imperials developed in the business much quicker than I did. They worked with Richard Barrett, who helped them a lot. They started playing the Catskills and getting a taste of nightclubs. Their repertoire changed; they started going after pop songs, learning modern harmony and studying the Hi-Lo's and the Four Freshmen. A gentleman by the name of Kenny Seymour sang with them for a while. He was brilliant at teaching them four-part harmony. The Imperials had become fine performers. But I was still going around doing "Tears on My Pillow." I stayed very stagnant, very rock-and-rollish. I took jobs singing wherever I could. But the clubs only wanted to hear the old music. Can you imagine that? I was already an oldie but goodie.

We were still friends, even when we broke up. We were

hanging out at each other's houses. I was going to gigs with them. People were always asking us to get back together. Ernest [Wright Jr.] had an apartment at the Mohawk Hotel in Brooklyn, and I used to go there all the time. One day we just said, "Hey man, let's do it." Two of the original members, Tracy Lord, the tenor, and Nathaniel Rodgers, the bass, had left. We got Sammy Strain, who'd been with the Chips, to join us, and he was with us for fifteen years.

What the Imperials did was to teach me what they were doing. I fell into their rhythm; they didn't fall into mine. As soon as we started rehearsing we knew it was going to be magic. We worked so much it was unbelievable. We worked everywhere, especially in the New York area—wherever there were teenagers or college kids. That was the audience that really dug us.

Murray the K put us on one of his shows at the Brooklyn Fox, second billing to Johnny Mathis. It's something I'll always remember for as long as I live. The theme of the show was: The Triumphant Return of Little Anthony and the Imperials. We walked out onstage and there were so many people, from Brooklyn, Queens, the Bronx, and all you could hear was screaming. They just loved us, and we didn't know we were loved.

When we first broke into Vegas, there was a group called the Checkmates working at Caesar's Palace who were performing at the level we should have been at. We were doing a lot of the vaudeville things, very show business, very slick and classy, but that was the era when they were just getting down into disco, and that's what the Checkmates were doing. We learned a lot from them. We'd be playing to a half-full house; the Checkmates had standing room only. You couldn't get in to see them. All the stars were going over there.

That's how you know you're doing well in Vegas, when

your peers come to see you. When you looked out in the audience and you'd see everybody from Connie Stevens to Johnny Carson. There were times I'd look up from sitting with someone like Muhammad Ali, and say to myself, "Oh man, here I am from Fort Greene, running in gangs up and down the street. I'm sitting next to these people, people of stature; I'm in their homes. I'm talking to Sammy Davis! Here's the guy I loved to watch and we're talking like we've known each other for years."

Real show business takes years. A lot of the young acts that were coming up didn't realize the kind of sacrifices you have to make in order to reap from it. The time is not your own. You sleep, eat, and think show biz. We became a disciplined group. Richard Barrett always instilled in us his discipline about performing. A disciplined person is a disciplined person. He will be exactly what he's going to be and that's it. The discipline came as the years passed. I'm a professional performer today. I know what I have to do to go out and entertain people.

Scotty Moore
An Uncanny Sense of Timing

Guitarist for Elvis Presley

I quit playing for twenty-four years. Other than a couple of record dates for Carl Perkins and Billy Swan, I didn't even play from 1968 to 1992. 1968 was when Elvis decided to go to Vegas. I said, "Well, hell, that's not happening anymore, so I'll just take care of business," and kind of got out of playing. I'd had a studio since he went in the army in '58; I started the studio in Memphis and then moved to Nashville. I also had a full-time tape-duplicating plant and then I got into commercial printing. I didn't miss it. I didn't think I did anyway. Now I wish I hadn't quit. Now I got stuff in my head that I can't get out through my fingers. But back in those days I felt like I was pushing too hard. It has to be a natural flow. So I have mixed emotions. I hear the stuff now and I can't play it; back then I wasn't hearing it.

I had just purchased a Gibson ES-295 when I was called to fill in with Elvis. While I was in the navy we were over in Japan, and there were these Japanese guitars that were copies of Fender's solid-bodies. They were real cheap. They made the frets out of beer cans, I guess. You'd have to buy one nearly every month because the frets would wear out. When I came out of the navy in 1952 I bought a Fender Esquire and a little

Fender Champ amp. I was used to playing in the navy sitting down, but standing up with the Fender I found that I couldn't hang onto it. It kept getting away from me. So I saw this gold ES-295 in a music store one day and I said, "I've got to have it." I kept that guitar through the Sun days, and then I discovered the L5 for the last session on Sun, "Mystery Train." That was really the best guitar I ever owned.

When we did the first stuff on Sun I was just beginning to get turned on to Chet Atkins and Merle Travis, trying to figure out how they kept that thumb doing something different from the rest of the fingers. On the first couple of records I was kind of doing a rhythm thing, and adding in a few notes, other than the little solo things I did. People still think I'm a thumb-and-finger picker, but I'm really not. I do it a lot, but it's different—the thumb does what it wants to do and the other fingers do what they want to do. I got a dumb thumb. Soundwise, I started off with the Fender Champ. Sam Phillips was using slapback delay on the records and I knew how it felt when the three of us went out jamming—it was so empty—and that delay he added made it sound even more empty. Then I heard a record of Chet's in the middle of 1954—I don't remember the title—where just his guitar had that slapback tape-delay sound. I said, "Wow, if I could do that at least onstage, just with my guitar, that way I could give people listening a semblance of how the records sounded." So I did some research, found out who was making it, and got one of those amps. It cost five-hundred dollars, which was pretty high in 1954. But I used that sound off and on until we signed with RCA.

We were out traveling it seemed like all the time. It started off with just three of us in a car and then we added the drummer, D. J. [Fontana], about a year later and it was four of us in the car, until D. J. started bringing one or two of his buddies along—

then it was two cars. Nobody ever thought of a bus back then. We finally ended up with a Cadillac limousine. While we were traveling, I'd listen to jazz all the time, but I never could really play it. I tried to get D. J. and Bill [Black], if we were going to be someplace for a couple of days, to take the instruments up to the room to jam, to practice, or whatever. "No, no," they'd say, "I don't think so."

Our crowds were large, but they weren't near as large as they were later with the Beatles and the Stones and such. I think the biggest crowd we had was twenty-eight or thirty thousand at the Cotton Bowl in Dallas. When the crowds were like that, I'll give you an example of what it sounded like. You know when you dive in a swimming pool and you get that rush of the water when you dive under, the crowd will get so loud your ears would shut down on you like that. Elvis fed off the crowd. Bill, of course, was clowning with Elvis. It was up to D. J. and myself to keep it together. If we couldn't hear, me and D. J. would watch Elvis real close, to see which way he moved. I made a statement one time to a news reporter. She said, "How do you guys hear?" I said, "Well, as far as I know, we're literally probably the only band that's directed by an ass." Actually, we really didn't have to worry, because somehow or another, the boy, I'll give him this, he had an uncanny sense of timing, and when we'd start a song, he'd never miss; he was right there. But it sounded good at the time I told it.

The 1968 TV show was the last I thing I did with him. I still had the studio at the time, and he asked me if I could just lock up for a couple of weeks. He didn't give me a clue of what he had on his mind—something new, something different, a little of the old stuff, I didn't know what. It hadn't been that long since Elvis had gotten out of the army. He had gone to Paris and a couple of other places, saw the fans over there, but he hadn't performed. He wanted to do a world tour, is what he really wanted to do. But none of that ever happened. And that was the last time I saw him or spoke to him. Next thing you knew he went and did Vegas. Parker diverted him into Vegas. I really regret that that tour never happened.

Now I make a couple of trips a year to Europe for a week, maybe two weeks at a time. I pretty much play the same set list over and over, the key songs, and I try to do a chronological set. I start with a couple of the early Sun things, up through the time I was with him. I do a few things with Ronnie McDowell; Ronnie will do a couple of the later things like "Hurt." I love playing blues, but I always try to do the songs fairly close to the way we recorded them so you can recognize them, then go off a little bit, but still in the same chord structure. Overseas we never get a request for any of the 1970s things; it's always two or three of the early Sun things and "Hound Dog," "Jailhouse Rock," "Don't Be Cruel," the key songs along the way.

I wouldn't say I was trying on a personal level to get recognition. I probably missed out on a bunch of bucks, or the band did, by not having a manager to fight those battles for us, but now I'm happy with what little recognition I've gotten. When other musicians say you've influenced them in one way or another, that's a good feeling. When we did the cut with Ron Wood on the *All the King's Men* album, I remember telling him when we were over in his studio in Ireland, I said, "You guys have got the ball now, it's up to you to carry it on forward." Not those exact words maybe, but words of that nature. And he actually teared up when I said that.

Emil Richards
I Used to Stand Right Next to Frank When He Sang

Session Percussionist, Los Angeles

In 1962, I went all around the world with Frank Sinatra. There were only six of us on his private jet and we were very tight. All of the big arrangements of Nelson Riddle and Neal Hefti, Billy May and Axel Stordahl were broken down into a six-piece band that had to sound like a full orchestra. A CD came out a few years ago of Frank Sinatra live in Paris in 1962. That was from the next-to-the-last concert of the ten-week tour and I gotta say, Frank never sounded better. He was at the peak of his singing at that time. I felt it later when I heard it because he went into retirement after that and when he came out of retirement he asked me to go to Vegas with him and Count Basie's band. I don't think he was ever singing bad, but after listening to that tape, and seeing a video of the last concert we did—at Albert Hall in London, when the queen was in the audience, as well as Anthony Quinn, Elizabeth Taylor, and Judy Garland—I realized he was just singing his butt off.

We worked every venue you can imagine, everywhere possible. I remember when we did the Acropolis in Greece, Frank said, "Maybe we can raise enough money to put a roof on this joint!"

Before the tour we rehearsed for a week or two at Frank's

house above Mulholland Drive. He knew his music and would definitely make suggestions, like "You're drowning me out here. I don't want you to be so far down that we can't hear you, but I want you to know that I'm cooking at the peak of my range and it's hard for me." He was very diligent in everything he did. On tour, if there wasn't a piano available, he'd vocalize with the vibes. I'd go to his room and roll the vibes in and he'd vocalize for an hour before the concert. When you're hangin' out with the boss an hour before the gig, you're up. You're in the frame of mind for doing the concert. Just before we went up he'd select the tunes he wanted to do for that show. He would pull them out of the book and have them onstage ready. Every time Frank would introduce a song, he would talk about the composer or the lyric; he would say something about the song that would make the audience appreciate what was coming.

Some people said that he couldn't sing, but they didn't know about music or musicianship or art. His breath and his diction and timing—there was nobody like that. I've worked with Sarah Vaughan, Ella, I worked opposite Lady Day with George Shearing doing all the jazz venues, but there was no-body like Frank. Nobody ever had the timing that Frank had. When he sang something real low like "Old Man River," I used to get goose bumps. Frank used to hold his hands behind his back so that he was literally pushing his chest out. "Tote that barge / lift that bail / you get a little drunk / and you land in J-AAA-III-LLL . . ." I mean, I'd get out of breath. I used to get goose bumps and cry and think what a thrill to be with some-body so good he could make you feel like that. I wish all my loved ones could have heard it. I used to stand right next to Frank when he sang . . . and those are the moments that I re-member.

When Frank came out of retirement, Elvis was at the peak of

his career and we were working Vegas and Frank was giving us this rundown. Somebody came in and gave us this telegram from Elvis, who was playing across the street at the M-G-M. And he was really drawing them in. But the telegram was humble and kind and it said, "Thanks for the overflow."

Frank laughed and said, "Look at this guy! Is he kidding? I'm the one with the overflow!"